The
Game
Changer

The Game Changer

INSPIRATIONAL STORIES THAT CHANGED LIVES

Inspired and Compiled

by
Iman Aghay

The Game Changer (Volume 5): Inspirational Stories That Changed Lives
©2020 by Success Road Enterprises. All rights reserved.

Print Book ISBN: 978-1-953806-04-8
eBook ISBN: 978-1-953806-05-5

Published by Success Road Enterprises | Spotlight Publishing™

Cover Design: Angie Analya
Cover Background Image: Adobe Stock
Interior Design: Soumi Goswami
Spotlight Publishing™ https://SpotlightPublishing.pro

Ordering information: Copies of this book may be ordered directly from www.mylifechangingmoment.com

Table of Contents

···•◆•···

Dedication

···✦···

To all the courageous entrepreneurs
serving the world with their excellence and
leading the way for a better world.

Introduction

······ ✦ ······

I've been working with entrepreneurs and other successful professionals for the past sixteen years. As a business mentor, I see the complex interworking of an entrepreneur's life. I have the privilege of knowing what goes on behind the scenes. I am humbled when I see what it takes for entrepreneurs to realize their achievements.

The Game Changer Book Series is a collection of these behind-the-scene stories—stories that most people never realize have laid the foundation for a successful business or company. These stories are personal, connected to the authors' hearts, and many of them are being shared for the first time with you, our reader. As I read this collection, I could not stop thinking about this old adage: *"Everyone you meet is fighting a battle you know nothing about! Be kind, always...."*

This book reveals some of the hardest times and darkest moments that entrepreneurs live through. Their experiences are real and deeply personal. Many of the chapters tell of bad choices and overcoming mistakes. However, all of them share something in common: a turning point—the turning point that changed the author's life forever. These stories are very dear to each author, and I am honored to be able to share their experiences with you. I hope that each of these stories touches you as deeply as I have been touched.

Iman Aghay

1

I Woke Up Like This

···•◆•···

Authentically Own Your Greatness

~ Iman Aghay

by
Sarah Lawrence

I woke up on a Sunday.

All my muscles between my neck and my thighs felt stiff. It took my breath away.

I reached for my phone, with shaky hands. I needed to check the date and time. In my fog, I had no idea what day it was, much less how much time had passed. It was September 19th, 12:23 pm. My hand fell next to me, holding my phone.

I started to process the last week.

The Tuesday prior, I had opted for surgery. A tummy tuck and breast lift. On the day of surgery, I was excited! I was ready to move forward with my new body and get rid of the pieces of me that I had disliked for so long. I was feeling confident, secure, and absolutely sure.

During pre-op, I was laying on the bed when something above me caught my eye. There was a picture of a dolphin jumping out of the ocean. It looked like paint by numbers. I was sure it had been painted by one of the staff's children. It seemed out of place, like they ran out of TV's and didn't want there to be a hole in the wall.

My internal narrative started to contemplate if surgery was paint by numbers. The surgeon had drawn on my body with a sharpie, drawing out each piece of me that he would cut, adjust, and sew back together. Planning his art, the way that a painter can see his picture long before it's ever completed. This correlation gave me some peace because there were parts of me that were out of place. The surgeon could see my body as this beautiful piece of art that just needed to be manipulated to its potential. He could see how my body, that I was ashamed of, could be tighter, stronger, and bring me more confidence.

This day would change my life.

I woke up on a Sunday.

As I was laying there, I realized that I remembered very little of the 5 days prior. I could remember leaving the surgery center. I could remember one of the days being in excruciating pain and my husband taking me to the ER. I could remember friends texting me, but I didn't know what they said. Essentially, I had lost 5 days.

I lifted my phone back up to my face. I started to look for evidence that I was alive for the previous 5 days. What I found was texts where I said, "I am not coherent," or texts that were, in fact, not coherent.

In that moment of realization, that my sense of awareness had been gone for almost a week, I became quickly aware of the tubes that were coming out of my body, the binders and bandages, and the machine massaging my legs, to prevent blood clots. Everything seemed surreal. I reached down to undo some bandages to look at my abdomen. It looked so flat. I had never had a flat stomach, and now I did! As my eyes went lower, I saw the incision that was covered in bandages and ointment. I removed a small piece to see the damage. It wasn't nearly as intense as I had anticipated, and I placed it back. My curiosity brought me to my chest. 4 kids and over 100 pounds lost, I had no idea my breasts could be so high! I finally exhaled. I felt good about the body I was left with.

Next, I needed to move.

I felt as if I was being resurrected, and it was up to me to cross the bridge back to the living. My brain had come back first, and now I needed to will my body back to life. My abdomen muscles had been sewn back together, and that process had temporarily taken away all of my core strength. It was as if my core essence, strength, and power had been ripped from me. I couldn't sit up or move in any position where I needed my core.

I called my husband to come in to help me sit up.

He came in and asked how I felt.

"Dead. How do I sit up?"

"Like this."

He supported under my arm and supported my body into a sitting position. Clearly, he had done this in the last week.

"You ok?" He asked.

"I don't know. I really don't know what to do."

He took the pieces of fabric off my legs, that was massaging them, and helped me to sit on the side of the bed. I made my way to the bathroom. I washed my hands and looked in the mirror. I looked small. I looked contoured, even through the bandages.

In the 5 minutes I stood there, in disbelief of the person I saw in the mirror, I suddenly felt a wave of nausea and dizziness. The colors of the room started to fade, and I felt like I was going to pass out. I slowly made my way back to the bed and sat down.

I had no idea how slow the path to true recovery would be.

Later that day, my 7-year-old daughter came bouncing in my room with all of her enthusiasm.

"Mommy!! You're awake. Are you better?"

"Not really, baby. But I will get there."

"Ok. Well, when you are better can we have a girl's night?"

"Sure, my love."

"Wait. You had plastic surgery? Why?"

Her question was another gut punch. I had three daughters. I was teaching them how to have confidence and go into the world with love, and power. However, I had just made the decision to lay on a table and let a surgeon cut off the pieces of me I didn't like. My daughter loved my belly, and my squishy arms, and how snuggly I was. I always made a point to truly show up in the world in a big and meaningful way. Yet, here I was, unable to even sit up. By my choice. By my choice to have a body that I believed would give me more credibility, and validity.

How do I reconcile the idea of loving who you are, unconditionally, when I put conditions on myself?

My answer to my daughter didn't really exist.

"Can we talk about this later?"

"Sure!" She responded and bounced out of the room.

That moment took the rest of the strength I had, and I began to ponder all of the decisions that brought me to this moment as tears streamed down my face. I had worked so hard to lose weight; my biggest obstacle had always been myself. I was addicted to food. I ate when I was happy. I ate when I was sad. I ate when I was anxious, depressed, laughing, or simply if a tasty thing caught my eye. My brain couldn't let go of the pleasure food brought me, and I often justified it by the community, family, and false satisfaction. At my highest, I weighed 305 lbs.

When I was 29, something had to change. My last pregnancy had made me bedridden and I couldn't imagine not being able to move through the world actively. I started to work out daily and changed my lifestyle. I got myself down to 218 lbs. But like every other time, I slipped once, and down the slippery slope, I went. By the time I was 33, I had gained back everything I had lost. I knew I couldn't keep fighting the uphill battle of my own mind. I opted for a gastric sleeve. I had gotten my weight down to 187 lbs. by the time I had opted for plastic surgery, about 2 years later.

The gastric sleeve was quick, easy, and internal. The result was slow but steady. It felt natural. The day I laid on the table to have a tummy tuck and my breasts lifted, nothing felt natural. Yet, I wanted it with every ounce of my being.

I would've sacrificed so much to feel normal.

How could I be so willing to hurt so bad?

I took a deep breath and thought about all the moments where I was reminded my weight defined me. I remembered weighing 99 lbs in 2nd grade (back then they weighed all the students for health checks). I remembered being in weight watchers by 11 years old. Then, as a pre-teen, losing so much weight that by the time I hit puberty, adult men, who were my teachers, would stare at me and make comments about my body. This clear act of sexualization was celebrated and ingrained in my mind as a success. I remember being 17 and weighing 256 lbs and knowing my worth was based on my weight because my peers made sure to tell me daily how they thought other girls would be more successful. After all, they cared more about themselves.

There wasn't a time in my young life where my weight didn't weigh on me. Years and years of being reminded of my Achilles heel could've only ended the way it did, for someone as stubborn as me. I wasn't going to back down. I was willing to do whatever I needed to.

Nothing hurt as bad as being fat.

I woke up on a Sunday.

I was brought back to the moment I lost weight on my own. I was brought back to the gastric sleeve. I was brought back to all those moments where I knew I couldn't exist in the world, as I was.

I finally got the only thing I ever really wanted: I had a normal body.

The truth is that no food choices or lifestyle could've ever fixed what was really happening with me. I had decided long ago that my worth was based on my weight. I understand, now, that this was so deep-seated in me, that I would've always slipped into the same vicious cycle of binge eating. I would've always slipped down that slope because only someone who has a healthy mindset around food would ever be able to maintain a healthy lifestyle. I needed to change my mind before I could change my body.

I didn't see a way out. I knew I couldn't trust myself. My path was the best, for me.

Now, I have a body that is still flawed with scars and stretch marks and is far from perfect. But when I look in the mirror, I love myself.

I love who I am so much, I see working out as a celebration, and making good choices as an investment.

I was able to change my mindset because I was no longer fighting myself. I was celebrating who I was, and who I could be.

I took a path that is not for everyone, but it was absolutely the right path for me. The process of surgery, and pain, and healing left me with nothing but my mind to figure out exactly why I needed this so much. In the end, it took healing my body and mind, to realize that the demons keeping me overweight needed to be stared down with a body I had absolute and perfect love for. The surgeries were a tool to make me stronger.

As we move through life, we all get judged. Every decision we make will have a judgment attached to it. Maybe it was your choice to become an entrepreneur. Maybe it was your choice of the number of children you will have or had. Maybe it was the donut you ate for breakfast, last week. There will a voice in the crowd who will swear you are wrong. There will be a voice in the crowd, only there to smell your wound and make sure you know exactly how broken you are.

Your strength will come from finding the decision that is in alignment with who you need to be. Plastic surgery was a tool for me to love myself and gave me the gift of time to stare down the demons in my mind that always kept me overweight.

I eventually answered my daughter.

"Baby, I did have plastic surgery. I needed it to heal. Not everyone does, but this was my choice to be the best version of myself inside and out."

Make a decision on who you need to be, and the path to get there. No one gets to live your life, except you. So, when you are told you are broken, it's up to you to fill the cracks with gold and become stronger than you ever thought.

Sarah is an award-winning speaker, writer, and organizer of TEDx Tenaya Paseo. She is a master communicator and collaboration ninja.

Over the years of her career, she has built over 300 public speaking stage opportunities for experts in different niche markets. She has worked with everything from personal development, health, non-profits, all the way to marketing, tech, and business.

Currently, she is the Operations Manager for Success Road Academy, an industry leader in the online market and training, specializes in online Course Creation for the expert industry. She believes in helping people develop a business around their life purpose.

Connect with Sarah: Instagram @superstarupgrades

Scan the code above with your smartphone camera to watch Sarah's message.

Or, follow this link:
https://youtu.be/F2oP1Hc8B00

2

How the Financial Danger Zone Left Me Homeless

··· • ◆ • ···

"Sometimes when things are falling apart, they may be falling into place."

~ J. Lynn, Fall with Me

by
Robert Bernard

It wasn't that long ago when I found myself living in my small compact car in a parking lot outside a Planet Fitness gym. I am a former aerospace engineer with a rare Master of Experimental Methods degree and another Master of Business Administration degree (MBA). I certainly had the smarts to be wealthy and can solve problems when there is a task to accomplish. Yet, I was constantly struggling. I was usually the smartest guy in the room—and the poorest.

How does that even happen? How did I find myself living in my car? These were the questions I asked myself until I finally got some answers.

If you are like me, you have read a lot of books and gone to seminars looking for ways to have financial freedom and retire early. I was always looking to make money outside of a job because jobs to me were like doing daily jail time. After reading *Rich Dad Poor Dad* and *Cashflow Quadrant* by Robert Kiyosaki, I certainly couldn't work for someone else for the rest of my life.

Like that other Robert, I value freedom above all else. This was one of the reasons I was homeless for a stint. And I will say, just because your role model did it (Kiyosaki and his wife were "homeless" for 2 weeks) doesn't mean *you* should. So, if I could make a suggestion, learn from this chapter, so you don't have to find out how comfortable (or not comfortable) your car is to sleep in.

My problem was that I was too smart for my own good. You will often hear me say that I was smart enough to be a rocket scientist and stupid enough to be an engineer for a career. Surely, I thought with my education and brains, I could become wealthy on my own. My ego blocked me from seeing my blind spots that were preventing me from moving into financial freedom. This cost me a lot of money and a lot of years of heartache that could have been avoided. So, here is what I know now...

Books were helpful because they educated me on the possibilities. They left breadcrumbs of potential but not actual answers. Things like the rich don't pay any income taxes. How is that even possible? Everyone has to pay taxes, don't they??? I also knew the rich prefer real estate as an asset class. I knew that I wanted to buy and hold real estate for a tax deduction called depreciation. I had concepts but no hands-on experience.

Traditional education has its place teaching the basics. However, my MBA program was designed to make better employees, not wealthy business owners. So, I specialized in entrepreneurship, taxes, and real estate inside my MBA program, looking for more answers to creating wealth. I was a real pain in the ass for my professors because I had read enough to understand the rich got excellent rates of returns and paid very little in taxes. I asked a lot of questions, and frankly, they just did not know the answers. *They weren't thinking about how to solve the problems it takes to be wealthy.* They were just out to make super employees. I did learn the true vocabulary of money and some great real estate tips from guest speakers actually doing real estate investing daily in the real world. I want to thank that professor for being wise enough to bring in experts and not try to teach it out of a book.

Robert Kiyosaki wrote that seminars are really where you learned about being rich. I did find this to be true. My level of education about being wealthy skyrocketed when I started attending them. I learned *how* the rich don't pay taxes. I was shown how to accelerate depreciation through cost segregation and then use a §1031 Like-Kind-Exchange to keep all the tax savings.

Seminars also revealed to me how the rich control assets without owning them, through trusts. Trusts provide fantastic estate planning and if done correctly, asset protection. Did you know you can put a house into a trust without triggering the due on sale clause that is in all current mortgages? The due on sale clause gives the bank the right to demand payment in full if you transfer title, even though you may have years left on your loan. Yup, Congress gave us that power with the Garn–St. Germain Depository Institutions Act of 1982. Knowledge is power, and I did learn the secrets of the rich.

I also learned the downside of seminars and coaches. Some seminars are just a series of sales pitches with no real info, and not all coaches are created equal. Usually, coaches teach seminars on one specific topic, giving you just enough information to be dangerous to yourself and your wealth. Some are just in it for the money and not the students. Some are just not ethical. Finding the right training and coach can be hard, and yet it makes all the difference.

For about 15 years, I had some successes with real estate. I had flipped a few houses, and at one time had 24 houses in my control that cost me under $100 apiece to acquire. I had passive income that gave me a nice life for a couple of years. Then disaster struck. I realized I did not have all the information I needed to hold on to my money. I found myself in the Danger Zone because of a misleading coach that purposefully didn't tell the whole story and compounded his omission with bad legal advice. I ended up losing all 24 houses and all that time and energy. It was a form of theft and a classic Danger Zone predator.

Then, I put all my eggs in one basket with a business partner that went south. We had signed up for one of those coaching programs I warned you about that was for itself and not its students. This time the Danger Zone really got me. I lost *everything*.

I didn't have a second source of passive income. I had been self-employed for too long and was over-educated to qualify for a good job. I couldn't even get in the door for an interview. And just to confirm what you might already know, ageism still exists in the workplace. It was a perfect storm to be homeless.

That is why, even though I was a rocket scientist with an MBA, I found myself sleeping for six weeks in my tiny car, which was fully stuffed to the point I could not lower the front seat. Of course, being an engineer, I had my homeless routine and systems down to a set of scientific procedures.

I was sleeping in the parking lot of Planet Fitness in South Florida because they are open 24 hours a day. It was reasonably warm at night, so I didn't have to keep the car running, and I didn't have to worry about freezing to death. Plus, I was using an aviation solution when I didn't want to get out of the car to go to the bathroom. But no matter what I did, including compression wraps, my ankles would still swell. Sleeping upright is hard on the body.

A positive was that in the same parking lot was a coffee shop, so I could go straight to 'work' when I woke up, without moving the car. I was using all my problem-solving capabilities, and it was still hell. I had hit rock bottom, and I didn't even have drugs or alcohol to blame it on, just lack of knowledge about the Danger Zone. I knew I had to create a new future for myself.

The good thing was that I had an end date for being homeless. I would be taking care of my then 92-year old grandmother for six months in Vermont, and that would give me time to figure out what went wrong and what to put in place so that would never happen again to me.

Over those six months, I realized I was missing a few critical pieces to have the success I had chased after for nearly 20 years. I went looking for clues on how self-employed people can overcome the ups and downs of business. I had been on a quest that led me on a journey of self-discovery and proven methods of income generation, retirement planning, real estate investing, and wealth protection, and those six months led me to the last two missing pieces.

Those last two pieces were having the right coach and the right partner. A coach who could give me step by step instructions and the accountability to make sure I was doing the work correctly. **Knowledge without application is pointless. Application without great coaching is dangerous.**

Personally, my highest priority in how I wanted to move forward was finding a great business partner. I know myself, and I work best in a partnership. Luckily, I found a great one who also became my life-partner and loves me. Then it was about the right coaches. Equally good news was that my new partner had been in the coaching and seminar training industry for years and gave me great insight into the right coaches for what I was trying to achieve. Now I could develop what I had been looking for all these years, a proven plan to generate passive income no matter what was going on economically.

With the help of my partner, Carolyn 'CJ' Matthews, we created the S.M.A.R.T. Ultimate Retirement Formula (S.U.R.F.)™ for our Master True Wealth System™. For small business owners like us, it is the fastest and easiest way to retirement. The 5-step formula ensures entrepreneurs take home more money, invest it to create passive income exceeding their expenses, and then protect it from the five major financial predators: taxes, lawsuits, wealth-draining fees, theft, and illness.

The first step is the **S**mart mindset. According to T. Harv Ecker, we all have a financial thermometer. Our minds work to lay out the foundation for keeping us safe for the rest of our lives. The problem is that financial 'temperature setting' quite often is much lower than we would prefer, and until we 'reset' it, you won't get the level of wealth and financial freedom you are looking for.

The second step is to **M**aximize the small business owner's financial engine. Here is where profits are maximized with proven business strategies that can be implemented in a simple way to accelerate your financial freedom. The goal here is to work less and have more money within the first year of using the S.U.R.F. Program™.

The third step is to **A**lign taxes to save the most amount of money. We set up small business owners so they can put up to ten times more a year into retirement programs that can save them up to $20,000 every year in taxes. This way they can keep more money to help them retire faster. We help them integrate their business taxes, income, and the goal of early retirement to accelerate their path to financial freedom.

The fourth step is *R*eally smart investment strategies. We help small business owners learn how to invest outside of the stock market. This way they can have more control, stable returns, and truly passive income. This is especially important for self-employed professionals if they are no longer able to work.

The last step is *T*otal asset protection. Most entrepreneurs or small business owners making over $100,000 are in the Danger Zone, surrounded by financial predators, and don't even know it! We teach asset protection the super-wealthy enjoy that you can swipe and deploy for yourself. This allows you to build your wealth without interruption and be able to leave a legacy. Like Warren Buffet said, "Predicting rain doesn't count. Building Arks does."

With this formula, I enjoy financial freedom, time freedom, and location freedom. It also brings me peace of mind that my wealth won't be taken or lost to the Danger Zone Predators. I am able to vacation for as long as I want, with whom I want. And every time I lie down on a mattress, I never take it for granted.

Robert Bernard is a co-founder of YourSmartWealth.com, a coaching and consulting company helping 6-figure entrepreneurs keep more money and protect their wealth from financial pitfalls so they can retire faster, smarter, and wealthier

Using proven integrative strategies of the rich that most small business owners don't know or have the time to learn YourSmartWealth.com gets you to financial freedom fast with the S.M.A.R.T. Ultimate Retirement Formula (S.U.R.F.)™ only found in their Master True Wealth System™.

Robert Bernard
Email: team@YourSmartWealth.com
Website: YourSmartWealth.com
LinkedIn: linkedin.com/company/YourSmartWealth/
Facebook: facebook.com/YourSmartWealth/
Twitter: @YourSmartWealth

Scan the QR code with your smartphone to watch Robert's video message.

Or, follow this link:
http://bit.ly/YSWYoutube

3

My Road to Reinvention

·····◆·····

"Life is what you make it."

by
Melissa Kramer

As I left the hospital maternity ward on a sunny September afternoon in 2011, swaddling my newest tiny miracle tightly in my arms with my husband at my side, I was riding a powerful swell of emotions. Feeling so complete in that perfect moment, it was unfathomable that just nine months later I would be hit with the devastating blow that would shatter my world and eventually lead me to discover the most important lesson of my life.

At the time, I thought I had succeeded in creating the ideal life scenario, adhering to the checklist of life accomplishments that was instilled in me from an early age. I had a successful career in advertising sales, a stately home in an affluent neighborhood, and my storybook family complete with two little boys and my husband of nearly eight years. I was doing everything that was expected of me, being the good girl I was raised to be, and having become successful in the way society told me I was supposed to become.

The irony of my marriage is that my husband and I nearly didn't get together. We met at a wedding in September 2001 and had an immediate attraction to one another, but we both had plans to relocate from Detroit in a matter of weeks. He had his sights set on Chicago and I was plotting to join my best friend in San Francisco. Then the terror attacks of 9/11 happened, causing me to question my ambitions and yearn for safety and security, so I opted to stay in Detroit where I felt comfortable. That young man from the wedding stayed in Detroit too. We started dating and were married three years later. I happily surrendered to the midwestern suburban lifestyle that we began to build together.

In 2011, we seemed to be living the proverbial dream. The life I saw in front of me looked picture-perfect. There was just one problem. I was only seeing what I wanted to see... until it was too late.

I don't remember exactly when I first noticed that things were different. I was under a great deal of stress in the months following the birth of baby #2. I was fighting to keep it all together while continuing the trajectory of my career and my home life. I felt like I was losing my grip. Then one day I noticed that my husband had stopped kissing me. No usual peck good morning or goodbye or good night. All gone. And it wasn't just the kisses that disappeared. I couldn't remember the last time we had sex, or he had told me he loved me. *Has he said it since the baby was born?* He avoided participating in family activities and he barely spoke to me (only if spoken to). As if that wasn't enough, I realized that he wouldn't even look at me. If I approached him attempting to start a conversation, he'd divert his eyes, avoiding any eye contact.

Once I started to notice these signs, it was impossible to ignore them. My awareness of the situation began to consume me, gnawing away in my mind, feeding my fragile postpartum emotions, and conjuring ideas that I had done something wrong. *It must be my fault. I've been so focused on the kids, and on my own stress... was I not paying enough attention to him?* So, I did what came naturally to me. I set out to regain control.

With dogged determination, I silently hatched my plan to fix what I surmised to be broken and win back his affection. My repair methods included over-the-top gestures of all kinds; massive cleaning and home repair projects, elaborately prepared dinners, endless surprises, and gifts that appealed to his key interests, fancy new golf accessories, another wine club subscription, a giant TV for his news, and sports viewing pleasure. I was willing to do whatever it took to make things perfect for him.

Nothing produced the results I was seeking. The harder I tried to make things better, the more rejected, invisible, and alone I felt.

I tried to get him to talk about it. I'd attempt to select an ideal moment to casually mention, "Hey, you seem like something is bothering you. Is there something wrong?"

Crickets.

"No. It's nothing. I'm just tired."

I vowed not to give up. I tried waiting for the right opportunities to present themselves, and I would attempt to engage him only to be dismissed again. This went on for months, and with each inquiry, he seemed to grow increasingly more frustrated.

And then it happened. June 2012, we found ourselves standing at opposite ends of the massive marble-topped island in the center of our kitchen. A potentially perfect moment to have a conversation!

This is it! This time, I am going to get him to talk to me.

My delivery was more assertive than usual, and I refused to accept his trite rebuttals. I wouldn't let him walk away from me again. I moved to the doorway to block his attempted exit.

"Listen, we keep having the same conversation. I know there is something wrong"

I pushed on.

"It can't be nothing. Things are different. I feel it. You don't kiss me. You don't look at me. You never want to do anything. What did I do? What's going on?"

It was like someone turned on a spigot and the words came flowing more freely than ever before. It felt so good letting it out, until...

He spoke.

'When I think about my future, I don't see you in it. All I think about is the boys, not you. I just don't love you..."

Crash. Shatter. My veins turned to ice and the earth started to sway as it split open, taking me down, swallowing me into a deep pit of airless darkness.

Then he added one final blow.

"And I have been feeling this way for a long time. Years."

Thud. That was me hitting the bottom.
Years? How could that be? Our oldest son was just 2!!

I was slapped with the devastating realization that I had been unconsciously participating in a fictitious charade.

Was my whole life a lie?

Was my marriage just a mirage?

In my attempts to fix the relationship and be the perfect wife, I never considered for even one second that things were beyond my ability to control and repair.

It was all too much for me to comprehend. I spiraled into a state of shock, leaving my body, suddenly seeing it all play out like I was watching a movie on fast-forward, moving rapidly like the sickening blur of a high-speed carnival ride spinning out of control. And in the center of the swirling chaos, there was an eerie stillness. That was the moment when I realized my world had changed forever. I was in the eye of the storm.

I was not prepared to handle what was happening to me as the shock took hold. For several days I remained stuck, a prisoner of my mind. I didn't sleep. I didn't eat. My lean body grew wan and fragile as I eroded to a mere shell of a person, floating through a dense, dark fog.

During those darkest of days, the only glimmer of light I had was my children. Even at the lowest point of my breakdown, my unconditional love and sense of duty to protect them prevailed. That force is what kept me going. I would channel my strength for them because they did not deserve to have a pathetic and broken sad sack for a mother. So, after several days spent lingering at the bottom of the self-imposed pit, what was left of me rose from the darkness and attempted to rejoin the world of the living.

With each day, the stinging numbness subsided a bit more and the fog eventually lifted its heavy veil. I was no longer in the eye of the storm, but I was by no means okay. The world I thought I knew had shattered around me and I did not know how to be in this new place.

How do I live in this life… now that I know?
How can I look at him knowing how he really feels?

I didn't know anything, I just had questions. And the biggest question of all loomed over me.

Now what?

My initial choice was to stay in my marriage. It felt obvious to me. I was not ready to give up. What about the checklist of life accomplishments? And since my husband showed no signs of taking any action, I considered there might be some hope. So, I tried to hold on.

I woke up very early one Saturday morning several weeks later, my mind in its then typical restless state. I could not fall back to sleep, so I decided to go for a walk. Walking and running had become my cherished active meditation. It was my time to clear my head and recharge. That morning, as the sun was just starting to rise, I found myself on my favorite densely wooded trail - a rare oasis in the suburbs. I observed the sun's rays beaming through the branches, turning the darkness into light, and I was in awe of the brilliantly golden leaves of the season illuminating my path. In one flash of spectacular light, I was struck with a profound realization. All this time I had been trying to control everything except for the one thing I could control... myself. I finally saw that before I could save my marriage or anything else, I had to save myself.

Thus, began my journey to save myself from myself.

I started paying more attention to how my perspective, attitude, and beliefs affected the things that were happening in my life. I read books that expanded my understanding of philosophy, spirituality, relationships, and self-improvement. Books like Don Miguel Ruiz' *The Four Agreements*, Marianne Williamson's *A Return to Love*, Eckhart Tolle's *The Power of Now, and* Lao Tzu's *Tao de Ching*.

I established three key understandings about my life experience that provided a foundation to make real change within myself.

1. Acknowledging that I was exactly where I was in my life due to every choice I had ever made.

2. Surrendering the tendency to try to control everything and simply allow, be fully present at the moment, and welcome the unknown.

3. Placing my intention and attention on what *I wanted* instead of *what I didn't want.*

Through these understandings, I grew to truly love myself and appreciate my experience more deeply than ever before and I began to radiate from within. I was no longer burdened with the belief that I had to meet certain ideals or expectations. I felt so much happier and lighter as I freed myself from the constraints of the life accomplishment checklist.

As I progressed with my inner work, I began to see my marriage for what it was and my crusade to fix it waned. Yet, I remained in the comfortable pattern of complacency that I had settled into for a while longer because I had not yet fully come to the realization of what I really wanted for myself and my children. Let's just say I wasn't quite "there", yet because I was still letting fear dictate my situation.

And then, it happened! The labors of my personal development paid off and my perspective radically shifted. The whole world looked different to me, filled with possibilities! I became clear about what I truly wanted, and I started making choices and taking actions that were more aligned with those desires instead of my fears. I was prepared to take a leap and fully embrace the unknown. It was time to do what needed to be done.

The day I approached my husband with my proposal was one I will never forget.

"It seems we are at a crossroad," I said in a clear and measured tone. "We've been going around and around for years and there does not seem to be any change in our situation. At this point, I see we have a choice to make. Do we choose to commit and really try to do something to rebuild our marriage, or do we choose to go our separate ways and get a divorce?"

He seemed completely shocked by my calm delivery of such a direct statement. I was no longer the frightened hysterical person slumped over the kitchen counter he remembered from the summer of 2012.

He started quickly. "Well, there really isn't anything to rebuild..."

Then he stopped himself, realizing what he was about to say and possibly bracing for another meltdown. His concluding words slowly rolled out. "So... I suppose... we... should separate."

"Okay, " was my single word reply. That was almost too easy.

After my divorce, I had many loose ends still to manage. Foremost, there was the major effort of making sure my kids were as okay as possible. Divorce is rough on kids, no matter how young they are. It rips their lives apart and rattles their sense of security and trust. I understand why many people choose to stay together "for the kids." I also knew that option never would have worked for us. I felt great validation knowing that my divorce was an opportunity for my kids to have a better chance at life because they could see their parents (or at least their mother) as authentically happy, exuding truth, love, and appreciation.

It sickens me to think about what my life would be like if I had never had that moment of awakening on that morning walk in 2012. Even though it took me a few years, I was saved by my choice to make a change. I also recognized that it was my resilience and fortitude that got me to a certain point on my journey of self-discovery and renewal. To truly move on and move into a new life, it was time for some additional support.

I found the most valuable form of support through the wisdom and experience of the guide I met in the summer of 2016. Enlisting his guidance and support illuminated the things that I was not seeing for myself, raised important questions I had not been asking myself, and saved valuable time and effort that I would have otherwise wasted if I had attempted to fumble through uncharted territory through my own trial and error.

He helped me navigate my way through some significant milestones in my reinvention including a major career change, exiting the corporate world to follow my passion and help others, a massive lifestyle adjustment, selling my giant house, and casting off most of my excess possessions to live more simply, and finally, leaving the Detroit suburbs and finding my heart's home in the glorious natural splendor of northwestern Michigan.

Even now, so many years later, he continues to guide me through my deeper existential exploration as my partner both in life and in the business, we are building to help others through their own life transitions. I know that if I had not become the person, I AM it never would have been possible for us to be together. It is something I am grateful for every day.

Today, I am joyfully living my dream and my passion for helping women - especially women who have been through a divorce as I did.

As a certified coach, I guide them to understand themselves better so they can thrive to live the life of their dreams. I'm dedicated to helping these women reinvent themselves because I know how it saved my life. What I was doing before was not living. I was merely existing. I only started to truly *live* once I embraced the three key understandings of myself, which brought me to learn the single most important lesson of my life.

Just six simple words:
Life is what you make it.

It is the not-so-secret secret that has changed the lives of those I share it with, and it is what helped me create the life of my dreams.

So, I'd like to invite you to ask yourself, have *you* chosen to make your life the life you want?

Melissa Kramer credits her reinvention after divorce for saving her life, and she now guides and inspires women through post-divorce transitions in her writing, public speaking, the YouTube channel @ *RealRADWomen*, and her coaching practice.

Melissa is based in northwestern Michigan where she and her partner create life-changing programs and retreats through their business Nowhere Tour, LLC.

Melissa Kramer
For more about how to work with Melissa visit www.radnewlife.com or
email: melissa@nowheretour.com.
Facebook, YouTube, and Instagram: @RealRADWomen

Scan the QR code with your smartphone to watch Melissa's video message.

Or, follow this link:
https://youtu.be/vAudRKwcXzg

4

A Confusing State of Affairs

...·+·◆·◆·◆·+·...

"If it is to be, then it is up to you!"

by
Basile Lemba

Are you one of the millions of people who find networking a challenging process?

Have you ever stood in the middle of a networking event wondering, "What's happening here?!" as your unmet expectations collided with a confusing reality?

I've been there.

One bright afternoon many years ago I found myself standing in a crowded room looking around hopefully for an opportunity to make eye contact. I was keen on starting the process of forming some good business connections as I was new in town, and the event organizer had promised that this business networking lunch would put me shoulder to shoulder with more than 200 people. My ticket had cost me $150 – a large investment for me at the time – but I was expecting to easily connect with between 20 and 30 people.

Ultimately, I would be introducing my services to these people.

This was a dream opportunity!

As the head of a new business, I needed to expand my network. I had previously been on the "networking circuit" in my new community, and this had found me going out to plenty of events that had very few people in attendance. These experiences had left me confused and a little bewildered at what people in this community took to be productive networking practices. There had to be a better way, and I expected this expensive lunch-time networking event to fill in the gaps of what I had been missing.

The day of the event saw me properly dressed and eager to meet people.

And it was with high expectations that I entered a room that was, as promised, jam-packed. I could barely move. The noise level in the room was very high. If you were two feet away from me, I could certainly have seen you, but I surely couldn't have talked to you. This was not proving to be the solution I had hoped for.

A few minutes after I arrived, a voice came over the P.A. system and announced: "Have a seat, we are now going to serve lunch." I squeezed myself into a chair. As we ate, someone came on stage and introduced the keynote speaker. He started talking and rambled on and on. Finally, 2:00 p.m. came and the guests started leaving to go back to work. I started scrambling to connect with people. A few minutes later the room emptied, and I wound up standing alone in the middle of it with three business cards in my hand.

I scratched my head and asked myself, "What just happened here?!" Tickets were expensive, and the place had been packed. While this had been a good day for the event producer, it was, for a guest like me, a total disaster. Suddenly, I had a realization: no one had made sure that attendees got what they paid for! Surely, we could do better!

I'm originally from Cameroon, Western Africa, and this focus on doing better has long been part of my vocabulary.

When I was 10 years old, my teacher, Ms. Rose – one of the boldest people I have ever met—took me and another student and moved us up to the next class, mid-way through our last year in primary school. Ms. Rose had thought we could do better, and fortunately, we did. Later I learned that her action had almost started a local war. She had had to get the principal, the parents, and the teacher to agree to that move, showing their approval by signing an agreement on paper. In that last school year, the other "accelerated" student and I had to take two national exams and pass both to get accepted into secondary school. I never really fathomed the effects, influence, and impact this would have on me as a child.

I spent eight months a year in boarding school while I was an adolescent. There I was surrounded by other students and teachers pretty much 24/7.

One Christmas break, I returned home to my family and told my mother about the bad things a couple of students had done to me. And, I added, "When I return, I'm going to..." I never got the chance to finish my sentence.
My mother interrupted me by asking:
"What period of the year are we at?"

"The end of the year," I replied.

"Don't you think that since we are starting a new year, you should just put that behind and start anew?" she asked.

I was dumbfounded because that was not what I had been expecting, I was thinking she would "be on my side." I did not say a word after she spoke, but I can remember that incident even today as if it happened moments ago. My mother's words made a lasting and profound impact on me. My mother expected me to do better. And so I did.

During those years in secondary boarding school, I was *constantly* in contact with other human beings. I heeded what my mother taught me and learned to communicate, connect, and deal with people of all types of personalities and characteristics. At that time, I did not see that whole experience as a learning experience. Only much later, did I realize, understand, and appreciate the value of it.

At age 15, I moved to Paris, France, where I finished high school and earned admission into the prestigious "Ecole National Supérieure des Beaux-Arts," or, as it is known in English, "The National School of Fine Arts." This is one of the most respected and influential art schools in the world and I felt deeply the profound privilege of being able to study architecture there. Paris is a beautiful cosmopolitan city where people from all over the world congregate and communicate. As an architecture student, I studied hard and walked the cobblestoned streets of this vast and graceful city. I stared up at the artistically built walls of old and time-worn buildings that coexisted with bold, modern ones. Paris is a city where the old and the new merge in a mutually beneficial relationship. So many great builders of the past had built on the work of previous generations to create ever more impressive places for people to live, work, and entertain themselves.

In Paris, I had the opportunity, again, to meet and speak with all manner of different kinds of people. While pursuing my studies I took a job in an architectural office. Things went well, and I learned a lot. One thing I did not enjoy, however, was a habit prevalent in architecture schools and businesses that was called "Charette." It basically means leaving the bulk of the work to be done only a few days before a project's due date. This creates a situation where students and architects alike wind up working around the clock, often for three days or more. It makes students and architects look strong to themselves. Perhaps it gives them a "macho" feeling.

I didn't need this kind of anxiety in order to feel fully embodied in my masculinity. I like things organized. Staying up for days just did not appeal to me at all. And I knew people could do better. So, I vowed to myself that I would study organization in the future so I could get things done properly and in a timely, efficient fashion.

Eventually, I moved to Florida, USA, and spent 10 years working in administrative positions where I became steeped in the laws of administration. Administration is a very organized discipline. After that, inspired by the idea of becoming an entrepreneur, I moved to Northern Virginia and started my own business.

The problem was that I did not know anyone there. Running a business means you need a community of people to whom you can present your business, products, and services. Then I had the idea of joining a local chamber of commerce, where I was able to make some positive connections. Many chamber members kindly invited me to other events where I could make additional contacts. One of these was the disastrous $150 networking event that had left me confused and disappointed.

I kept attending these networking events because there didn't seem many options available but in truth, I was not happy with the whole scene. I was feeling something was not quite right, but I couldn't put my finger on what it was.

Could I do any better?

I needed more information.

So, I went to numerous business owners and professionals and surveyed them. I asked them the following questions:

1. When you go to a Networking Event, what would you like to see happening?
2. When you go to a Networking Event, what don't you want to see happening?

I tallied their responses and used that data to create a regular series of networking events that were exclusively focused on the things these people wanted.

Called the "Breakfast Club," the event quickly became very popular and I have run it now for more than 16 years. Some of our attendees have been coming regularly since we started, and we are continuously bowled over by the rave reviews new attendees give us. In fact, in all the time we've been running the event, we have never had a single request for a refund, and I'm gratified that attendees have found value in the events we host.

There was still something missing, however, something I hadn't yet identified. For over a decade, the people coming to the Breakfast Club had been asking me to write a book and create a course on networking. I never did this because I saw books on the subject in bookstores and libraries. What more could I add to the field? Could I do it better?

Eventually, I created another survey for business people and I asked them the following questions:

1. Do you drive a car?
   To which most people replied, "Yes."

2. How did you learn how to drive?
   The answers were:
   a. "I went to a driving school."
   b. "Someone taught me 'how-to,' or
   c. All of the above.

3. Do you network or attempt to network?
   a. "Oh yes."

4. How did you learn how to Network?
   a. "Eu, eu... I just walked into the room."
   b. "Someone pushed me into the room."

Clearly, people were not being trained to network effectively. Nor did there appear to be the slightest degree of organization inherent in anyone's "system" for networking.

We wouldn't take a set of car keys, hand them to a 16-year old and say to him, "Go ahead, drive." But that is pretty much the deal we all got when it comes to networking.

Three things were now crystal clear:

1. People want to learn about networking
2. They have never been trained on how to do this in an organized fashion
3. They would like to do it better.

I've looked up the definition of "Networking" in dictionaries before and I've found them to be incorrect. In fact, if you were to apply what a dictionary suggests you do in order to network effectively, you would fail. In actual fact, networking sits squarely at the foundation of relationship development, and becoming an expert in this area this helps to dramatically improve social and familial relationships, as well as business results. Effective networking can benefit anything a person does.

You could say people have never been taught how to network because the subject has never really been codified before. This also means that the information that is out there is, at best, a roster of "successful actions" and at worst, "opinions." If people had workable networking know-how available to them, I reasoned, they wouldn't have been clamoring for assistance with the topic for so many years.

Understanding and grasping the true state of affairs, I went to work, using everything I had learned in 40 years of experience in Africa, Europe, and North America. I put together a workable networking body of knowledge that spells out:

1. The Cardinal Rules of Networking
2. The purpose of networking
3. The correct networking mindset
4. A workable definition of networking, and
5. The five keys to successful networking

With that, networking has now come into its own, and it is a science. The Small Business Administration (SBA) reports decade after decade that 95% of the businesses in the United States do not make it through their first five years. That saddens me because when you get right down to it, a business has two main functions:

1. Delivering a product or service.
2. Acquiring customers.

The first function is not much of a challenge for most businesses. The second, however, is, and it remains a problem due to the lack of workable networking know-how out there in the marketplace. I've devoted most of my working life to untangling the networking needs of entrepreneurs and other small business professionals. If you've been struggling to profit from your valuable networking hours, I urge you to not give up on what's possible. I know you can get better at this!

Are you ready to try?

Basile Lemba teaches small business owners and others to maximize their networking efforts so they can more easily achieve financial success while growing through the personal development opportunities strong relationships can provide.

Realizing that effective networking can dramatically improve people's quality of life, Basile provides consulting services and group programs, and he runs the BL Networking Breakfast Club and the bi-annual BL Small Business Expo where business owners can network, learn, and get results.

Basile Lemba
International Leading Authority in Networking
CEO/Founder of the Networking Institute and BL Networking Breakfast
Executive Producer, Author, Coach, Speaker, Host.
Email: Basile@basilelemba.net Cell: (571) 263 4190

Scan the code above with your smart-phone camera to watch Basile's message.

Or follow this link:
https://youtu.be/Ny1kMWGYQA4

5

"Is This It?"

Often when you think you're at the end of something, you're at the beginning of something else.

~ Fred Rogers

by
Kathy Denise Hicks

Have you ever wondered if there is more to life than what you are living? Just like the other day, I was in the fast-food line to get some lunch. I ordered a large drink, and when I got it, it appeared to be a small. I began thinking, "Is this it? Is this all I get? I thought I ordered a large, and this is not a large!!" I am sure we have all had that feeling of thinking there has to be more. That I deserve a large and not a small. That I am getting ripped off!! This can't be all there is for me and my life. I think about those poor folks on their death beds, wishing they had chosen differently during their lives and thinking about all they will be missing out on.

Throughout my life, I know the thought of "Is this it?" has entered my mind a hundred times, but it pierced my gut one dramatically life-changing day when I thought my time on earth was over. This is the story of how that day affected my life.

We were sitting down to an exquisitely set dinner. Well, it was on the second story of a typical horse barn. The stairs leading up to the loft apartment were wooden and rickety. This particular day was to be a celebration for a number of reasons. I had just arrived back from a European trip, and it was the first game of the World Series. My host had gone to great lengths to prepare this feast.

As we were sitting down to dinner and getting ready to enjoy our first bite, 'it' happened. I say 'it' because, at that particular moment, I didn't know if it was an explosion from an air attack, or gas tank or perhaps a car. During the next 10 seconds, 'it' became clear what was happening. I glanced at my dinner companions, and we each had anxious, questioning looks on our faces. Movement of the whole floor began - side to side. I noticed a hanging crystal on the window and fully expected either the crystal or the window would shatter.

My heartbeat out of my chest and my mind raced with abnormal thoughts, such as, "Am I going to get out of this? Is someone going to find us buried in this barn?" And the question many probably ask on their death beds, "Is this it?"

My attention snapped back to the life-altering moment. Our dinner plates were launched from the table, recently filled wine glasses shattered on the floor, and appliances toppled over from the sheer force of the rocking motion of the wooden building. Ten seconds of pure terror felt like an eternity. My thoughts continued, "I haven't even married yet, started my new job out of college, nor have I had a chance to be a mom. How can this be all there is for my life? There has to be more!" I then had the unthinkable thought, "Am I going to die? Maybe someone will revive me." And of course, "I don't want to die! There has to be more!"

The day was unusually hot and still. The baseball game was between two rivals that hadn't played against each other in the World Series "forever". The time the quake hit was 5:04 pm, which would have been during rush hour traffic, but because of the Series, there was no traffic on the freeways. It was an abnormal day that changed everything about the way I saw life.

We had tried to get up from our seats during the shaking, but it was impossible to move. Frozen in our seats we rode out the earthquake. The shaking finally stopped, and we glanced at each other with adrenaline pumping through our veins. Our first impulse was to jump up and run to the door, but we felt pinned down from the weight of the shock. In the space of probably 20 seconds, we dislodged the debris blocking the door and scrambled down the damaged stairs. We bolted to the open-air just in time to feel an aftershock. Being at a working ranch countryside, we found a field away from fallen structures and stopped to collect ourselves and try to process what had happened.

My mind rejoiced that we had survived this nightmare of a natural disaster, but little did I know, my personal nightmare was just beginning.

All was well, or so I thought, until the recurring nightmare began haunting me, night after night. It was always the same realistic dream. The earthquake would start, the beams in the living room would dislodge and fall, and my roof would open up to show the sky. I found myself waking up several times a night, walking into the living room, seeing beams on the floor, and then fully waking up and realizing that I had just been dreaming. At first, I tried to push the effects of the dream aside, but it started occurring throughout the night, interrupting my sleep and ability to think and perform my duties at work.

My mood about my job shifted. I had started my first 'real' job shortly after the earthquake. Excited to have many new things to focus on, I kept busy and distracted for a few weeks. But soon, I began to dread and hate my job because of the stress and lack of sleep. I began to ask myself again, "Is this it?"

Not only that – I began to get anxious about going home and going to sleep. I began to feel depressed and exhausted. I didn't want to sleep and wanted to avoid dreaming the dream. I was determined to stay awake for most of the night and have small naps to avoid any deep sleep that would allow dreams. This went on for about a month, and finally, living life became too difficult. Balancing work and the lack of sleep was overwhelming. I began contemplating suicide as an option to deal with the problem. Thankfully, these thoughts were fleeting. I knew I needed help, and oddly enough, I realized that I again started asking the same question I had asked on the day of the earthquake, "Is this it?" I had wanted a *large* meaningful life but was living a *small*, meaningless life.

Life as I knew it had to change, I couldn't keep living this way. I needed sleep and rest. I needed to have purpose and meaning, and maybe this was most important part of what I needed.

So, I decided to get help. I began to focus outside myself. There had to be someone to help me. I got some counseling and began to unlock several personal issues that kept me isolated and alone. I then joined a support group, which had me work with a sponsor. I began learning about how to have healthy relationships. I finally realized I could actually benefit from outside help. Both of these resources began breathing life into my existence.

The first major epiphany that I embraced from these early interactions with my support team was that I didn't create these problems, and I couldn't solve them all. The earthquake was a natural disaster. I didn't cause that. My reaction to the earthquake was predicated from how I had dealt with stress from childhood. I had had night terrors my whole life. It was just a fact of life.

Knowing that I didn't cause this problem, and I couldn't cure it, freed me from thinking I had to figure everything out. My whole life had been spent trying to figure everything out and appear perfect, free from worries and trouble. What a huge relief it was to discover I *didn't* have to be perfect and know everything.

The next idea that I began to accept was to allow myself to believe in something bigger than myself. Call it creator, universe, or energy source, but I had to have something to put my faith in. I was raised in a formal faith system, so this concept wasn't new to me. I had decided at this point to disregard any religious training I had been introduced to at a young age. But deep down I needed to know I was put on the earth for a reason. I needed to know that what I do matters. That what I feel, and think is important and that I could make a difference in the world. I will never forget the peace that I experienced when I decided to trust that the universe was designed to have me in it. That I was a part of an unfolding plan and that I was co-creating the divine vision of my life. I started to have dreams that I could participate in creating a life of purpose and meaning.

As I grew and changed, I also began personal development habits like prayer and meditation. This discipline not only helped my spiritual awakening but also helped alleviate the nightmares. They return occasionally, and I have many crazy and humorous stories about my dreams. For the most part, I am empowered in my dreams and am able to interpret many of them or at least have support to guide me if I have struggles in this area.

During this process, I slowly learned to like who I was and who I was becoming. I will never forget the day I looked in the mirror and actually realized those self-loathing feelings and thoughts were gone. They had slowly subsided as I began realizing that I was important and was contributing to others around me. As those around me really began to see the real me and acknowledge the value they saw in me, I eventually began to see and acknowledge that value in myself.

This has been a slow process and may never be over, but I gained huge progress when I started helping and serving others. I became aware of how my story affected and helped others. That by embracing all of my experiences and sharing them with others about how I overcame difficult circumstances, others were inspired to keep going. I taught at women's groups and homes, and they began having successes. I became so encouraged and full of life.

Lastly, having explored the question "Is this it?", I have been given a new and exciting life. I am free to dream about the future again. Just like a child who knows no limitations, I have started to envision a life with a new purpose. I am so hopeful and optimistic. My desire for you, as you ask the question, "Is this it?", is for you to hear a resounding "NO!". There is always more to learn, more room to grow, more love to share, more ways to be, and more opportunities to contribute to the world. You are uniquely designed and created to exhibit your unique gifts and talents to the world. Being you, and allowing others to experience you, brings *more* to the world. I encourage you to let your real self be known and loved, allowing the world to be a fuller and richer place with your contribution.

> *"The flower that blooms in adversity is the rarest and most beautiful of all."*
>
> *~ Walt Disney - Mulan*

Kathy Denise Hicks, a California transplant from Texas, is a lifelong entrepreneur/writer who recently pivoted from Civil Engineering to build an online fitness and health business. She uses her engineering background to help many create their dream body through science.

As a personal trainer/corrective exercise specialist, Kathy chases her dream of helping others accomplish wellness goals such as being pain-free, having more energy, and attaining their ideal weight.

Kathy Denise Hicks
Email: kathy@blueprintfitness.net
Web: https://blueprintfitness.net/
Facebook: https://www.facebook.com/coach.khicks
Instagram: https://www.instagram.com/aussiehicks/?hl=en
Linkedin:https://www.linkedin.com/in/kathy-denise-hicks-12138262/

Scan the QR code with your smartphone to see Kathy's video message.

Or, follow this link:
https://vimeo.com/422615651

6

The Downside of Getting Rich Quick

··· ✦ ✦ ✦ ···

Money often costs too much. ~ Ralph Waldo Emerson
An investment in knowledge pays the best interest.

~Benjamin Franklin

An investment in knowledge pays the best interest and
then using it pays the most money.

~ Carolyn CJ Matthews

by
Carolyn CJ Matthews

Did you ever play that game with your friends, "What is the first thing you would do if you won the lottery"? I'm sure we've all thought about it when the big lotto prizes are in the news. It's the "If I won $1,000,000" question. Or nowadays it's probably more like $10,000,000 since a million dollars just doesn't go as far as it used to! Just imagine if you did win $10,000,000 or $20,000,000. TWENTY MILLION DOLLARS!!! What IS the first thing you would do?

A lot of people say things like, "Quit my job, pay off my house, go on vacation, buy a new car." What most people don't say is, "Pay taxes, protect it, and educate myself on how to hire professionals who will go make more money with my money, so it doesn't dissipate away." Don't feel bad if you didn't think that either. Just like you, it's only because they don't know what they don't know. They haven't really experienced it or known someone who has.

Those poor suckers who won the lottery don't know that they instantaneously went straight into the Danger Zone of problems and financial predators, including financial professionals with private agendas, con-men that target you, and sadly our own government's complicated tax laws that whittle it away. Not to mention friends and family members, including some you haven't heard from in ages, guilting you into borrowing money (with no plans to pay it back).

The worst part is that it doesn't even take a million dollars for these things to happen. Just being a moderate success, earning six figures or more a year, and BOOM—suddenly you fall into that Danger Zone of losing money, watching it disappear, and not knowing how to stop it. How do I know? Because it happened to me.

No, I didn't win the lottery, and it sure as hell wasn't $20 million. It was only in the $1-million range – but it was enough to fix a lot of money problems and cause a whole new set of money problems that I never saw coming and wasn't prepared for. We see it in tabloids and never think it could happen to us, but it does, and more often than you think. The family strife and infighting, the strange and unexpected loneliness and guilt about having more money than your financially struggling friends, the con-men, the host of professionals who really are not looking out for your best interest, and of course, surprising tax laws that you didn't even know existed and are not in your favor, isn't just limited to the celebrity gossip channels.

When you get any kind of significant money (the definition of significant will depend on you), you immediately level-up to a new playing field and along with it a different set of rules you don't have any practice with. It's kinda like knowing how to play a sport because you read a book about it, and then someone throws you in the professional game overnight. If you were not aware of the Danger Zone or even saw it coming, then it can be a very steep learning curve, like what happened to me.

You are probably curious about my lottery story. What it was like to have enough money to quit my job, buy a new car, pay off the house, take a vacation, and live my dreams (at least for a little while). Mine wasn't quite as nice as winning the lottery. You see, someone had to die for me to receive that money. Yes, I inherited. The crazy thing was that I knew it was coming, thought I had prepared perfectly, *and still wasn't prepared and fell into the Danger Zone!* We thought we had dotted the 'I's' and crossed the 'T's', but really it was a drop in the bucket of what we **should have** been prepared for. We just didn't know what we didn't know, and I had to find out the hard way, by the school of hard knocks.

First a little background. I was raised with my maternal grandparents in San Francisco and Marin County after my parents divorced when I was four. My family wasn't uneducated by any means. My grandfather was extremely smart (Magna Cum Laude, University of North Dakota), a hard-working accountant, stockbroker, and a trainer for Dale Carnegie. My grandmother, beautiful, shrewd, and sharp as a tack, was an immigrant from a formerly wealthy family. She had been allowed to immigrate during World War 2 because the US was looking for women who could work. She sewed parachutes, put wicks in bombs, and after meeting my grandfather, took English classes so they could communicate. She became a stay at home mom and hairdresser. They were classic working middle-class Americans for their time. They had saved their way to wealth, and along with my grandfather's company retirement (and gold watch) and his military retirement, they went into their Golden Years completely secure.

When my grandfather died, it was very well planned, much more so than most people – the funeral service paid for, plot picked out, and my grandmother financially taken care of – except for one little thing. No one in my family had needed to pay attention to making the money make money. My grandfather was the one with those skills. He had created the plan, and we never talked about it. His plan was the traditional 'live off the interest of the capital, and if it doesn't make any money, dip into the nest egg, spend it down, and hope you don't run out of money before you die' system. Of course, in the end, the big plan was to leave whatever was left over to the kids as you went over the rainbow.

Now I'm going to share a family secret, and before I say it, I'm going to also say I love my mom. There is something about my mom that doesn't allow her to do adulting very well. Basically, it's very high anxiety, which may have been caused by a traumatic brain injury when she was about 8 years old. She has had this issue most of her life. The hardest for her is that it doesn't allow her to make 'major' decisions easily, if at all. To add to the problem, she also doesn't want to take any suggestion you give her after she asks, because it overwhelms her. Things as simple as picking paint colors or tile can be agonizing for her with anxiety, causing her to literally take months to make a decision and sometimes not at all. So, you can imagine how it would be for her in even normal but stressful life situations, like buying a car or making a larger financial decision like deciding where to invest money.

My grandparents knew this, but they came from a time where any kind of potentially "shameful" issue was kept locked away and never spoken about. Today it's a completely different attitude—this type of anxiety is openly discussed and admitted to amongst strangers along with what latest medications work the best for them. But in my grandparents' day, it was hushed. So, they planned an additional part of their legacy – enough money for my mother to be taken care of into her old age.

The last 14 years of my grandmother's life was spent protecting that legacy, however, she feared and had guilt that she wouldn't do a good job. So, she tapped me for support when she began finding her way through the miasma of financial learning to grow and protect that money. We searched for answers, even though the financial world changed drastically. E-Trade was breaking into the market, but many people didn't have computers yet. New alternative investment products came out, or old financial products were used in a new or different way (like life insurance as your own bank), tax codes were changing all the time, and there was so much we just didn't know.

Remember, we didn't really have Google yet, where you could have the answers you needed at the tip of your fingers with reviews and comments to help you make a good decision. We didn't have any connections to even ask – I mean ZERO – so we had to open the phone book, make appointments, interview potential advisors, and then take the risk that they were telling the truth. Frankly, we didn't even know where to start except at a bank, which we later figured out *wasn't* a good place to start. It wasn't like either of us had been in business for ourselves, nor did we really know anyone who had.

Over time, we got a family attorney who specialized in trusts and taxes. We had to find a CPA and create a relationship to figure out taxes and a broker who would help us with buying and selling stock. In the process, we needed to learn how to decide to keep or sell stocks that we knew nothing about. Slowly, we found our way out of the dark. As we went through this process, my grandmother discovered she had cancer, went through chemo, remission, cancer again, remission, and then, sadly, it came back, and she just couldn't kick it. Like I said, we were prepared and ready, or so we thought.

When my grandmother died, it was in a hospital with family surrounding her. We were devastated and grieving. I was in a daze through the funeral and burial, and as I went back to sit in her house that she had lived in for 60 years, I thought that we were settled and would be financially fine with all that inheritance. But that's not what happened.

My first inkling of trouble was my mom letting me know she was upset that the estate was being split evenly. I wasn't the Trustee, but I was a beneficiary along with her, splitting the estate directly down the middle. Remember the financial problems we don't know are coming? One of them is family. Money can tear families apart, simply by having more than they are used to but still thinking it's not enough and not 'fairly' distributed. There are ways to fix that, but I didn't know them back then, so the *deep emotional toll of inheriting this money went on for a long time.*

My grandparents and I were very clear that the responsibility fell to me to manage the family money to make sure that my mom had enough to live on for the rest of her life. But they also wanted me to have financial help, since I was a single mom. Besides not being prepared for the family strife, here is the mistake we made, AND IT WAS HUGE! Essentially, we were land rich and cash poor. We had a decent amount of cash, but not enough to pay the estate (death) taxes and have something to live on. Remember, we lived in San Francisco and Marin County – both very, very, expensive for living, and housing was some of the most expensive in the nation. The two houses were worth so much that their value essentially broke our 'bank' when the taxman came calling

In trying to prepare for the eventuality of my grandmother's death, we didn't get that we had to adjust our plan. Unfortunately, we set it and thought everything was fine. Not one of our advisors told us additional or alternative ways to lower or protect against death taxes. They were each very siloed in their fields, with little cross-pollination of expertise.

I was about to pay dearly for that lack of knowledge and protection. I had leveled-up to that new playing field with new rules.

The biggest shock came when the CPA sat me down and showed me the tax bill. Yes, if you have money and you die, you (well, your family) must pay taxes. I'm not sure of the history of the reason for death taxes and how they came into being, but it's ridiculous, and I'm still mad that we must pay them. Here's the thing – if you are poor you don't really have to pay death taxes, and if you are rich, you've been educated, mentored, and already protected, so barely any death taxes are paid. It's the regular hard-working folks who followed the 'system' of getting a job or creating a business, buying a house, and saving some money in investments for retirement who get burned from the surprises. **It's only because they don't know the secret systems of the rich that they could use too.** All my problems would never have happened if I had just known that information.

To fulfill my promise to my grandparents and protect my mom from a disruption in her home and life, sadly, after trying to find ways to keep the house, I ended up selling the family San Francisco home of 60 years. I moved, sold, or gave away everything in it. The process was a dismantling of the lives of loved ones. It was as if there'd been another death in the family. The grief and guilt were intense. The question plagued me, "How did I end up here, selling the home I grew up in, after all that preparation?" It was depressing, and I cried a lot. I felt like a failure.

Selling my grandparents' home covered the cost of the death tax and gave us some extra cash to work with, so that both my mother and I would have something to live on. The intense emotional and financial cost of that experience changed my life and put me on the trajectory of learning as much as I could about the protection options available to people just like you and me. Not the richy-rich and not the poor – the in-betweeners. Successful people with enough money to be in the Danger Zone. Protection from financial predators, exposure from a small car wreck that may not have even been their fault, a health challenge that closes their business, and yes, death taxes. All these things are preventable if you know the strategies that can protect you.

Here is the challenge – just like me when I started this journey, you don't know what you don't know, and I'd like to help you with that. My wonderful partner Robert Bernard and I have collected our mutual knowledge into what we call the S.U.R.F. Program™ and Mastering True Wealth System™. We also do a discovery/analysis call that will help you get clear on what knowledge you may be missing.

At a certain point, you must treat your money as its OWN business. That's right – it's not a hobby or something you just keep in savings or the stock market. You need to get learned, schooled, and educated about you and your specific financial situation. Don't think you need a lot of money saved up to do this. If you have bought a house, if you earn over $100,000 a year, or if you might inherit, this information is invaluable to you.

Life turned out pretty good for me, eventually, but it was a long hard road. Hard for me, hard for my son, and hard on my relationships. And it could have been so much better with just a bit more knowledge. My wish for you is that you get the knowledge you need to have and protect the most magnificent life for you, your family, and your future. May this information help you on your journey to the life of your dreams.

Carolyn 'CJ' Matthews is a co-founder of YourSmartWealth.com, a coaching and consulting company helping 6-figure entrepreneurs keep more money and protect their wealth from financial pitfalls so they can retire faster, smarter, and wealthier

Using proven integrative strategies of the rich that most small business owners don't know or have the time to learn YourSmartWealth.com gets you to financial freedom fast with the S.M.A.R.T. Ultimate Retirement Formula (S.U.R.F.)™ only found in their Master True Wealth System™.

Carolyn CJ Matthews
Email: team@yoursmartwealth.com
Website: YourSmartWealth.com
LinkedIn: linkedin.com/company/yoursmartwealth/
Facebook: facebook.com/yoursmartwealth/
Twitter: @YoursmartWealth

Scan the QR Code with your smartphone to view Carolyn's video message.

Or, follow this link:
bit.ly/SURFCoupon

7

The Face of Industry 4.0

· · · ◆ ◆ · · ·

"Pain is inevitable, suffering is optional."

by
Behnaz Gholami

Have you ever looked at the workday yawning in front of you and wished you could feel at least a little excited about the tasks that lie ahead?

Has the uncomfortable feeling that your work is not meaningful *enough* ever crawled up your spine and taken up residence in your mind?

Have you ever caught yourself yearning, a little wistfully perhaps, that your work could be more fun and colorful?

Well, you are not alone.

Corporations everywhere are full of people who feel disconnected from who they truly are and what they could be doing in the world. And they are full of people who are terrified of asking themselves if their life, in general, has meaning.

I know this because I was one of those people.

One dark winter morning as I was preparing for work, I stood at the stylish bathroom sink in my ensuite bathroom, washed my face, and held my breath as I looked up and suddenly caught a glimpse of myself in the mirror. The woman staring back at me on this quiet day was a stranger and I realized, with a shock, that it had been a long time since I had seen myself for who I truly was. I looked at the curve of my cheekbones and the worry lines forming along my forehead. I saw pretty dark eyes that looked dull and serious, and not even the hint of a smile lit my face. Where had the real me gone? When had she been replaced by this solemn imposter?

"Who is this girl?" I whispered. And, more to the point, I wondered, "Who am I?"

The endless work-day stretched out beyond this chance meeting with the stranger in the mirror and when I finally fell into bed late that night, I cried silently for hours. Floods of grief-stained tears poured from my body. I felt I had become a dead soul struggling to animate a living body and I was terribly confused! Why the hell was I even feeling like this? Where was this tsunami of emotion coming from?

Like many women the world over, my entire life up until this point had been about being a good girl. I had tried hard to adhere to what the community around me told me I should do. I come from a religious community and a disciplined family. Growing up, approval and comfort stemmed from how well I could respect and obey the laws, regulations, and benchmarks that were standing by ready to judge how "good" or "bad" I was. As a child, I had an effervescent personality and a rebellious nature that conflicted with expectations of how a girl should be. Could I ever win the approval of the people who considered these standards important? For me, it was very tough.

At the moment of my birth, my country was being torn apart by war and the city where my parents lived was being bombarded. It was a traumatic time for many and in the turbulent war-soaked years of my childhood, girls could not laugh loudly, and boys would not cry, even quietly. They called us war kids.

Despite all that, I was fortunate to have a relatively safe childhood, marked, though it was, by religious and moral debates, and restrictions on what one "should" be doing.

From the early years of middle school onward, I felt an urge to change things at school. I had so many creative ideas! I was a playful girl who loved colors. I loved group activities and dancing and singing. I was quite a rebel on the inside, yet a good student even so. As my personality evolved, I kept coming up with new ideas to improve my surroundings. But as time went on, I stopped pushing the limits and stayed more within socially acceptable boundaries.

My teenage years were a time of restriction. I was taught that satisfaction in life was only available to those who adhered to particular social and religious rules, who competed with others over the country's limited resources and opportunities, and who, ultimately, beat everyone else in the high stakes games of success being waged at every turn.

I began suppressing my natural effervescence and became quieter, seeking more and more approval. I tried hard to tame my rebellious soul. Such a conflict this created within me! Many of my family members were rebels as well, although they were conservative people who were comfortable staying within their legitimate boundaries.

I did not have much choice over the clothes I wore to high school and university classes. I remember the rule was that we could wear only dark colors and hefty fabrics. I remember once I was banned from my math class because I had decided to wear white clothing!

Girls were not supposed to draw attention to themselves, and we were supposed to be humble and unnoticed in society. Pretty, colorful clothes were signs of vanity and arrogance. I was quite a tall girl but tried to bend while I was walking, so I could remain as invisible as possible to society's judgmental eyes. For many years of my life, I did not know how it felt to have the wind play joyfully with my long silky black hair or to feel the sun kissing skin I did not have to hide. The boundaries of what constituted a "normal" life for me were dictated by my community's rules about how I *should* be, what I *should* do.

My circumstances were really not so unusual when you think about it. People in every culture in the world are heavily influenced by what passes for normal in their immediate family and community.

This all becomes worse in workplaces and corporate cultures. Humans are reduced to human resources and are treated like any other business resource. To survive in this environment, people feel they need to seek approval and play it safe. The path to success is usually reduced into specific steps, behaviors, politics, and performance. To be successful and accepted, people really have no choice but to stick to what the system wants. There is less room, generally, for thinking outside the box. Likewise, business systems, services, and processes are not designed to serve people and enhance their experiences, but to define how people behave.

Even years before I was to become a corporate employee, however, the "normal" in my life rarely made room for what I needed, what I wanted, and where I felt my path should lead me. Looking back upon those years now I realize I was quite a brilliant student. I tended to ask "why?" a lot and I doubted many of the rules and beliefs that were presented to me as truths. But honestly, the desire to be seen as a "good" girl was more potent than finding answers to my questions. And somewhere along the line, without realizing it, I left my true self behind on the way to adulthood. I stopped sparkling and asking "why?" And I stopped looking in mirrors.

My family unconditionally approved of my decision to pursue my education outside of the country, for which I was grateful. I wanted to change the world by becoming a scientist. This was the most legitimate path for a rebel! Earning a Ph.D. was the ultimate path to becoming a scientist and changing the world, and the journey took me more than a decade. I kept moving forward and looking ahead. I was in stinging competition with the entire world, which was nothing new for me since my home culture had pitted people against everyone each other in the drive for scarce resources and even scarcer approval. I had the added motivation of wanting to prove that nothing is impossible for a girl from the Middle East.

It was inevitable that 12 years spent careening competitively through the gauntlet of learning, adapting, and achieving, would steer me back onto a path of questioning what I had thought to be true in life. I had a Ph.D., I lived and worked on four continents and I racked up many achievements of which I was proud; I traveled the world. I sat with many so-called important people in business and science, many CEOs, vice-presidents in Fortune 500 companies, and top scientists from top business schools. I attended and presented at many significant conferences and gatherings in my field. I was successful.

And yet there was a void within me which caught me off guard: despite my successes, I did not feel seen and understood in my place of work. My deepest needs for authentic recognition were still unmet. As it turned out, I had not changed the world by becoming a scientist. I felt bitter, angry, and disappointed most of the time. I felt that I did not fit in. I had not been a good fit in my Homeland because of a rebellious soul that questioned many beliefs and systems. I did not fit in other countries and other workplaces because I felt that I was not "one of them." I was either too soft, too feminine, too happy, too subjective, or too creative. I wanted to enhance human experiences at work. I wanted to bring color and fun back to the workplace. I was a square peg in a round hole. But as usual, I was inclined to suppress myself, so I would be at least minimally welcomed in my surroundings.

Living in different countries, I managed to partially live my authentic self, outside of my work. But work and career are key parts of my life: I live through my working days. I could not help but seek meaningfulness in my work every time I opened my eyes to start a day. I came to realize that I was no longer craving other people's approval but rather was I craving *empathy*. I wanted to be seen for who I really was. The nature of my work repeatedly drew attention to the nature of human beings in the workplace. It drew attention to our humanity. But few decision-makers in any of the corporations in which I worked seemed to care about these important heart-based topics.

I realized I had grown tired of fancy business slogans, organizational reports, and articles about humane organizations, all of which remained little more than words on paper. I was tired of quick strategic fixes and superficial plans.

After the day when I looked at myself heroically in the mirror and saw no-one there, I experienced a dark period of passiveness and grief. And then I decided to begin a journey of self-discovery. I reviewed all the happy moments I had experienced during a decade's journey around the world. I meditated, went to therapy sessions, studied many books and articles, changed my diet, changed my workout routine, and started practicing gratitude for small things in my life. I tried to face my fears, stand up for myself, speak up, and take responsibility for everything that happened to me. I began to defer to my intuition and focused on what made me and the people around me happy. I started to reflect on the changes in my workplaces.

I realized that the times when I had felt authentic and happy in my workplaces had been times of co-creating solutions for important business problems with employees, customers, and stakeholders. They had been times when I had been able to speak up and share my perspective and my beliefs. Or when I had listened carefully to what people really needed and wanted. They had also been times when I had learned from my mistakes and dogmas and changed the way I worked. I remembered the moment I had designed a service that generated 90% uptake among customers. I had also curated a strategic workshop for thousands of employees, which many people acknowledged had been the most creative and effective workshop of their lives. I had changed a system that helped the business increase its ROI by focusing on human experience and satisfaction. On another occasion, after years of struggle, I had helped a leader resolve a complex issue in their business. And there had been that time I had been able to inject meaningfulness into the heart of a corporation by leveraging human sciences, gamification, design, and mindfulness.

In short, the best moments of my work life had been times of discovery, co-creation, collaboration, iteration, learning, and course correction.

I realized that every single person has the right to speak up and tell everybody what they think and need. Employees, stakeholders, and customers need a genuine, empathetic listening process and some help with course-correcting. People need to be treated as people, not money-making machines. I realized that I had been reduced to a money-making machine. And, in reality, the meaning of life pretty much depends on how each of us feels doing our job and contributing to the world.

I strongly believe that businesses cannot merely put human beings in a crystal frame and ask them to shape and grow and be productive and engaged. We all need to be discovered. This belief helped me discover my calling: to help people be their whole and best selves at work as they manage change, and to help businesses grow, and save millions of dollars by enhancing human experiences. My mission is to bring human sciences and design into organizations and make the world a better place to live, especially in the industry 4.0 era so people can reach their full potential, and businesses can benefit from the extraordinary power of humanization.

I am thriving as I deliver on my mandate. My creativity has returned. There are many creative ways to enable people in corporations to blossom and grow, and I have committed myself to put human beings first in everything I do in my workplace consulting. People need to be discovered and respected for who they are so we can have more engaged employees and customers, and we can have more successful businesses. I am not squelching myself anymore, and I have empowered myself to help others, leveraging the strength I gained through my personal journey and the knowledge and skill from my education and work experience. I now like the person I see in the mirror.

Whether you are a professional, an employee, an entrepreneur, or a leader I invite you to ask yourself whether you have been suppressing vital aspects of who you are, just as I used to do. Does the person looking back from your mirror truly reflect all you have it in you to be? Are you excited about your workdays? And, more importantly, can you take your full self to work? Are the services, systems, and processing in your organization effectively working? If the answers to these questions do not thrill you, then maybe it's time to look a little deeper. Maybe it's time for a change so you can thrive too.

Dr. Behnaz Gholami is a social scientist and researcher, a service designer, and a change strategist. She is internationally experienced in successfully developing and implementing organizational change management strategies and other business services based on human-centered design and multidisciplinary pragmatic methods and scientific approaches such as design thinking, neuroscience, and psychology, gamification, mindfulness, and workplace design. Her mission is to put human needs and desires at the center of all business practices.

Behnaz Gholami
https://dizengroup.com/
https://humansideacademy.com
https://www.linkedin.com/in/drbehnazgholami/
https://twitter.com/DrBehnazGholami
https://medium.com/@drbehnazgholami

Scan the QR code with your smartphone to watch Behnaz's video message.

Or, follow this link:
https://youtu.be/W3l5McduIIk

8

Busting Through Barriers

from Bullied Youth to Business Growth Strategist

· · · ◆ ◆ ◆ · · ·

*"There's a little caged bird locked inside of you who wants
to escape from the prison of your existing life and soar like
an eagle to something Better. That bird wants to unleash
you into the full expression of your true potential and
fulfillment in life... you alone hold the key to its Freedom."*

~ David Grinder

by
David Grinder

This story is dedicated to anyone who has ever felt that people are or were "preventing you," "holding you back," or "blocking the path" on your journey... to being fulfilled.

I crawled under the dining room table and clutched my cat while terror seemed to flood through my very veins. I was four years old and alone, and I was ill-equipped to handle the paralysis that came with this all-too-common situation. My dad was a traveling salesman and he was only home on weekends; my mother had mysterious things to do in the big world outside the walls of our Chicago apartment. I don't think either of my parents realized the impact my fear of being found by the "Bad Guys" actually had on me. But whenever I was alone in the apartment, I would be scared out of my mind. Down in the cave the dining room table provided, I would put my arm around my cat, and sit frozen in fear.

I hoped we would be able to survive this ordeal together. My cat was my companion and my protector as we sat and hoped the Bad Guys wouldn't see us, although I feared they would probably hear my heart pounding or my body shaking. I don't know what I would've done all those days if the cat hadn't been there with me.

When you're completely alone, in those dark times, not knowing what to do or how things are going to turn out... Who do you reach out to?

This sense of being alone in the world followed me as I grew up, and I often felt that someone or something was always trying to prevent me from being happy or getting what I wanted. It wasn't just one event that made me feel that way; it was the way my entire life unfolded. Maybe you've felt that sense of always having to fend for yourself, too. In school, it seemed like I was always on the outside looking in, and I never felt part of the group. I was verbally and physically bullied – constantly.

In Kindergarten and First Grade, a much larger older boy would run by me every morning as I was walking to school and push me down. At the end of every school day, my next-door neighbor—a much older kid—would be waiting back at home to terrorize and threaten me. I hated going to school—knowing the bully would be coming—but there was no escaping it. I couldn't avoid the bully outside my front door, either. Not having a father by my side every day to teach or mentor me, I didn't know what to do or how to be.

As a five-year-old. I just accepted the situation. I was going to have to endure whatever life threw at me. This belief stayed with me for years.

One day, my dad announced he was changing jobs and we would be moving to rural central Wisconsin. I would finally be free of the bullies I had been unable to vanquish! Mere days before we moved, the next-door bully got chickenpox. I summoned all the courage I could muster from the depths of my seven-year-old heart and went and stood outside the picture window at the front of his house. I stood there, separated from him by a thin pane of glass, and I watched as he cursed and threatened me, his face all broken out with the ugly red blotches of his condition.

This was my chance for a little payback! I walked closer and closer to the window until I was just a couple of feet away. I raised my arm and pointed at my nemesis, and then I began to laugh, loudly and hysterically. His cursing changed to death threats, which was fine with me – the window protected me, just like the cat had done years earlier. I had stood up to the bully and I'd be gone before he could get me.

Despite that one moment of victory, the bullying followed me throughout grade school. I was punched and yelled at for being a "city slicker." One boy, wanting to help me, advised me that I just wasn't cool and he offered to steer me in the right direction. Being "cool" and fitting in was one way I could stand up to bullying.

The strategy didn't work perfectly, however.

Later, in high school, when I was talking to a friend at a party and feeling relatively "cool," a bully sucker-punched me several times, right in the face. My head twanged back and forth with the weight of his blows...fortunately the few drinks I'd had helped numb the pain. Out of the blue, a State Champion wrestler grabbed my attacker, lifted him up, and threw him across the room. I had never met this guy before, but for some reason, he had decided to step up and protect me. I was speechless…my "cat" protector had become a "lion."

Over the years that followed, there would always be a bully wanting to fight me, threaten me, steal from me, damage my possessions, or get me fired. But mysteriously, someone was often there to support me…a teacher, someone's brother, a friend, a stranger.

Once, though, a co-worker actually tried to kill me. While on a job site one day, I saw something out of the corner of my eye come hurtling towards me: it was a 5'-long pointed metal bar that slashed through the air like a spear. It would've gone right through me if I hadn't turned, a split second before impact. It missed me. The boss went on to fire me over the incident, telling me I was upsetting people. I couldn't believe it! I had been minding my own business, and working hard, but the crazies had won again. It seemed like I was never able to catch a break from the hound of Hell that was after me. I was convinced there was a target on my back, that Somebody was trying to snuff me out. I was not going to survive, and the bird caged up inside me was never going to be set free.

What do you do, when you feel trapped, that what you want in life is being denied you… when happiness and prosperity just don't seem attainable?

I got a new job working for a delivery company and, as before, I set myself the task of being the hardest worker there, knowing promotions and raises were inevitable if I just kept at it. I was bound to catch a break. I was certain, *this* was my breakthrough job! One day at work, the boss called me into his office. He said he had to watch the numbers and had decided to cut my hours and hire an additional part-time person. Two part-time people would ensure I had no overtime, it was cheaper for the company. "All this, over a few hours of over-time."

I was devastated. My job performance and the value I brought to the company were of no concern. I couldn't believe it! I felt I was being pushed down and held back yet again! There's no way this was happening! I was barely paying my bills; part-time hours would be the end of me. This finally broke me. I was in my own twilight zone, not sensing the world around me. I spent two hours trying to work while my head was in a daze, but I was too full of anger and frustration, I couldn't focus. Completely unable to work, I just stopped.

We're taught to get an education, get a job, and work hard, and that one day it will pay off. Well, it didn't.

I thought back on all the jobs where I had believed that working hard would bring success. Somehow, something was always getting in the way of my payoff. Struggling seemed to be inevitable. Success was always being choked out of me. I'd been hearing "NO" for years now. No promotion, no raise, no appreciation, no escape. I couldn't buy a house or a newer car, nor afford a vacation. Everything was an ordeal.

This was the last straw. I finally came back to the present and said to myself in anger: "I'm tired of other people being in control of my situation. I'm tired of bullies determining my future. I'm tired of always getting let down. This must end NOW."

I realized that my happiness, my dreams, and my future, were all up to me – that I alone am responsible for my success.

What's more, I thought, a job doesn't fulfill my dreams, a boss isn't responsible for my success, what other people do won't bring me happiness. I must pursue these myself. I came up with a plan. I decided to use the same courage that had fueled seven-year-old me to walk up to

Chickenpox kid's window. I would laugh at these circumstances. I would walk away from this place, and this job, from this emotional stress. I would get another job to pay the bills, then launch my own business, which would put me in control of achieving my dreams. I had a wife and four kids by then, which would make this all very difficult, due to lack of time, but I decided I was going to do this. That I HAD to do this.

After my next delivery stop, I pulled over and took a break. I started calling companies out of the phone book. One business granted me an interview right there over the phone. Within a week, I had a new job, a good one. Step 1 was now accomplished.

The secret to your Freedom is to Decide and then take Massive Action, NOW – that's the Key.

Now for Step 2: start a business focused on something I could be good at and would enjoy. I had always had a passion for electronics and I had studied this complex field at various institutions over many years. I had an aptitude for it, and worked hard at it, so I was almost always at the top of my classes. I loved designing and building things and had even made my own stereo amplifier from scratch. Computers were just coming out at the time, and it was clear to me that networks were going to be a requirement for every business going forward. And electronics were the foundational studies for computers! I had a big head start in the area: I decided to develop a business around computer networks. This would be a perfect fit for me but I would need to enroll in online schooling, so I could keep working and pay the bills.

I found a great computer school with classes I could take remotely. I studied during work breaks, at lunch, at night, and on weekends. I was on a mission. Even my coworkers' harassment over my decision to eat lunch alone didn't bother me. Studies came first. The opinions of others weren't going to distract me. I built my own computer from pieces, then started building computer networks. It was exciting!

I had always felt the real me was trapped in a cage... my soul would cry out, desperately wanting someone to unlock that door so I could break out and soar to my potential. I finally sensed that I might be escaping.

Meanwhile, the job was so good, that I was able to buy a house and get that newer car. It took me one-and-a-half years to fast track my studies, complete all my education and training, and get my initial IT Certifications. I found a mentor and later started a technology business, while continuing my technology and business education.

And who would I serve?

With a history of having been bullied, told "no" at every turn, and always feeling pushed down, I understood business owners' need for a "Protector" to stop the Computer Network Bullies and this became the focus of my business. Everyone who had come to my assistance in the past had generated a desire within me to do the same for others. I couldn't have found a better fit. Past experiences had turned me into a fighter, and now I could combat the issues that wreak havoc on people's business networks. Besides having found a talent match, I had now found my Mission match...something I was passionate about.

Today I help, support, and defend small businesses against the bullies that prevent success... internet, software, and cyber issues, system crashes, the loss of data and revenue due to downtime, and as a result, the loss of a business's reputation. To clients, I've become both "Cat" and "Lion" – supporter and champion – to ensure they stay up, running, and online so they can keep their revenues flowing and their business profitable. Most of all, this enables them to seize opportunities and make advancements without worrying about their technology.

I've worked with some large companies and government agencies and some of what I learned corporately highlighted the root causes and blind spots common with all small business owners as well. So, I've created a customized program for small businesses, to help them become more successful and more profitable.

My passion is to always have the best interests of a client in mind, with a focus on executive strategy first; then I align the technology with their business goals. I'm enormously fulfilled in the work I do today. But it took me getting to the point of saying "Enough is Enough" to transform my mindset.

What changed my game was this: I made a decision, then I took fast action. I stuck to the plan and didn't give up when things got tough.

My past forged the tools I needed to be an entrepreneur...to stand-up, to fight, to go against the grain, and to never give up because "This is just the way it is."

The boy who was alone and paralyzed with fear, who had to fight and claw for everything, is now sought for his valuable insights and foresight. I've grown into someone who brings clarity to companies that are seeking to grow and increase their profits. Fear is no longer part of my experience.

I'm here to stop the bullies in their tracks.

··•♦•··

Special Thanks to all the Protectors (too many to mention) who helped me or had words that encouraged me throughout the years. And to three successive Mentors who helped forge my career, after I made my "Last Straw" mind-shift decision: Todd Risen, Erick Simpson, and Mark S. A. Smith...inspiring me to be more than I am.

David Grinder helps small business owners mitigate the negative impact of system crashes, internet, software, and cyber issues, and the loss of data and revenue due to downtime.

He has developed a customized program for helping small businesses first solidify their executive strategy and then align their tech to support it. If you want to become more successful and more profitable please go ahead and connect with David.

David Grinder
Telephone: 928-388-6058
Email: david@y3kitservices.com
Website: https://www.y3kitservices.com
YouTube: https://www.youtube.com/channel/
UCB4DQFV_dFFd9WB1m_Gv0Dg/videos

Scan the QR Code with your smartphone to watch David's video message.

Or, follow this link:
https://www.youtube.com/channel/
UCB4DQFV_dFFd9WB1m_Gv0Dg

9

Vibrant Leadership

···•◆•◆•◆•···

*I don't know what your destiny will be, but one thing I
know: the only ones among you who will be really happy
are those who will have sought and found how to serve.*

~ Albert Schweitzer

by
Teresa Blount

I finished my morning run and opened the door to my house to be
greeted by the deafening sound of silence. The walls no longer
echoed the sounds of "Mom," the sounds of motherhood that had
expressed so many aspects of my life.

In what seemed only a moment, like the blink of an eye, years had
passed and I had become an empty nester. Where had those years
gone? The children one by one had left and the empty nest was
beginning to feel more like an empty hole. The "What Now?" and
"What Next?" questions that had begun as a whisper were becoming
an ever-increasing roar.

The chaos of busy-ness was giving way to the bottomless pit of emptiness. What was I going to do now? Especially since I had also just closed the business that I had been running for 20 years!

I always knew that the children would leave. And I always wanted them to leave with the freedom and independence to pursue their dreams and find their own unique brand of happiness. I had anticipated the sadness I would feel and even did my best to prepare for Act II of my life.

During their years at home, I had gone to college, earned a degree, founded a fine arts school, and furthered my studies in piano, painting, and dance. I thought I would be prepared for this stage of my life… but I was wrong.

I couldn't understand the dilemma. I had grown up in a military family as the oldest of six children. My childhood life had been about transition, change, and responsibility. Military life had meant moving from one culture to another—usually in the middle of the school year—and being the oldest of six meant that family dynamics were always changing as siblings were added. Military life also meant my dad would be deployed for a year at a time, and extra responsibilities always came my way when he was absent. I was a competent young girl. I could handle almost anything.

When I was 14 years old and in high school my dad was deployed to Korea and the rest of the family moved from Germany to the small American community where my mother had grown up. It was a dramatic move for me. I transitioned out of the largest military school in Europe to a small country school where everybody knew just about everybody else. When my dad returned safely to us a year later, he retired and we moved for a brief time to the unique culture of New Orleans, Louisiana, and then soon back again to small town USA as my dad transitioned to civilian life.

It was a chaotic upbringing that mirrored the inner chaos so common to the years that border adulthood. And I decided somewhere along the way that if I ever had children, I would want to bring as much stability and calm to their lives as I could. I would help them become the greatest version of themselves possible. I would dedicate my life to enhancing theirs.

I met my husband during high school. He had been born in the area and had grown up in a family whose livelihood was tenant farming. And the steady "same" of his life attracted the continual "change" of mine. I had often heard people refer to marriage as "settling down" and I was ready to "settle down," to find calm amidst the chaos. We married while I was still in high school.

My idealized perception of marriage as a reprieve, a place of "calm amidst the chaos" surrendered to the chaos of marriage and motherhood... and the calmness brought by feelings of deep gratitude and love. Becoming a mother was a pivotal experience in my life and I surrendered to the needs of my family and a profound commitment to their wellbeing.

As long as my children were the North Star of my life, I was deeply connected to what mattered most to me. I had something bigger than myself to live for. I had a reason to be on my "A Game."

But with them gone, and also having just recently closed the music school I had run that had been so much a part of their lives, I found myself standing at a crossroads that felt like a dead-end.

As the days turned to weeks I began to feel myself spiraling into a fog of doubt and uncertainty about the future. And I began to look back for what felt familiar and felt safe. The past seemed full of the joy of new discoveries and fresh adventures.

Without realizing it, life was becoming more and more about the way things were, than about how things could become.

Have you ever felt that way too?

And then one day while replaying memories of past successes I heard a Whitney Houston song that has long been a source of inspiration for me. It's the song titled "One Moment In Time" and the lyrics that especially resonated with me in that moment grabbed me by the heartstrings and pulled me to my feet.

Each day I live, I want to be
A day to give the best of me...
...
My finest day is yet unknown.
...
I want one moment in time
When I'm more than I thought I could be..."
And I woke up.
I woke up to the realization that...
I didn't want to just plod on, content to let life just happen to me.
I didn't want my life to be about the way things had been.

I didn't want to stop growing and start feeling "less" – less sure of myself, my dreams, and my purpose.

I wasn't ready to resign myself to "growing old gracefully." I didn't want to accept a diminishing connection and decreasing purpose as the years passed.

I knew I had more to offer, and that if I didn't take control things would not get better. And I also knew that I would never be content to live with the nagging guilt of knowing that I wasn't living my dreams...It just wouldn't be enough.

I realized that these years of my life were not the end of something old... they were the beginning of something new. I adopted a "from this day forward" mindset.

A "from this day forward" mindset that began by looking back, "back to the future." I looked back to find the best way to live forward. And as I looked back, the memories began to inspire hope as they became the springboard for new dreams...dreams! And I found myself facing forward from the very mindset I had begun embracing almost 25 years earlier...

I had become a mother at the age of 18, with nothing but dreams and the determination to be the architect of a framework of "Nothing but the Best" for the tiny first life, and the lives that were soon to follow—my children, who from the beginning believed in me more than I had ever believed in myself.

"Nothing but the best" was not about things my children might possess, but about the opportunities that would be available to them to become the best of whom they were capable of becoming. I realized when they were very young that you can't take someone somewhere that you haven't been... and I knew then that it would take all and everything that I had to become all that I could be for my children's sake, and mine...and it would be so worth it.

As the years passed, my dreams morphed into reality and without realizing it, being a mother led me to develop the skills that would fuel my choices later in life. I stepped into the reality of my children's lives and shared in their experiences. I learned what leadership is.

I wanted to share in the experience of my youngest daughter's passion for art, so I studied art myself. While leaning into that endeavor I painted portraits of all three of my children. I wanted to share my love of music with my children. So I decided to improve my mostly self-taught piano skills by going back to school for a music degree. That led to the beautiful experience of receiving an income from my music school and an adventure that allowed my children to be involved in my work. The opportunities that resulted from this led to the eventual graduation of my oldest daughter from The Juilliard School for the performing arts.

Diving into my parenting experiences also led to the fulfillment of another dream that I had held all through high school. I had wanted so badly to be a cheerleader all those years! And thanks to my son the dream finally came true. He loved playing ball outside with his dad and it was pretty much a nightly occurrence. He wanted a cheerleader and I was finally on the squad... in fact, I was the entire squad. He insisted on it... I only wish they could have played in the back yard instead of the front.

And as I contemplated the past, I realized that being a mother, a teacher, and a business owner had been my platform for learning how to lead others to their greatness. I learned that the true secret of leadership lies not in motivation, but in inspiration and that real leadership is a "done with you" project that honors the principle that people support what they help create. I learned to keep the main thing the main thing and let the important issues trump the urgent ones, whenever possible. And I learned that people are the most important of all. What's more, I learned that people are not broken, and they're not bent...only unfinished. I learned to hold space for others' greatness.

From that wisdom, I realized that what I needed now was a plan, a strategy to reclaim "forward" momentum in my life.

I decided to return to school and finish my graduate studies in counseling and psychology. I knew from past experience that school would provide the structure, support, and accountability that would make commitment easier, and it did.

I went on to obtain my license and opened a counseling practice. One day a colleague in the office asked who my ideal client was. Immediately I knew the answer: it was anyone who had not yet allowed their "issues" to turn into "problems"... It was anyone who wanted to become their best and continue to grow into the next level of their own unique greatness... my ideal client was a coaching client.

I continued to study, research, and experiment. I tried lots of things. Some worked... some didn't. Through the years I discovered the strategies and principles that made the biggest difference, the needle movers. And I designed a process for living an engaged, energetic, and productive life... a life where how old you are has nothing to do with the number of years you've lived and everything to do with your ability to participate in life, to love and be loved, to rediscover your creativity, and build healthy connections with family members and friends.

I became what to me was the highest professional expression of leadership: I became a coach.

I had reimagined my life and discovered the secret that changed everything for me, and I wanted to help other women get there too. Today I love helping female entrepreneurs 40+ marry the joy and enthusiasm of their youth with the wisdom and discipline they have achieved. We work together to reach their highest levels of clarity, courage, energy, productivity, and influence. My children are still a vivid part of my life and a key part of my sense of who I am here to be. And they continue to inspire me to become a higher version of myself, one who faces the future with energy and excitement. There was a time when I didn't feel this was possible for me.

And you?

Teresa Blount is a Certified High-Performance Coach, a licensed professional counselor, and an entrepreneur. She loves helping purpose-driven female entrepreneurs, ages 40+, take their personal and professional lives to the next level.

Her signature program, **Vibrant Leaders Blueprint**, provides a proven step-by-step plan to empower clients with the knowledge, skills, and tools to live, lead, and serve at their highest level, both personally and professionally.

Teresa Blount
Connect with Teresa:
teresablount.com
https://www.linkedin.com/in/teresa-blount-ab195572/
https://www.facebook.com/groups/agelesslivingwithteresablount

10

I am brilliance and Greatness Just Expresses as Me!

·· • ✦ • ··

by
Juliette Bastian

D o you ever wonder, "What makes me special? What's my life's purpose?" For a long time, the answers to those questions felt as elusive as the rarest gemstone to me. As a child, I daydreamed about what was to be my 'special'. I pretended to be a dancer on American Bandstand and Soul Train, a one-name celebrity like Cher, or the lead of a singing group—Diana Ross of the Supremes, Michael Jackson of the Jackson Five, or even Marie Osmond, the youngest sibling of the Osmond family. Because my last name is Bastian, I was convinced that I was related to a TV actor named Sebastian Cabot, and he just didn't know about me yet. In my reality, however, there was nothing extraordinary about me.

As a kid, I didn't have a care in the world! I had a great childhood, parents who loved and provided for me and my sisters, a private school education, and we lived in a beautiful house in a great neighborhood. All I had to do was what was expected of me—get good grades, go to college, and get a good job.

I left home when I was 19, not because I had to, but because my mother pampered me. Deep down inside, I knew I would be in trouble if something were to happen to her. So, at the ripe old age of 19, I got my first job, moved out, and focused on getting a degree. I knew three things: I loved to dance, I could sew, and I wasn't like everyone else!

After leaving home, I did what was expected of me and faced many challenges along the way. I was determined and went to college, got good grades, and then a good job. I used my degree, hard work, and dedication to my job to build an illustrious career with all the bells and whistles. Along that journey, I did a lot of comparative analysis with what others were doing, and my interpretation of the results were never in my favor. I was never good enough!

My first professional job was as an accountant. Everyone in the office studied for and passed the CPA exam, except me. For three months, Monday through Thursday, after a full day at work, I would drive 45 minutes each way to a CPA prep course, praying that my old car would make it to and from the class. I took the exam three times and got close but never passed. I realized that it was not really what I wanted to do and felt such a relief when I decided not to pursue it. Besides, I didn't like the 'ledger green' color anyway!

When my Grandmother passed away and then my cousin was killed in a car accident shortly thereafter, it was quite shocking to me to realize that everyone will die someday. I found myself moving past the sentiments and lovely writings about "how short life is" and "telling people you love them while they're alive" to asking the question, "Is this all there is to life?" Was the answer, "I'm just going to wake up each day, go to work, go home, and then someday die?" I asked myself, "What was the point?"

Based on that, I was even more determined to make a difference and to work hard at my current job so I could be the best at what I did. I decided I wanted to be one of the executives that met in the huge mahogany-paneled board room. I wanted to have the prestigious title and the six-figure income, so I didn't have to live paycheck to paycheck. I achieved that and more.

Due to my hard work, I was always selected for 'special projects' – which I loved! I worked directly with elected officials, national and local leaders, and other executives. I made a huge difference and always achieved results. The week before my 45th birthday, I was unanimously appointed to an executive position making more than I ever dreamed I could. I was the first African American appointed to that position in the state.

I'd made it! But it wasn't what I thought it would be. I had hit the glass ceiling, working long hours, and feeling like a hamster on a wheel. The janitors would kick me out every night around 10:00 pm. I would drive home, work until midnight, and wake up to repeat the cycle. I worked six and a half days a week, many of the holidays, and I didn't take any vacations. I forced myself to relax on Sundays by driving an hour to the beach, hauling my briefcase filled with work files, a beach chair, umbrella, and water, to sit for two hours and 'relax' while working. I must have been sending out 'spiritual smoke signals' because my world changed overnight.

One day, one of my employees confided in me that they had been asked to do something unethical by a politician's staff member. Long story short, because I spoke to the politician about the incident to protect my staff, I became the political scapegoat. A few days after the conversation with the politician, I had an ally come into my office, close my door, and suggest I seek legal counsel because something was about to happen that wasn't going to look good for me.

Shortly thereafter, I was put on administrative leave to give me time to prepare a response to a complaint that had been filed. But I didn't have a copy, nor would they provide one when I requested it, in large part because it had never been written. I was ordered to meet with an investigator, who proceeded to rudely interrogate me and use intimidating tactics to twist anything I said to something derogatory or negative. What ended up in her report didn't represent anything near the truth.

I had newspaper reporters calling me. A call to the Sheriff was made requesting any 'dirt' he had on me. I had representatives from the NAACP and local African American community leaders showing up to support me. I never sought attention, but if I had, this was definitely not the kind of attention I wanted. I was mortified. I searched my mind over and over again, trying to figure out if there was something I could've done differently. What did I do wrong?

I didn't even tell my family. I was so embarrassed that I had brought shame to the family name. My family found out when my niece saw an article in the newspaper. Of course, they rallied around me, but I was devastated. I tried to remain stoic throughout the entire ordeal, but inside I belittled myself and believed it was something I had done wrong.

I hired an attorney from my limited savings. She negotiated a deal which was not in my best interest and then quit two days before my hearing. I had to obtain another attorney – who advised me to walk away to do greater things in life instead of tying up years of my life and eating up my savings to win something that was politically driven. I followed his advice.

So, suddenly I had no job, no identity as to who I was or what my value was. All I'd known for 25 years was this organization and what its needs and values were. What was *my* purpose?

I'd never thought about what I wanted my future to look like. I had given control and devoted my life to something else, an institution, and other's opinions about what I should do.

I was lost. I didn't have anything—no job, no interests, no friends that were there to support me, no goals, dreams, or desires. While I loved to dance and sew, I couldn't figure out how I could make any money from these activities. I had discovered that all the years of apprenticeship under my mother's tutelage resulted in me being a great fashion designer and seamstress. One year, during my career, I set a goal to make a new business suit for each day of the month! Every Monday, I debuted a new suit, and it became an anticipated event at the office. For many years, I'd used my Christmas vacation to make my New Year's Eve dress, just in time to attend that most important year-end holiday party.

I took dance classes, and once my fellow dancers found out I could design and sew anything, I began making dance costumes in preparation for performances and events. Now, these were all successes, but I didn't see it that way! Even though the love of my life told me repeatedly that this was truly a gift, I just couldn't see it. I had this inner voice reminding me that this would not pay the bills, and I would never be as good as my mom, who taught me how to sew just as her mother had taught her. Could this really be my purpose?

After a while, I had to figure out how I was going to make money, and I vowed never to rely on one stream of income again. It was in that moment that I realized I might be this thing they called an entrepreneur. I didn't know what that term meant, let alone what it was about. But I knew I would be okay, just as I did when I left home at 19. I just had to figure out *what was my purpose?*

I spent a few years trying different things based on the opinions of what other people told me I would be good at doing. And I was, but I didn't enjoy it, and marginal success only served to reinforce my self-doubt and belief that I really didn't have something of value to contribute to the world. I spent time and much of my savings attending seminars, workshops, and classes on personal development and the "What's My Life Purpose?" topics. I was busy doing a lot of things but had nothing to show for it.

Then I had one of those infamous AHA! moments. I realized I am the CEO of my life! My Accounting Department takes care of my finances, my relationships are handled by Human Resources, and "Me, Myself and I" are my core team that make things happen to bring in money while fulfilling my Vision. I just needed to figure out what "My Life's Business" or "My Purpose" was. What made me unique? What made me special? Why do people like to be around me? What do they see in me? How could I help others? What did I daydream about? Can you relate to this?

With this new level of awareness, I decided to do a different kind of comparative analysis of my life and discovered I was onto something! I did a SWOT (Strengths, Weaknesses, Opportunities, and Threats) analysis on my life! If my life (my most valuable asset) was my business, then why not do what successful businesses do? Businesses are established to provide a product or service to make the world better. They leverage what makes them uniquely qualified to present that asset and are paid to do so. I had learned about successful business strategies, so I began working on applying those principles to my life. I finally figured it out!

That's what led me to create a unique approach to discovering my life's purpose, designing a life I love, and developing a simple action plan that keeps me focused on achieving my dreams and goals. What I know now is how to treat and nurture my most valuable asset—me! I still work hard at being the best. The difference is it's the best me! I dance regularly, I'm an accomplished fashion artist with many years of experience creating fashion designs for creative artists, performance wear, red carpet events, and special occasions, with unique creations that inspire and adorn the body temple, and I live a life that honors me!

Now I know my life's purpose! I love to support people all over the world to design the life they love, by showing them how to discover their unique beauty and showing them how to polish their gemstone to reflect the highly prized and well-beloved person they are.

Juliette Bastian's passion to help people achieve their best is the inspiration behind the creation of G'JEM (Greatness Just Expresses as Me).

As CEO /Founder, Juliette brings over 30 years of business, organizational development, communication, change management, and creative expression experience to all her endeavors. After a 25-year career in the corporate world, she suddenly found herself transitioning to an entrepreneurial lifestyle and struggling for clarity around her life's purpose and her dreams.

Juliette created a unique approach to discovering your life's purpose, designing a life you love, and developing a simple action plan that keeps you focused on achieving your dreams and goals. In addition to enjoying her passions of dance and fashion, she now supports people all over the world by reminding them of their unique beauty and showing them how to polish their G'JEM to reflect the highly prized and well-beloved person they are.

Connect with Juliette
Email: LifeWorking4u@gmail.com
Schedule a Call: https://calendly.com/LifeWorking4u
Web: www.LifeWorking4u.com

Scan the QRcode with your smartphone to watch Juliette's Video Message.

Or, follow this link:
https://youtu.be/L_EEpBHhzK0

11

Why Most Dreams Don't Come True

····◆····

Life's battles don't always go to the stronger or faster man.
But sooner or later the man who wins is the man who
thinks he can.

~Bruce Lee

by
Jason Surat

The journey of my baseball career was one with ups and downs, wins and losses, learning and implementing while playing a game of failure. I began my journey with a dream coupled with an unwavering belief that I could accomplish that dream. Have you ever had a dream so real, so clear, you could see every detail as if it already happened? That's how I felt when I fell in love with the game of baseball and set out on a journey to become a professional baseball player.

I remember when my dream took root inside my soul as I fell in love with baseball. A pair of brothers I knew asked if I wanted to join their men's league baseball team—like those you see being played on weeknights and weekends. I had no real baseball experience. I never played as a kid or in high school. I was around 21 years old when they invited me.

Little did I know that experience would ignite a dream and a passion in me that would lay the foundation of my character for the rest of my life.

Obviously, I said yes, and the journey began. I already possessed a foundational belief that you could achieve anything you put your mind to. Once I had committed to my belief that I would play professional baseball plus a crystal-clear vision of me on the field at a professional stadium, in a white uniform, in front of thousands of fans, I began to work out the steps. The more I said it out loud, the more I felt it become real. I started looking into other people's eyes and telling them I was going to play major league baseball. Almost every time, I was met with laughter. People would ask, "What makes you so sure?" I told them I was different. The difference was how badly I wanted it.

It's that feeling when you believe in something so much that you can't explain it to people, but you knew it was going to happen. All I could do was smile and tell them I just knew. During the season, I became obsessed and was willing to sacrifice everything to make it happen. I realize now I had decided. The meaning of the Latin root of the word decide means to 'cut off' all possibilities except for one. I had decided that any other outcome than my dream coming true was unacceptable.

The importance of that step cannot be overlooked. Not only was I lacking experience, but I was way too old in baseball's perspective. That didn't matter. I went back to college at the age of 23 and made my first college team. Not because I had any skill or talent, but because the coach said he'd never seen anyone with so much determination and heart. He wanted my character to rub off on the rest of the team. I knew the only thing I could control was my effort and that I had to give it 110%. He allowed me to join the team with the understanding that I would not play in any games. The choice was mine.

Have you ever looked back and realized the moment of a decision that shaped your destiny? In my first year, I saw a ton of improvement. So much so, that near the end of the season I started some games and got playing time in others. At the end of the season, the coaching staff awarded me with a plaque for the most improved player. I was turning myself into a ballplayer!

After two years at junior college, I needed to figure out how I could keep getting better. To plan my next steps, I knew I had to ask myself better questions. How could I practice all year round? How could I immerse myself in the game? Who had gotten the results I was after in a short time? Could I get help from a specialized coach? I quickly realized I needed to surround myself with better talent and find a place where the weather was warmer almost all year round.

I chose to move to California. The weather was warm all year round, and California was known for turning out the most professional ballplayers to the major leagues. Two weeks before my move to California, I hurt my left shoulder, my non-throwing shoulder, diving for a baseball in the left-center field gap. It was bad. Bad enough that I had to come out of the game I was playing in as part of a competitive summer league. What had I done? I didn't know how badly I'd hurt it other than how much pain I was feeling. More importantly, what was I going to do about trying out for the college team in California?

My dream was too big, I wasn't about to let an injury stop me. I rested my arm and told myself I would figure it out when I got there. I landed at a small Division 3 school, California Lutheran University, located in Thousand Oaks. I was nervous during the time leading up to tryouts. If I didn't stand guard at the door of my mind, questions like, "What did I get myself into? What happens if I don't make the team?" would creep into my thoughts. There was no room for fear to sink in.

I knew the less I sat with fear, the less chance it had to control me. I had to work with the fear, not to mention the pain I was still feeling in my arm. When a vision is so clear and determination is so strong, what stops most people is just a hurdle for those who've made that decision—those who are committed and passionate about seeing their vision come to life.

I made it all the way through tryouts to the final cuts again. This time there was no fortune in my favor. I got cut, didn't make the team. It had nothing to do with the shoulder, which still hurt by the way. My hard work and determination just did not pay off this time.

I was devastated. My worst fear had come true! How was I going to go forward? Why did this happen to me? Those were the types of questions that first entered my mind. The disempowering kind. The ones that amplify the terrible feelings inside. These questions do not help us. It's human to feel the initial pain, but when you live there is when you get into trouble.

Questions that empower us are the questions that help us move forward. Ask better questions, and you will get better answers. I took it for what it was, a chance to learn and get better, then try again next year. That's exactly what I did, after my shoulder healed. I stayed in shape by working out with some of the guys during their season.

In the summer, I flew back to New York to play in that same competitive summer league. Things started looking up again. I had a good summer season and came back to California in the fall ready to claim my rightful spot on the team. This time I had no injuries, more baseball experience, and more confidence. I was back, baby! And this time I had a better idea of what to expect. Experience had been one of my best teachers up until that point.

Again, I made it all the way through to the final cuts. Unfortunately, I was met with the same results. I got cut again. This hit me even harder. I had given up everything I knew, from my family, to my hometown, my friends, and everything familiar in my life. Didn't the coach know what I had sacrificed? Didn't he know that I wanted this more than anything I've ever wanted in my life? Didn't he know what I had been through to get where I was?

That's when I fell back into an old pattern of disempowering questions. "Maybe this isn't for me? Maybe I don't have what it takes? Maybe I am not good enough?" I actually gave some thought to just giving up and finishing my degree at CLU, because I liked where I was, and I feared more change. But then it hit me. Once college is over, I could never go back and play college baseball. What was I thinking?! What I didn't realize was that setbacks often make us think more about the how, instead of the why. When you get caught up in the weeds of the how, you set yourself up for doubt to creep in.

But breakdowns often become the catalyst for breakthroughs. I got my focus back on my why. Discipline is important to get you going but it isn't enough. Staying connected with your why is what pulls you through the dark times.

I snapped out of my funk and called another college that was on my list when I first came to California. After my call with the coach at the new school, I transferred to my third college in pursuit of my dream. Fortune was back on my side. I made the team at Whittier College. I was now a Whittier Poet!

It was time to get back on track and keep getting better. It wasn't the exact situation I wanted, but I stopped focusing on the how. It allowed me to be more flexible about which path I took to achieve my dream. Where focus goes, energy flows.

Whittier was part of the same division as CLU, so it made for interesting games when we played each other. The CLU coach knew I'd transferred, and it was fun to see the guys I knew.

I continued to get better, gaining more experience at Whittier and seeing how different the competition was in California compared to New York. The most important thing was that I found a way to continue and found out how resourceful I could be, a useful skill when you feel as if there's no other way. It's usually not a lack of resources—it's a lack of resourcefulness.

As college came to an end and I was getting ready to graduate, I needed to figure out what my next step was. For most college baseball players, that would be the end of the line if you weren't getting drafted. But I wasn't done. I still had the fire, and I was only getting closer. Or was it closer to the end of the line? Again, it was important to see things how they were, not worse than they were.

From here on out, there was no more college. By then, I was nearly 30 years old. They said if you hadn't made it by 25 or 26, your chances to become a major leaguer were zero. I paid no attention to what "they" said—that didn't serve me. Now it was time to see how my skills lined up against a bigger spectrum of competition. I was scared, and this time I felt more alone than before because I had just left the brotherhood of college baseball.

I kept moving forward regardless of the fear. Fear is a good thing. It can protect us. But fear can also be a bad thing. It can paralyze us from taking that next step. We must learn to dance with fear if we truly want to make our dreams come true.

I got my biggest break when I got the chance to play semi-pro baseball for one season with the Blythe Heat, a semi-professional independent-league team. I was in the white uniform, on the field of a professional stadium, in front of a couple thousand fans, playing third base when we made the last out to win the championship in 2008! What transpired leading up to that moment on the field was something I never saw coming.

Our team had been off to a bad start. Our record was 0-4 when our manager, Jeffrey Leonard, a 14-year major league baseball player himself, called a team meeting out on the bleachers before our next game. We all sat down while he just stood there with his arms folded, staring at us. Finally, one of my teammates shouted, "What's up coach?"

"Has anyone heard any good jokes lately?" Coach said. We all looked around, confused, as we too were feeling the pressure of the season. Then he said, "That's because you guys are the joke." That hurt like getting hit with a 90-mph fastball during an at bat. He was telling us we were the laughingstock of the league. We went on to lose that game too!

We were 0-5 to start the season, but we never gave up. We went on a winning streak, and toward the end of the season, we had to win our final two games to get into the playoffs. What was worse, the very last game was against the first-place team that had only lost one game all season! Our chances were not looking good. However, not only did we win the final two games to get us into the playoffs, but we beat that same first-place team to win the championship! My dream had come true as I threw my glove up in the air to celebrate and ran toward the dogpile on the pitcher's mound.

The lessons I learned from that journey have laid the foundation for my life. I realized that I always knew what I had to do to make my dreams come true. I had a crystal-clear vision of where I wanted to go, and I made a decision to go all-in for it. My foundational belief that humans have infinite potential when we put our minds to something led me to take massive action.

Massive action led to results, some good and some bad, but my mindset allowed me to learn from those results, instead of living in the moments of the bad results. I implemented what I learned right away, in some cases from pitch to pitch during an at-bat. You have to be willing to immediately course correct when you aren't getting the results you want.

If you surround yourself with like-minded people who've achieved what you want and make sure you aren't the most capable person in the room, this will push you out of your comfort zone. Get comfortable being uncomfortable. Seek out coaches and mentors and stay connected to your why when setbacks make you worry about the how.

Self-confidence is muscle, and you need to keep working it out. Don't make things worse than they are—see them for what they are and not worse. Today, you can find my name right alongside all the other professional major league players immortalized on the baseball reference website www.baseballreference.com. For me, that was a dream come true.

Over the years, I found that the more complex something is, the less likely we are to execute on it. When I started to reflect on why most people don't achieve their dreams, it came down to one simple answer, they just didn't want it bad enough.

Reference:

https://www.baseball-reference.com/register/player.fcgi?id=surat-001jas

https://en.wikipedia.org/wiki/Blythe_Heat#:~:text=The%20
team's%20uniform%20logo%20was,5%20in%20the%20
Championship%20Game.

https://en.wikipedia.org/wiki/Baseball-Reference.com#:
~:text=Baseball%2DReference%20is%20a%20website,in%20Major%20
League%20Baseball%20history.&text=Baseball%2DReference%20
is%20part%20of,million%20unique%20users%20per%20month.

Born in New York, Jason Surat was always a big dreamer. It wasn't until his early twenties when he fell in love with the game of baseball that he would form the foundation for his success. It was through his journey of realizing his dream that he recognized the patterns around success. Applying these patterns to his professional career Jason carved out accolade after accolade in sales performance awards. After years of perfecting his craft, Jason has dialed in his experience and has realized that true fulfillment comes from helping others. He has embarked on a mission to inspire others to believe in themselves and their ideas.

For more information:
Website: www.jasonsurat.com
Email: info@4pillarsolutions.com

12

Daddy's Girl?

········◆◆◆········

*"If you are not intentionally connecting with someone,
you are probably pushing them away."*

~Marilyn Sutherland

by
Marilyn Sutherland

My mom was loving, generous, kind, caring, self-expressed, and communicative. In her presence, I always felt loved and nurtured. In many ways I'm like my mom; I, too, love to touch, hug, and talk. When I married and became an instant 'stepmom' and 'grandmother,' I modeled how to be with my teen and 20-something adult children, and my first (of eight) grandchildren based on how my mom treated me. She died unexpectedly a week after my wedding. I was grateful my mom was able to attend my wedding and share my day. And I was heartbroken she didn't get to witness me as a mother. She would have been proud of me.

My passion as a Relationship & Communication Coach for Love and Leadership is fueled by lessons from my parents. From my mom, I learned to intentionally connect with others from love. Now I use that approach to coach professional women to claim their value, voice, and power, and to master critical relationship and communication skills most of us were never taught. My clients have breakthroughs like being vulnerable with people they love, asking for a raise they deserve, focusing on praise rather than criticism, and setting and holding boundaries with respect. As a result, they create effective, fulfilling, and nurturing partnerships in their personal life (romantic, family, and friends) and work life.

I believe the loving qualities my mom taught me are just as important in our work relationships as they are in our personal relationships.

The lessons I learned from my Dad were totally different.

Does "Father Know Best"?

When I was a little girl, I remember watching the TV show "Father Knows Best." I so wanted my dad to be like that TV dad – sweet, warm, affectionate, and kind. And I so wanted to be daddy's girl... but I wasn't.

He was born in 1910, was 19 when the Great Depression started, and 29 when he signed up to serve in the Army. He served for more than four years in Europe. When General Patton landed at Dad's base, he came out to where my dad's squad was working shirtless in 100+ degree weather. Patton commanded my dad to have his squad put on their shirts. Dad stood up to Patton to protect his men; he didn't want them to have heat stroke.

My parents met just before World War II and knew each other mostly through letters they wrote during those four years. They married a few months after the war. Mom told me dad expressed his feelings in his letters but, after they got married and he settled in, she knew he wasn't a talker.

Dad was a good provider, hard-working, never complained, and a man of his word. He was usually a quiet, contained man although when he laughed, his face lit up. Most nights, Dad would sit in his recliner, content to read a book and watch TV (especially golf) all evening, and never say a word. Starting in 7th grade, if I needed to ask him a question, I would stand between his chair and the TV while he was reading, hoping to get his attention when he looked up to watch the TV. When he saw me, he would say "You make a better door than a window." I knew he wanted me to get out of his way, yet my feelings were hurt. I felt like I was a "thing." I wanted him to see **me**.

When you felt invisible to someone you loved, how did you feel?

Has someone said something they thought was funny, but it was hurtful to you?

When I was in junior high, my dad's friend, Tony, hired him to be a supervisor of materials at a company in a nearby city. Dad left early Monday morning and returned home every Friday afternoon. Dad often stayed with Tony's family or at least had dinner with them weekly.

When dad's mom died, Tony and his family came for the memorial. When his daughters saw Dad, they ran to him and he stood with a big smile and arms wide open to hug them. I had never remembered my dad doing that with my brother or me.

Oh no! Not only was **I** not daddy's girl, but these **other** girls were! I sobbed. After everyone left, I yelled at my dad for showing them more love than he showed us.

Have you ever yearned to get the love and attention you wanted?

Revelation
In college. I majored in psychology and sociology and had a revelation! My dad was doing the best he could!

With that understanding, I appreciated the relationship we had. If I called home, dad usually answered. I enjoyed our short chat before he would pass the phone to mom.

In my early 30s, I participated in a personal development program to explore a new career. I got that and so much more. During an exercise, the leader asked us to pick a relationship where we had resentment or disappointment. I immediately thought about my dad.

I was shocked! The resentment I thought I had released in college was still there. My unfulfilled, unrealistic expectations for Dad to be like that TV father had been blocking me from accepting the love he did offer. In fact, I was pushing him away and deflecting the way he loved me because he didn't follow the script in my head.

At that moment, I was able to forgive my dad for not being the father I wanted, release my resentment, and accept him exactly the way he was.

For weeks after, I wanted to share with Dad the shift I had experienced when I called home, but every time, I stopped. I had forgiven him, but the truth was, he had done nothing wrong. He was just being himself. He didn't need my forgiveness; it was my expectations that were the problem.

The Real Shift
What happened a few months later when I visited my parents for a week was unbelievable. One evening toward the end of the visit, I was in my old bedroom, sitting under the covers with papers spread out on top.

As Dad came up the steps, he said gruffly, "The TV's too loud!"

"Dad, would you mind turning it down, so I don't have to mess up these papers." He came in, lowered the volume, then started to walk out. Halfway out, he stopped, his back to me, and said clearly, "I love you."

What? He often said it in response, but I never remembered him saying it first until that moment.

Then he started walking out. "Dad! Wait!"

He turned around and I pointed to my cheek. "Kiss me here?" I opened my arms wide. He gave me a big kiss on the cheek, and we hugged. I whispered "I love you" with tears in my eyes.

Even though I never said anything about my forgiving him, my energy was different after I accepted him just as he was. Finally, he felt safe to express his love for me.

When nothing was blocking the love between us, I could be myself—fully-expressed, loving, and funny. I started building the relationship I wanted with him and stopped waiting to be Daddy's girl. I already was!

After that, I could be playful and ask for what I wanted because I knew he loved me.

Where do you have disappointment that someone has not met your needs?

When they don't respond the way you want, how do you push them away?

The Golf Shot

In my 40s, I signed up for golf lessons. I thought it would be good exercise and something I could share with dad. After a few weeks of lessons, I drove to my parent's house to visit over spring break.

The next morning, my dad said, "Let's go out and see what you've got!"

I stood on the grass right behind our house and he stood on the upper level of our driveway facing me. He pointed to the small space between his feet and told me to put the ball there.

"Dad, I've had three lessons. And I certainly haven't learned how to hit a golf shot 12 feet out, 10 feet up, and drop in between your feet."

"Marilyn, go."

The first ball sailed past him. The second ball wasn't high enough, but the third ball landed right between his feet! Amazing!

Guess what my dad said...

"Do It Again!"

"Dad, that was amazing. Can't you just tell me "Great job, honey"?

"Yeah. Great job. Do It Again!"

I laughed ... That's my dad and I love him.

Lessons I Learned from Not Being "Daddy's Girl"
Who I am is a relationship and communication coach. I draw on all my training and experience, personally and professionally. What drives my passion has been shaped by what I learned from my parents. Here are four lessons from this story:

Give up expectations
In many relationships, people are doing the best they can. Give them and yourself some compassion. Expecting is like demanding someone to do what you want. The results are upset, suffering, and resentment. Instead, request what you need in a way that acknowledges who they are for you. Ask for what you want, be willing to negotiate, and if they decline, thank them for considering it and find another source. We all have a right to say "no" to another's request.

Did you ever hear the saying "You can't get blood from a turnip?" Wanting my dad to talk to me like my mom did was unrealistic. I learned to ask for what I wanted in a way he could hear it (humor, love and/or respect) and appreciated him for whatever he did. Knowing he did love me, I could listen from love.

Do you have expectations that are blocking you from recognizing the love you do have?

At work, showing you care about people and value them creates a true team where everyone supports each other. Coaching employees is investing in them when it's done from caring and commitment.

Respect yourself

We cannot gain confidence in ourselves by waiting for others to reassure us. Of course, as young children, it's important for someone to love us or show us they care. However, at some point, the most important person to believe in you is you! What others think is their perception and it doesn't make it our reality unless we let it.

Do you give people power over you by caring more about what they say and doubting yourself?

I knew that third golf shot was like a hole in one. I didn't need Dad to say it!

Intentionally connect

We can't control what others do, but we can connect with love, caring, and/or respect in every interaction.

When we connect with intention, we are present with them - listening, being curious, and, reflecting what they say to be sure we understand. Being present includes looking at them, not at the TV, a book, or your phone.

If we're not *intentionally* connecting, listening, or speaking, then we are almost certainly pushing them away. When we are paying attention, if we say or do something that is not kind or loving, we can see when we hurt others and correct the situation immediately.

Many people are not intentional; they are in their own world. If we feel someone is disrespectful, we can speak up and clarify their intention. Speak with loving-kindness and find out what they meant and why.

I use the analogy that at any moment we are either adding bricks that build a wall between us (and so are they), or we're removing bricks and tearing down the wall so we can have a deeper connection. Don't wait for them to remove the bricks!

This applies to our business relationships, too. Even though we don't talk about having loving feelings for people at work, we do want our colleagues and clients to "Know-Like-Trust" us and want the people who work for us to love their jobs and trust us as leaders.

You can always ask yourself: "Am I pushing them away right now?"

If you are not 100% sure, then the answer is "Yes!"

Forgive them and yourself
When I forgave my Dad, he had not done anything wrong. He didn't know he was supposed to be like that TV father. I also forgave myself for expecting him to be the way I wanted. When I forgave, I was free and so was he. I could hear him say "I love you" and let in his love.

Where might you be clinging to resentment to punish them when really you are punishing yourself?

For most of us, the way we engage with others is based on the "survival habits" we developed in childhood. Recognizing our habits from the past and forgiving ourselves is important.

For example, hiding under the bed when your parents fought (or whatever you did to survive difficult situations) doesn't work as an adult. Fear of confrontation has leaders hide in their office and people isolate from family at home. Even if things work out on the surface (we feel safe), we are not satisfied and fulfilled when we are reacting from the past rather than creating the future.

When we interact with others from love, all our relationships can be fun, nurturing, loving, fulfilling, and fabulicious!

To have love, be loving
When I gave up expecting my dad to be a fantasy dad, I intentionally connected with him in a loving way.

I forgave my Dad for not meeting my expectations, accepted how he loved me, and respected him for who he was. I forgave myself for resenting him and let it go.

When I was fully loving to my dad and grateful for who he was, I expressed my love for him freely and felt his love.

Then I knew I was Daddy's Girl. He didn't have to tell me.

Marilyn Sutherland provides "leadershipandcommunication magic for your personal and business relationships" as the founder of Love Lead Connect. Her passion is for people to see communication as a source of the heartfelt connection we yearn for and the successful coordination of action with others.

Marilyn is a graduate of Presence-Based Coach Training and a relationship expert at YourTango.com and Goddess-Getaway. com

Her #1 Amazon Bestseller book "Why did you load the dishwasher like that? 9 Whopping Mistakes That Push Love Away?" shows you how to redesign both your actions, and who you are, in your relationship in love, work, and life.

Connect with Marilyn
Email: Marilyn@LoveLeadConnect.com
All Social Media Links: https://linktr.ee/Coach
Website: https://LoveLeadConnect.com
Facebook: https://www.facebook.com/marilyn.k.sutherland.1
LinkedIn: https://www.linkedin.com/in/marilynkodishsutherland/
Instagram: https://www.instagram.com/marilynksutherland/
Amazon: https://www.amazon.com/-/e/B07BS414ZB
Your Tango Relationship Expert Profile:
www.yourtango.com/experts/marilyn-sutherland

Scan the QR code with your smartphone to watch Marilyn's video message.

Or, follow this link:
https://vimeo.com/469615019/403bcef298

13

How a Postcard Changed My Life

······◆◆◆······

by
Domenico DiIulio

"The Academy is looking for students like you to attend and upon graduation serve in the United States Coast Guard."

Its message was simple, but that's the postcard I received in the summer of 1969 that changed my life.

"Why me," I asked myself. "Who else received a postcard like this?"

I was intrigued by the opportunity the postcard presented and by the Academy's location on the banks of the Thames River in New London, Connecticut. It certainly was a far cry from the western Illinois prairie near the banks of the Mississippi River I was used to.

The postcard came when I was entering my senior year of high school. Although I was focused on the upcoming academic year, football practice was in full swing that August, and I had yet to entertain any thoughts of college. The postcard changed that.

I talked with several classmates and discovered that many of them had received an identical postcard. I asked them if they were interested in the opportunity. This was during the height of the Vietnam War, and many of them replied the same thing. "Why would I want to go to a service academy and commit to an additional five years in the service?"

I, on the other hand, was thinking, "Why not?"

After all, only six short years earlier I had watched Roger Staubach, the Heisman Trophy-winning quarterback, lead the U.S. Naval Academy to victory over Army and to meet Texas in the Cotton Bowl for the national collegiate football championship. I had dreamt of becoming a Midshipman and emulating Staubach. However, the dream had gone dormant as I researched more about the Naval Academy in Annapolis and discovered that political appointments were required to attend. Self-doubt had crept in.

"How can I even consider attending Annapolis since I have no political connections?"

Eventually I decided I wouldn't pursue a political appointment. And so my dream of becoming a Midshipman faded further into the back of my mind.

Then the postcard from the U.S. Coast Guard Academy arrived and resuscitated my dream. It mentioned that no political appointments were required for entrance into the Academy. That got my attention. Plus the Coast Guard was also a sea service, albeit much smaller than the Navy. Despite the fact that the only time I had seen an ocean was on a family trip to California two months prior to the postcard's arrival, the opportunity to go to sea appealed to me. So I decided it was time to bring my old dream back to life and focus on the Coast Guard.

"Let's see what happens, " I told myself.

So I filled out my name and address on the detachable return postcard and dropped it in the mail. A couple of weeks later a course catalog and a one-page application for admission to the U.S. Coast Guard Academy arrived. I read the course catalog from page to page many times. I completed the application and sent it off.

The application process continued over the next several months of my senior year. I submitted more detailed forms, requested letters of recommendation from my teachers, and took the SAT, even though I had taken the ACT the year before, since the SAT was the only college entrance exam the Academy accepted. With each passing day, I was thrilled that I was still in the running for an appointment. But when the middle of March 1970 came and went with no appointment from the Academy and with graduation only a few months away, I needed a back-up plan.

So I applied to the local college which was literally only three blocks away from my high school and miles away from New London, Connecticut. This choice would allow me to stay close to home and play football with a championship-winning small college team. The quarterback of the local college team was Ken Anderson. Maybe he wasn't Roger Staubach, but Ken met with me and discussed their program, and I was grateful. I became a longtime fan of his, and nobody was more pleased than I when he went on to become the quarterback of the Cincinnati Bengals for several years and led the team to the 1982 Super Bowl.

As the oldest of five boys, I grew up in a competitive and loving environment. Each of us boys was always vying for the attention and approval of our father while our mother constantly doted on us. Together with our father, we were the focal point of our mother's world. As a high school senior, I felt that her attention was often overbearing. I couldn't even talk to a girl on the family phone without

Mom listening in and subsequently asking me "Twenty Questions" after I hung up!

The postcard beckoned to me like a magic genie. The thought of leaving home and going off to college far, far away became more appealing than ever. It would mean I would also be giving up my position as the leader amongst my brothers, and I welcomed that. Little did I realize the implications until many years later.

By mid-April, I finally received notice from the Academy that I had been accepted for enrollment and that an appointment would be forthcoming. The opportunity to attend a small military college over a thousand miles from home had just gone from a dream to reality. I was beyond excited the day the Cadet Appointment Certificate arrived!

Filling out that postcard so many years ago was the first step of a journey I couldn't have imagined in my wildest dreams. I've served my country as a Coast Guard officer. I've learned navigation, seamanship, and leadership. I've sailed across the Atlantic with over a hundred of my classmates aboard a 295-foot, square-rigged sailing ship to participate in the 1972 Olympics in Kiel, Germany. I've served as a Coast Guard exchange officer aboard a Navy frigate. After a taste of the Navy, I was thrilled to return to the Coast Guard, secretly glad I hadn't attended Annapolis.

During my Coast Guard career, I commanded three cutters that enforced fisheries laws along the west coast of the United States, countered drug smuggling efforts in the Caribbean, and responded to several mariners in need of assistance. In my later years in uniform, I taught the very same navigation, seamanship, and leadership classes I had attended as a cadet to the next generation of Coast Guard men and women.

In service to country, there is no higher honor than to lead a United States military delegation to discussions with another country. In

1998, the Pentagon arranged talks with the Vietnamese Defense Ministry regarding search and rescue protocols and insisted upon a Coast Guard Captain to head the delegation. I was that officer. The talks in Hanoi were the first military-to-military talks between our countries since the end of the Vietnam War. I was proud to have played a key role in laying the groundwork for the establishment of the Vietnamese Coast Guard two years later.

Over all my years in service, I always found a prominent location on my office wall to hang my framed Cadet Appointment Certificate. It was a reminder of the postcard that had started it all. However, life in uniformed service is a career, but not a lifelong career. On our life's journey, we often define ourselves by the opportunities we act upon, the careers we select, the jobs we do. For many of us, our careers define who we are. Yet it's only when we pursue our passions that we discover who we really are. Building a career aligned with our passion provides the greatest opportunity to have an impact on our world. I had built one such career. Now it was time to do it again.

When my father's estate was settled in 2015, I became a part-owner of the family business, together with two of my four brothers and my mother. While I had long ago left town and pursued my career in the Coast Guard, both of my brothers had worked in the business for decades. With my new minority ownership stake, I became interested in many facets of business operations and decisions.

I hired a business coach. He offered to include my brothers and assist them in their personal growth at my expense. They turned the offer down. I decided I would continue on to learn the ins and outs of business with my coach and share what I had learned with my brothers when the time was right. In my latter years in the Coast Guard, I had spent a great deal of time in strategic planning for employing armed forces against an array of adversarial threats, including potential future threats. Similar thought processes are used in strategic business planning. I soon discovered that business principles apply uniformly across organizations, whether those organizations are governmental, not-for-profit, or private entities. Business is business. I became energized by the what-ifs in business development. I found that by working with others in collaboration, I enjoyed exploring business goals and objectives and framing solutions.

I saw an opportunity to apply these skills in our family business. In the spring of 2018, I was in the office with my brothers and a couple of other key employees. Meeting independently with each of them, I opened each conversation with this question. "Do you believe we can double gross sales in two years?"

Their answers were revealing. My nephew, the lead salesman, was very enthusiastic and had many ideas on how to accomplish the goal. The production manager was also enthusiastic and also had a number of suggestions to make. However, my two brothers, the key decision-makers, were hesitant and less than enthusiastic, to put it mildly. They were happy with where the company was. I was not. Gross profits had been steady year over year, but they had been essentially flat the previous three years. As I explained to one of my brothers, it was a clear warning sign that the company wasn't growing.

Apparently, I had asked enough questions and had applied enough pressure. Six months later, late on a Friday afternoon, I got a call from the production manager. He told me that my brother who served as Chief Operating Officer was talking to some consultants who were pitching their services, and it appeared he was about to sign a contract to hire them. I thanked the production manager for the heads up, hung up, and started fuming.

I felt slighted that I had found out what was going on from the production manager, without being informed or consulted by my brother before hiring outside experts. Within the hour, I called my brother, and he informed me that he had indeed hired the consulting company, and the kick-off meeting was scheduled for the following Monday morning.

"You're welcome to attend if you want."

Welcome? Want to? Are you kidding me?

"I'll be there," was my curt reply.

The weekend proved to be a necessary cooling off period for me. I was happy to know that finally, my brothers were taking action to examine the company from top to bottom, as I had urged.

I arrived early Monday morning to meet with the consulting team, consisting of the project manager and the prospective on-site consultant, and the tax strategist prior to the formal start-up meeting. In our brief preliminary conversation, the project manager and I discussed their company's purpose and my role in the family business. When he likened my role to that of the activist investor, he nailed it.

The program manager opened the meeting by thanking us for hiring them to help our company. He described how their consulting company seeks to help first-generation, family-owned *companies* transition into second and third-generation family-owned *businesses* by documenting the company's structures, policies, and processes. He continued by mentioning that the consulting team's efforts would include pursuing a strategic planning process and establishing goals and objectives "much like your brother Dom has been suggesting since he knows what he is talking about when it comes to these business practices."

I was feeling pretty good about myself and wasn't prepared for what followed. The program manager then turned to me and asked, "Do you know why your brothers don't listen to you?"

Without waiting for a reply from me, he simply said, "Because you're their older brother!"

And that's when I got it. Family dynamics are a funny thing. My brothers wondered what I could possibly know about business, let alone the family business since I had gone off to the Coast Guard decades ago. They viewed me as a government worker who had scant knowledge about the business. And now, here I was, the older brother and a minority stakeholder, urging them to improve the sales and profitability of the business – all for the collective good.

Our family business remains a story in progress, of which I will always be a part to the extent my brothers accept my participation. However, the day the meeting took place between my brothers, the consultants, and myself, changed everything as if a bright light was flipped on. I became energized by the program manager's comments as if a second postcard had been presented to me. That moment was a Game Changer. I discovered that I'm passionate about making this world a better place one business at a time through coaching, consulting, and motivating others to better their businesses and the world around them.

What are *your* postcards? What are *your* game changers?

Dom DiIulio is a Virginia-based Coast Guard veteran turned business owner, entrepreneur, investor, coach, and consultant. Dom entered the business world when the family business transferred ownership to several family members including him. He recognized the need to get smart in business and hired a coach. He also invested in a craft brewery and now serves on its board of directors.

Working with each company he contributed to their strategic planning efforts to update business plans and hone management practices. In the process, discovered within himself a new call to serve the small business community. He is driven by the intense desire to enable small business owners to achieve their vision and purpose.

Dominic DiIulio
email contact cherrytreepartners@comcast.net
Facebook Link https://www.facebook.com/dom.diiulio/
Linked In https://www.linkedin.com/in/domenico-diiulio-50950842/

Scan the QR code with your smartphone to watch Dominic's video message.

Or, follow this link:
https://youtu.be/Yoy2ykEwx5k

14

A Healer's Journey

···•◆•···

by
Parvin Ataei

I glanced at my watch as I climbed up the stairs to the tiny room I was renting with my brother and I looked around. He wasn't home yet, which was odd, and I idly wondered where he was. I had spent a hectic day at the university where I was learning to become a licensed medical doctor and I was worn out from around-the-clock routine that included classes, lab work, and more. I was looking forward to a quiet evening.

Especially *this* evening.

Just a little earlier in the day, while I had been in the medical school's anatomy lab dissecting cadavers, I had been overcome by waves of debilitating nausea that seemed to have nothing to do with either the gruesome sight of pickled body parts or the caustic smell of preservatives. I felt weak and light-headed, and barely able to hang onto my senses. What was the matter with me? I was usually much more grounded and stable!

My dearest wish in those days was to become an MD. As a daughter born into an ancient tribal family in Iran my parents had hoped—like most of their peers—for a strong and manly son to take over the family name and work on the farm from which my parents were then scratching a living. One day a son would support his parents in their old age. He would link them to his own children, who would proudly bear the family name in turn. In my parents' culture, a son is a source of pride and a promise for the future. A daughter is a disappointment.

When I was three years old I saw my grandfather—who I adored—limp across the yard on his way to our house. I was a tender-hearted little girl and I didn't want to see my wonderful grandfather suffer. So, when he showed me the bruise on his shin, I applied some saliva to my finger and then gently touched the dark purple spot on his leg. Although I didn't know it at the time, saliva has anti-bacterial properties. Grandfather smiled lovingly at me, and said, with some surprise, "It's all better!"

I instantly became hooked on healing and decided right then and there I would do whatever I could to bring wellness to others. This desire only strengthened when I was 14 and my favorite uncle had to have his leg amputated, a casualty of the severe case of diabetes he had been suffering with for years. It was a horrifying experience for our entire family. Did you know that today one person in the United States dies every seven seconds because of an unhealthy diet and high blood sugar? It is a tragedy that I have dedicated my life to reversing.

But as a young girl, that was all in the future. And so, with the goal of qualifying for medical school, and possibly gaining my parents' forgiveness for having been born a girl, I studied hard. I wanted to show them I was as good as any boy. As the years had passed my mother had given birth to more children, among them two prized sons who had saved my parents from the shame of having a female as their first-born child. I loved my siblings very much and I was proud to be the older sister in the family. I was responsible and maternal, dependable and capable.

Iran was in a state of upheaval in those days, with a dreadful political revolution underway in which many people died. We were also invaded by our neighbors in the country to our west—Iraq—and we struggled with yet more death and misery. My family members and I spent many restless nights waiting for bombs to drop on our home, potentially catching us unprepared as we slept. We lived in a state of constant dread as we had moved by then to the capital city of Iran—Tehran—so my father could expand the business he had started when he had decided to change the direction of our lives from farming to construction. During these troubled times, we escaped back to the country at night to avoid the worst of the warfare. With great difficulty, I managed to get my high school diploma. Unfortunately, the war had shuttered the doors of all of the universities in Iran. If I wanted to become a doctor, I was going to have to study in another country.

A chance meeting with a young woman who was studying medicine in India was all it took to set me on the trail of obtaining my Doctor of Medicine in that country. I applied for entry into one of India's most prestigious medical schools—Bangalore Medical College—and I was accepted – one of the proudest days of my life!

Life in India was very hard. I was lonely and working all the time. I had no friends and I was adrift in an unfamiliar world that I did not understand. What kept me going was the thrill of finally working on the grand project of becoming a healer. I was going to save lives someday!

With the war going on back at home my parents were worried. While I was safe in India, my younger brother, then 13, was on the verge of becoming eligible for military duty. All men in Iran must serve in the army when they turn 18, even today, but with our country torn apart by the war, the government was allowing ever-younger males into the army. On the field of battle, Iran was fighting for survival. But the cost was too high for my parents to bear. This was their younger son. And he had reached the age where he was legally permitted to choose to pick up a gun and stand in front of the bombs and bullets of his government's enemies. Alireza was just the kind of boy who would volunteer for the heartbreaking task of defending his country.

Terrified by the thought of losing their son, my parents packed my brother up with his most precious belongings and sent him to live with me in India. I had always been responsible and caring. At the age of 19, I was already making my way in the world. I was a fierce protector of my family and I was engaged in the precious fight to save lives and protect the sanctity of life. From my parents' point of view, living with me was the safest path for their son.

Or so we all thought.

My brother and I went on to form a close little family unit in India and for the most part, we got along well. I was thrilled to have him move in with me. Finally, I had someone to talk to and care about! We were both in school and I had just started looking for a larger apartment for us so we could each have more space. I had grown to find more and more things to love about my brother – his easy smile, his positive outlook, his sense of humor, his strong feeling of family, and the gentle way he handled small animals. He had become fascinated with motorcycles and had found one to carry him around the streets of Bangalore with joy and passion. He loved the freedom being in India gave him. He loved the novelty of his life.

The day I returned home from another exhausting day of medical training to wonder where he was, also turned out to be the day he had taken a turn too quickly and spun out into the middle of a busy street on his motorcycle. While I had been dissecting cadavers, the dear body of my precious brother had been strafed by the assault of a traffic accident. As I was entertaining the idea of changing into more comfortable clothes to more readily enjoy an easy evening at home, he was lying in a bed, in the very hospital where I was pursuing my medical studies.

Just then, someone knocked on my door.

I answered it to find the landlord's distraught daughter staring at me with tearful eyes and behind her, a policeman. I don't know how I drove to the hospital that night. I don't remember what I said or did after I saw the lifeless body of my beautiful brother lying there alone and untended. I was devastated and felt shattered by the loss, and by the guilt I felt. My brother had been under my care! I had failed him, and I had failed my parents! I don't remember how I made it back home again, or the sequence of events that took me to Iran for my brother's funeral and the series of ceremonies that invite the departed into the afterlife.

I do remember one of my aunts remarking that I would now, of course, give up this foolish idea of finishing medical school. Something shifted inside me.

"NO!" my soul seemed to scream. "I want to be there when someone else's brother comes in with an emergency! I couldn't save my brother's life, but I CAN save someone else's!"

And so, despite all the advice of family members and friends, I went back to resume my studies. It was terribly hard. Every room in that hospital reminded me of my brother and his tragic accident. I passed many night shifts in the same room where his life had ebbed away. But still, I kept on, determined to become the first female doctor in my tribe and the first doctor—male or female—in my family.

The years passed. I ultimately graduated from medical school, a proud, proud moment in my life. I met a wonderful man who lived in Los Angeles and after a steady long-distance romance, we married, and I moved to his home in the United States. I had begun to work on the challenging task of obtaining my California medical license when I became pregnant with my first child. Almost overnight, it seemed, my "MD" designation became a "DM"—Doctor of Motherhood! And when my second child was born, I was well and truly committed to a career as a mother: how could I possibly resume the hectic life of a medical doctor with two precious lives of my own to care for and protect?

Like many women, motherhood placed me at a crossroads. While still passionately dedicated to healing, I needed to find a path as a healer that would give me the flexibility to parent my children with the dedication I felt in my heart I needed to express through a full-time presence in my kids' lives.

That's when I turned to studies in the holistic field. Growing up on the farm back in Iran, I had shared with other members of my tribe and my family an honoring of a natural way of living without any medicine and using just herbs for illness. Balancing motherhood and course work, I studied meditation and tai chi. I became a certified holistic health coach through the Institute for Integrative Nutrition, the world's largest nutrition school. I studied the physical, emotional, and spiritual aspects of addiction, as well as the 12 Steps to Recovery. I studied more than 100 dietary theories with the world's most progressive holistic teachers, including Dr. Andrew Weil, Dr. Mark Hyman, Dr. Oz, Deepak Chopra, Joel Fuhrman, MD, Harville Hendrix, Ph.D., Bernie Siegel, MD, and Barry Sears, Ph.D. I studied quantum consciousness and integrative psychology and became certified in the Hoffman Quadrinity Process, which integrates body, intellect, emotions, and spirit.

When I opened my business, Radiant Wellness, in 2014 I was excited to integrate the skills I had learned as a healer of the human body with the skills I had learned to improve all aspects of people's lives. I bring a particular focus to my work to the key importance of eliminating sugar from our diet. The amputation of my diabetic uncle's leg had a profound and lasting impact on my world view, and I am especially dedicated to helping other families avoid the devastating impact of this terrible disease.

Today, I am a long way from that determined girl who wanted to win her parents' approval. I have learned that healing takes many forms and comes with much grace. I have forgiven myself for many things over the years that have witnessed my personal transformation. My past left me with wounds that I thought would never heal. Only now do I realize that I have healed myself through my journey of healing others. It is through resilience that we overcome adversity and through following our passions that we thrive And I invite you to welcome greater healing on all levels of your life, as well.

Parvin is a fully-credentialed medical doctor, with a Bachelor of Medicine and Surgery (MBBS) from Bangalore, India. She is a board-certified Holistic Health Coach in America.

She earned her certificate in Quantum Consciousness and Integrative Psychology from TakshaShila University. She is agnostic and practices meditation and tai chi.

Parvin has completed an extensive health coach training program with the Institute for Integrative Nutrition, and she is a faculty guest speaker at USC.

15

When Life Gets Out of Control

···•◆•···

"College doesn't have to be a DEBT sentence."

~ Denise Thomas

by
Denise Thomas

As a teenager, my boyfriend gave me a promise ring for my 16th birthday. My very worried dad asked my mom, 'What does that MEAN?!' Mom replied, 'Nothing. It means she'll be his girlfriend until something better comes along.' At the time, I was offended. As an adult, I know she was right.

It was a rocky relationship. I came home from a date late one evening, crying. My dad had stayed up watching television; I'm certain he was waiting up for me. I told my dad the boy had broken up with me and I could tell he was mad at the boy for making his little girl cry. Dad hugged me tightly and said,

"You are still in control. You are still in control."

I was too distraught to have a discussion, but I was confused. I didn't know what he meant.

I was NOT in control.

Seven years later, I had a new ring on my finger. This one, a pear-shaped diamond in an intricate setting. My new husband was out of town on a business trip and I was studying for my college midterm exams when I got a call from my aunt. She and I were not super close, so her call was extremely out of the ordinary. She NEVER called me.

"Hello?"
"Denise, its Aunt Vicky. Is your husband home?"
"No. He's out of town. Why?"
"Can someone else bring you home? Your mom is in the hospital. It's bad, Denise. it's real bad."

I found a ride and on the long drive to the hospital, no words were spoken. But my mind wouldn't rest. As I stared out the window I thought of all the things that would need to be done.: Which family members to call, my dad's HR department to ask about health and death benefits, and probably, funeral arrangements.

When I arrived at the hospital my dad fell into my arms sobbing.

"I was holding her. I was holding her."

My oldest brother, who had just graduated with a degree in medical technology arrived shortly after me and we visited Mom's room together. My brother's reaction said it all. She was hooked up to machines of all kinds keeping her alive. And he knew what each one of them meant. He collapsed at the foot of her bed. There was no hope.

I was NOT in control.

My mom's sudden death was devastating. So many thoughts ran through my head:

> A newly married woman just finding her way around a household needed her mom.
> I wanted her to see me receive my college diploma.
> I would need her when I had my first child.

But I didn't fall apart when mom died. There was too much to do. As the oldest of four, I had to help the family get back on their feet. They didn't know how to wash clothes or use the dishwasher. Mom had done everything. Hardly knowing what I was doing myself, I worked to get them into a new routine. We learned to run a household together.

It was over a year later that I finally allowed myself time to grieve. And then I told God what I really thought of His taking my mom so early. I didn't pull any punches and I used some words that would not have been appropriate to say in church. I was so angry that I sought out a priest to ask,

> "What gives God the right...?"

He helped me to see a new perspective:

> "Your mom had a brain aneurism. Perhaps God felt it was better to heal her in heaven rather than on earth."

It took some time for me to process it, but as I considered what he had said, I realized he was right. Had mom survived, she would have been in a vegetative state, unaware, and unable to function in any capacity.

I was learning to see the silver lining.

A few years later, my husband and I were in the midst of building a kitchen and I was used to transporting building materials in the minivan. A four-inch wide 6-foot long piece of granite stood on its edge across the threshold at the side door of the van. Since I couldn't reach my son's car seat by leaning in, I had to climb fully into the van, and over the granite, to unstrap him and carry him out. Only this time I forgot about the granite. I backed up, lost my footing, and fell backward. As I grasped at anything in reach to prevent myself from falling to the pavement, I lost hold of my son. With his head now hurtling toward the concrete, I stopped my own fall just in time to reach out and seize one of his ankles. We both froze there, caught in a moment of time, with his head just an inch above certain death. In that moment I distinctly heard God say,

"You are NOT in control."

Yeah. Despite my past familiarity with NOT being in control, that moment was still a rude awakening. I'm Type A. I like control. I make plans. I get busy fulfilling those plans. But in that moment, as I gathered my son back into my arms, I began to realize that control is an illusion. Of course, I make choices that impact my outcomes (which is why I wear a seatbelt and you should too), but that does not mean that I can control whether the woman in the SUV next to me is texting while driving, or whether the man in the truck in front of me has a heart attack.

Case in point: I'm always running late.

For context, when my daughter was in preschool my friend asked her what time she went to school? She didn't know how to answer that, so my friend posed the question differently.

"What does your mom say when you leave for school?'"
My daughter replied, "We're late!"

And for those of you without children, let me explain that lateness is not something I prefer. It's just that when you have kids, it doesn't matter if you start preparing to leave the house 2 hours prior. Just as you're walking out the door, someone will need to go potty (even though you asked if they needed to go 5 minutes before) or won't be able to find their left shoe ("They were JUST on your feet!").

So in typical fashion, I was running late to drop my daughter off at ballet class. So late in fact, that she was trying to put her own hair up in a bun while we were driving. That's when we turned a corner and saw a car that had flipped several times off the road. It was exactly like ours. The accident had occurred just moments before as the police and emergency vehicles hadn't yet arrived. It was my daughter who said, "Mom, that could have been us."

We were NOT in control that day and it might have saved our lives.

It's moments like that day in the car and like my mom's passing that started to teach me to appreciate those times when I wasn't in control to look for the positive in times of despair or frustration. However, sometimes, seeing the glass as half full hasn't been instantaneous. Sometimes, I have to swim around in that glass for a while, until I can find a way out. And sometimes swimming, can feel an awful lot like drowning.

Have you ever been so broke, so bankrupt that you have to sell your pot that you're currently cooking your dinner in? I've been there. My husband had been laid off, the stock market had crashed, and there I was standing in my kitchen, ladling food from pot to plates, so someone could pay me a few dollars and walk away with my pot. Well, their pot now. I didn't even have time to clean it properly. Along with everything else in my home... or the bank's home... the pot was gone. A few days earlier, I had had to watch someone drive away with my two beautiful dogs. That absolutely broke me.

I have never felt less in control.

We would be unable to put our kids through college or to co-sign for student loans. It took years before I realized that without those financial hardships I would not have done the research to find out how 30% of college students graduate debt-free, so my kids could do the same.

Of course, there are times I've doubted and wondered if I'm 'making up' a silver lining, an excuse, or reason that puts a person's actions or a situation in a better light.

My dad was sick in the weeks leading up to his death. I was nearly 3000 miles away and we talked on the phone daily. He always said he was okay. He sounded okay. He had been in the hospital several times during those weeks, but he always went home. Several family members asked him if they could call me and tell me to come home. He told them "No". It was only my sister who told me I needed to come home right away. I did book a flight to visit, but I don't know why I dismissed her urgency. He sounded fine. Less than 24 hours later, on the day I had planned to fly home, he passed away.

Though I was distraught, I realized perhaps I wasn't meant to remember him in that condition. Am I making up a silver lining? Maybe. I'm okay with that. Instead of being angry with myself or my dad, it gives me peace. Seeing the glass half full removes the bitterness and anger that many others suffer by always seeing it half empty.

When I was a teen, I didn't know what my dad meant when he said, "You are still in control".

But what I grew to understand is that, while I may not have control over the circumstances, I will always have control of my response to them and in how I perceive them.

There will always be times when 'life sucks'. But when you allow yourself to stay in the glass, the bad is all you will ever see. Every day, every moment, you have a choice. Learn to look for a new perspective. Look for the good. Teach it to your children. Remind your friends and family.

"You are still in control."

Dedicated to my dad. I miss you.

International best selling author, TEDx speaker, and coach to parents of college-bound teens, Denise Thomas' mission is to inspire, educate, and equip parents who take an active role supporting their children to live a life of financial freedom.

Denise is a 20-year homeschool veteran having homeschooled her two children from Pre-k through high school. Both attended their first-choice college on 17 scholarships exceeding $199,000, walking out of college with cash in hand.

Denise Thomas
Connect with Denise Website: https://GetAheadOfTheClass.com
Youtube: https://www.youtube.com/channel/UCkuItB4TG32sauvocyyJDpQ
Podcast: https://podcasts.apple.com/us/podcast/debt-free-degree/id1527024935
FaceBook: facebook.com/GetAheadOfTheClass/
Linkedin: https://www.linkedin.com/in/denise-thomas-debt-free-college-coach/
Pinterest: pinterest.com/deniseldthomas
Instagram: @getaheadoftheclass

Scan the QR code with your smartphone to watch Denise's video message.

Or follow this link:
https://youtu.be/405uVbZKH-8

16

Living with Purpose

Turning Adversity Into Success

···✦✦✦···

"It's what you learn after you know it all that counts.

~ John Wooden

by
Kevin Sturm

One Wednesday, late in May of 2019, I received some news that turned my world upside down. After four years of giving my heart and soul to a company that I was excited to work for, I received a call from my boss notifying me that I was being terminated from my position. Although the separation was made a bit easier, as I was asked to stay on for three months to transition, the shock and disappointment of the action was still painful. I was roughly one month from my 62nd birthday and the job market for aging executives was less than stellar.

As I started my job search, I discovered that many of my network connections were already enjoying retirement. Rather than continuing to cultivate a network, I had focused on my job responsibilities and therefore lost contact with most of the people who could lend immediate support. My network had atrophied and was not immediately available to soften my landing and assist me in finding my next role. With mounting college debts and a substantial mortgage obligation, retirement was not an option and I could not just fade slowly into the sunset. It was not the first time in my career that I was forced to scramble for a new position, as the telecom bust and its associated bankruptcies in the early 2000s had given me plenty of experience. This situation, however, felt different and I was more than a little apprehensive.

My immediate knee-jerk reaction was to attempt to find a similar position that would provide comparable pay and allow me to continue to provide for my family in the manner we were accustomed to. That was the path I had taken following previous bankruptcies and seemed like the pragmatic approach. I began immediately scouring the job boards and applying to literally hundreds of postings. After several months of a combination of rejections or crickets, I was forced to reconsider my situation and the options available.

Have you ever spent years climbing the proverbial ladder of success, sacrificing much of your personal time, only to discover the ladder was leaning up against the wrong building? I had climbed that ladder believing that I was on the path to success, yet the train had been derailed and I was left wondering what I had accomplished. To the outside world, I looked to have touched all the necessary bases of an accomplished life. I had a nice house with a two-car garage in an upscale neighborhood and was blessed with a great family. I had made a decent living which allowed me to provide for my family. When I looked beneath the surface, however, I wondered whether I had really capitalized on my abilities and created the impact that I believed I was capable of.

As I was reviewing my career, I realized that I had always taken what appeared to be the path of least resistance. I had avoided pursuing an entrepreneurial route due to perceived high risk and settled for what I felt was a more stable situation, working for others. I had taken a more traditional approach and achieved a level of success. What was lacking was the feeling of fulfillment that only comes from tackling a difficult challenge and doing something that caused me to stretch my capabilities. Something that I was passionate about and allowed me to make the type of impact that I thought possible. My real identity had somehow become lost in the bureaucratic corporate environments that I had toiled in for years. What was missing was my purpose. What was my reason for being and what was I truly passionate about? To discover that I had to go back to my roots and reexamine how I arrived at where I was.

I grew up in a small town in western New York in a family of eleven children. I was the second oldest child and the oldest of seven boys. My father was a high school physical education teacher and a three-sport coach. My mother ran the house and made sure that we all were fed, which, in a family that size, was a monstrous task, especially on a teacher's salary.

We had a tremendous home life and my parents instilled in us a set of values that still form the core of what I live by today. We did not have many of the things that others did, but we had what we needed, and I never felt cheated. Chaos generally reigned due to the number of people and conflicting egos, but we learned the value of teamwork and as the oldest male child, I learned how to lead and build teams at an early age.

When I was growing up it was common for kids to have heroes, most of whom were sports superstars. For as long as I can remember, however, my father was my hero. He got me hooked on sports, spent hours coaching me and developing my skills in multiple sports, taught me to enjoy the games, and more importantly how to act when competing. I loved playing and loved winning, however, learning to lose gracefully was a more difficult lesson.

From my father, I learned the value of sacrificing for the good of the team and that there was far more to athletics than just winning and losing. He had a sign on his office wall that read, *the measure of a coach is not his won-loss record but what becomes of his players.* He lived by that philosophy. I was continually amazed by the relationship that he established with his players and the respect and admiration that his players rendered him. He was able to push them to perform at their best while maintaining their enthusiasm and creating a fun atmosphere. It was not unusual for players that he had coached years before, to drop by the house just to check-in. When my father passed away early in 2016, it was incredible to see how many of his former players came to pay their respects. His impact was measurable through the loyalty of his past players.

I developed an extremely competitive nature early on and hated losing at anything. I strove to be the best in sports, academics, eating, crossword puzzles, and even Tiddly Winks. No matter the forum I wanted to win. I delivered newspapers and mowed lawns and competed against myself to accomplish the tasks faster and better each time. While I admired my father, I also recognized that there were many things that we were not able to do on the salary of a teacher and coach so decided early on that I wanted more; a bigger house, newer cars, the freedom to choose where to spend my time and my talents. I wanted to enjoy the "trappings" of success. Upon reflection, I now realized that I let my ambition and desire to be the best and have the most, direct me to a path that was neither purpose-driven nor aligned with my values. At that time, however, I did not have the benefit of experience and the wisdom of hindsight which I have today.

After a four-year stint at the United States Military Academy and five years as an Army officer, during which time I gained a tremendous foundation in leadership and team building, I was ready to pursue my vision of becoming a corporate executive and make my mark on the business world. I was accepted into a prestigious management career development program at NYNEX (now Verizon), advanced quickly, and capitalized on a company change to accelerate my career or so I thought.

At that point, I had surpassed my vision of what success looked like. I had the title and the responsibility that I envisioned years earlier and was on the path to more. Unfortunately, the economic environment turned, failed telephone companies littered the landscape, and I held seven different positions over an eight-year stretch resulting from corporate bankruptcies, acquisitions, and restructurings. During that period, I spent more time looking for the next job than doing what I enjoyed which was building teams and developing leaders.

Following the turmoil associated with the telecom bust, I pivoted and found a landing spot in a new industry and spent an additional thirteen years as an operation's executive in multiple companies. Career and salary advancement slowed but I still loved managing people and building high-performing teams. That is until the rug was pulled out from under me that fateful Wednesday in May. I was disappointed, humiliated, and when my initial job search efforts ran into a brick wall, I felt defeated. I had two children in college, a mountain of college debts, and a rather large mortgage to contend with, and no real prospects for my next position in the corporate world. I had reached a major nexus and there was no clear path forward.

So where did that leave me? I had secured titles and authority, earned a comfortable salary, and climbed the corporate ladder only to discover that those material gains were nice, but not sufficient to fulfill my desire to make a meaningful difference. I had sacrificed years of working 60+ hour weeks but had relinquished control of my destiny to others and had not made the impact I believed I was capable of. I knew I was capable of more.

I believed that I had untapped potential, and I would not be satisfied until I exhausted that potential and could live without regret. While I enjoyed the prestige of authority, I realized that the times I felt accomplished were when I was working with my people coaching, teaching, and developing them as leaders. My successes were the result of establishing a vision, molding teams, and developing the skills of the people within the organizations. At that point continuing down a similar path with an undefined company no longer held any allure. I wanted to make a life as opposed to just making a living.

Despite a somewhat tumultuous professional life, I have been blessed with a great family, a wonderful wife, and five terrific children. My children all participated in organized athletics from the time that they were five years old to the end of their high school years. I had the privilege of coaching all of them throughout that period and ended up coaching approximately 80 different teams over a 20-year period in a variety of sports.

Year after year, I was able to work with many of the same kids and it was gratifying to watch them grow and develop as leaders and teams. My teams rarely won championships and I often joke that I had lost more games than all the other coaches combined. At the same time, my players enjoyed the experience, returned year after year, and their performance continually improved. Through their participation in organized sports, they developed and honed many of the values that will afford them the chance to have a successful life filled with joy and fulfillment. For me, it was rewarding to know that I was able to positively impact their growth as young adults and hopefully position them for success in the future.

As I took stock in my career, I realized that my passion was in helping people manifest the greatness that was in them and my purpose was to develop leaders. I was at my best and most happy when I was coaching others. Although I could certainly accomplish that in the corporate world, I was neither assured of getting the right role nor willing to accept the limitations that the environment demanded. I wanted to do it on a bigger scale and have the freedom to do it my way and make the contributions I believed that I was capable of.

For years, I had dreamed of running my own business but had allowed the fears of failure and the unknown, prevent me from taking that leap. Faced with the dual realities that my services were not in demand in the corporate world and that I wanted to do it my way, I found the courage to take the leap of faith and go into business as an entrepreneur and business coach. I understood that my corporate positions were merely vehicles that enabled me to work with and teach future leaders. I knew that I could develop more leaders by focusing on that mission rather than doing so on a part-time basis.

While I certainly enjoyed the operations world and solving problems, I was happiest when I was acting as a coach and mentor. I loved having the opportunity and the ability to help others discover and achieve their potential and reach their goals. Whether on the basketball court, soccer field, or in the corporate meeting room, my enjoyment came when people had a breakthrough and were able to accomplish something that they previously thought impossible. I had taken a rather circuitous path, but I finally paid attention to the cues which had been there all along.

Armed with that new insight I have taken a new direction in my career. One that will enable me to impact more lives and contribute on a bigger scale. I am now assisting business leaders to hone their leadership and team-building skills, develop clarity around their business, and create customer advocates who will buy from them again and more importantly refer them to others to buy. Roughly 80% of small businesses today fail within the first three years and those failures have an impact on the owners and their families, their employees, and the communities they work in. I have seen first-hand the implications of those failures and want to reverse the trend. I know that by developing the capabilities of business owners to better lead their enterprises, we can reverse the trend and take innovation to the next level.

So, what do you do when you are thrown a curveball that you didn't expect? Well in my case I went back to the beginning, rediscovered my *Why*, and launched a new venture to make a difference on a bigger scale. I moved my ladder up to the right wall and redirected to what my calling was all along. Starting a new business venture during a pandemic has been challenging to be sure, but it has also provided me with an opportunity. Many business owners need help to find their way through the current turmoil to reinvent themselves. I have been able to help some of them do just that. I have enjoyed watching them transform when they discover how they can forge a new path forward.

With the wisdom of hindsight, I now realize that I always wanted to be a coach and walk in my father's footsteps. I am finally on that path. Since that fateful day in May 2019, I have grown a great deal. What initially seemed a devastating loss became a blessing in disguise taking me back to my roots and pointing me in the direction to make a real difference and live the life I was destined for.

> *The task of leadership is not to put greatness into humanity, but to elicit it, for the greatness is already there."*
>
> *~John Buchan*

Kevin is an accomplished executive who has been leading business transformations for over 30 years. During that period, he has grown start-up businesses, turned around moribund operations, resurrected failing programs, and completely transformed the culture at each stop in his career.

Kevin has led operations organizations for telecommunications, medical device, and IT Consulting companies with responsibility for P&L ranging from $5m to $50m and has been able to achieve world-class results by focusing on 3 main priorities: Attracting, developing, and retaining employees who are empowered and engaged, creating customer advocates, and embedding a continuous improvement culture and creating high-performing teams.

Kevin Sturm
https://hellophello.com/hi/kevinsturm
https://www.linkedin.com/in/kevinjsturm/
https://kevinsturm.focalpointcoaching.com/
https://www.facebook.com/GameOnCoachingCorp

17

The Ring

····◆◆◆····

Kirvin's favorite lines were:
Princess Leia "I love you," Hans Solo "I know."
"You will never age for me, nor fade, nor die."

~ Shakespeare in Love

"They say when you meet the love of your life, time stops,
and that's true."

~ Big Fish

by
Toni Munoz Kaufman

As of this very moment, there are people all over the world who are just like you and me. They are either lonely, they are missing somebody, they are depressed, they are hurt, they are scarred from the past, they are having personal issues no one knows about, they have secrets you would not believe. They wish, they dream, and they hope.

Right now, they are sitting here reading these words, and I am writing this for you, so you do not feel alone anymore. Always remember, do not be depressed about the past, do not worry about the future, and just focus on today. Even a broken mirror, when glued back together can still show beauty. If today's not so great do not worry! Tomorrow's a new chance. If you are reading this, be sure to share this to make others feel better.

Christmas Eve, 2017

It is not a very pretty ring, there is not a single solitaire on the top, it does not look expensive, actually, it was all we had at the time, around $500. The ring is nothing fancy. It is a cluster of diamond dust and little pieces of diamonds.

Kirvin and I were on our way to celebrate at my little brother's home in Tomball Texas, Anthony was in his second year with a liver transplant and we had just found out that he had Prostate Cancer. My little brother was the person I could talk to, he understood, he was my strength and I was his go-to when he needed it. We shared so much, we were the two youngest and we stuck by each other, especially when he got sick.

August 2017

What nobody knows except my children is that after Hurricane Harvey, we had just completed repairing the house from the April Tax Day Flood of 2016 and I just couldn't take 3 more weeks of 20 mitigation drying fans going on round the clock day and night, another round of fire ants and bed bugs and watching the claw pick up everything that I owned from the sidewalk, while the entire family lived in two upstairs bedrooms with a makeshift kitchen in the middle room and a bathtub full of dishes to wash each time we tried to cook anything.

But more than that and after 30 years of marriage to a functional alcoholic who spent most nights and all weekends sitting alone in the garage with his music playing until he would drink himself into a diabetic coma and then we would have to call 911 or pour syrup down his throat to get his blood sugar back up above 27 to save his life. By this time, I had lost so much respect for my husband that I did everything I could to be away, dedicate myself to my work, launch a new company, dedicate myself to study and learning, and doing everything I could to not feel. My anger was always there, my failure, my guilt, and my inability to control what was supposed to be the most important part of my life was going nowhere. I chose to miss weddings and family events because I knew he would get drunk and embarrass me and I did not want to deal with the humiliation.

I was comfortable. I was miserable. So, I traveled a lot. However, our sons did not. When I was gone, they kept the watch on dad, listening for noises in the night, understanding that if he went into a diabetic coma he could die, so my son slept in the same room, stayed in the same house, and in the process, gave up his life and girlfriend to ensure that dad would wake up the next day. We all believed that Kirvin's depression and addiction were going to ultimately kill him. I moved out.

So, there we were, in Walmart on Christmas Eve, looking for last-minute presents while Kirvin was looking in the jewelry section, I finished my shopping and got back to the counter where Kirvin stood with a box in his hand. Baby, he said would you marry me? Are you crazy I asked? I will not live with a smoking alcoholic and before you are allowed to move into the new house, you have to clean up. Now please keep in mind that our past 30 years were riddled with broken promises to me and the kids of sobriety and no more smoking. We were all hurt so many times. Baby, I'm ready, he said, let's try this again. After all this time, I was still in love with this man, so just for Christmas and in front of the families, I said, yes.

2018 was a different sort of year, Kirvin had been keeping his promise, started seeing a nutritionist, worked hard trying to keep his diabetes in check, he tried the insulin pump and chewed nicotine gum, and overall started getting really healthy. He never bought beer, did not drink any alcohol. He was going to the doctor; he was losing weight. We were so proud of him.

But then, he could not stop losing weight, it was changing him in ways that didn't make any sense. And then the pain in the right hip started. After a blood test which included a PSA panel, his readings were at 57, more than 50 points above normal. Kirvin had stage 4 prostrate cancer that had metastasized to his bones, spine and hips. On January 19, 2020, Kirvin passed away on on our last cruise, onboard the Carnival Magic.

We were so very proud of Kirvin, I just have to share the eulogy written by our son:

Hello, for those of you who don't know me, I'm Todd, Kirvin's youngest, and I'd like to tell you a little about him today and paint as clear a picture as I possibly can of a man who often preferred the company of a good book and a radio than most others, escaping into the worlds and realms and possibilities of galaxies far, far away.

While I adored my father, I'd understand if you told me you had complicated feelings about him, I think most people who knew him well might, and it's okay to feel that about frankly a complex man.

In high-school and college, I was deep into superhero comics, and despite how audacious and ridiculous their backstories may have gotten, it was always so easy for me to believe them. Why wouldn't I? I had heard about my dad's back story. Kirvin was born in Kwigilingok, Alaska. He was raised in an Inuit Village and then a Hopi Indian reservation, eventually, his family ended up in Austin, TX where the children were separated from their mom after she was confined to the state hospital. He was sent to a series of children's homes until ultimately he arrived in Mission, TX at the Rio Grande Children's Home. He graduated salutatorian of Sharyland high school, class of 1970. A brilliant man with an incredible mind and a smile you could spot from across the room, he was nominated to the Air Force Academy by Congressman Kika de la Garza, and ended up narrowly missing going to Nam because after all of his pilot training, he grew, and it does say this on his records, three inches too tall to be a pilot.

He had three sons, Benjamin, Josiah, and Lawrence from his first marriage. He married Toni in 1987 and moved to Austin with her children, Andrea and Mikael, then came Erik and Todd.

Kirvin and Toni founded The Computer Help Desk and Microsoft Support Unlimited, where he served as CEO and COO for ten years. He was a wildly intelligent man and had graduated from the University of Texas, RGV, with a BA in political science. He'd receive his certificate of energy risk management from the Bauer School of Business at the University of Houston and would become a Certified Information Systems Security Professional (CISSP).

His work ethic will always be burned into my mind. The first signs we got that he wasn't doing well was when he started needing to come home early, or not go in at all. That's when you knew something was really up, he knew the importance of being on time, of doing a job well, of being a reliable asset to the people around you. My father was infinitely reliable, as long as it was something he didn't mind doing. The sort of security you get from your favorite winter sweater, you knew where he was, you knew what he was probably doing, and you knew he loved you. Even when he had a hard time showing it, which was often.

Superheroes, of course, have their flaws too. The dark sides of waking up every single morning, going to work to make the world make a little more sense for the family you have back at home, but trying to find a sense of happiness that frankly is sometimes easier fought for than kept and held onto. Few people get to see Iron Man's alcoholism. Few people get to see the depression on ink and paper in the small squares of the comic strip.

There are demons and villains that we all fight on a daily basis, but I think a hero is only ever shown to be as powerful as the villains they conquer, and so it would be remiss of me to try and downplay the havoc that they wreaked.

I know my own and my sibling's memories, even the happier ones, have at the very least, a beer goggle tinge, but I bring this up because I can say, with a shining certainty, that this was a war that my father won. It may have taken years, but for the last few, my father had successfully overcome his alcoholism, even his smoking habit, and he did those before he had been sick. He was getting healthier, and he had a renewed will to live these past few years, and that, perhaps makes this all just shocking.

But now I'd like to take a second to talk about the softness of this superhero. Of a man who, although he could not help you with your homework unless you could take some yelling would let your friends stay over as long as they needed a place. Who taught me the importance of working hard and testing out your theories. Who taught me that it's okay to not take life too seriously and that sometimes it was okay to laugh it off. He wanted to retire and run away with me to the Renaissance festivals I work at and would tell me about his plans to get a manual crank snow cone machine and dress as a monk.

A man who was real with me, but supportive. And who, even when I put him in some particularly tough situations to be in as a father, I'd have to say passed with flying colors, even if just in his own quiet way.

I'll miss going to events with you, dad, just to leave over an hour early under the guise of 'wanting to beat the traffic' and knowing that we'd both just actually rather be at home.

The Kaufman family crest is an imposing field of black with a single silver anchor adorned on the front, and I often think of my father's idle musings of being a sailor. His love of Horatio Hornblower, admiration of giant wood vessels and even coming as a pirate captain to my themed wedding, I have to say that I am at peace knowing he passed while out over something he'd had a lifelong passion for, because I honestly don't know how many of those he may have truly had, and I like to think of him doing now all the things he ever wanted to do. Seeing all that he wanted to see. And at the same time, I feel closer to him now, because I know there's a part of him that is now always the sun on my back, the wind on my face, and my favorite warm winter sweater. The warmth of his love.

Thank you.

You can be happy anywhere you are, you don't need anyone's approval, you are enough, you are strong, other people can be part of your journey, but they can't and never will be a destination. Never put your happiness in another person's hands, it doesn't work like that, it's more like a state of mind, but you get to make it, not anyone but you. You can be happy in a small cottage, you can be happy in a big city, as long as you are a friend to yourself. You're loved and worthy, don't allow others to make you believe otherwise.

Only you know yourself well, they see just a picture of you their mind made. But it's not you. Not exactly. You're capable of anything your mind can think of. If it's there - you know it's possible. You're the center of YOUR universe, you can do anything you want. And yes, you're strong enough to achieve it. You just are. Even if you're scared or insecure, trust me, and trust yourself. You are capable. You set your own goals.

Remember: the point is to be happy. You can never dream too big or too small. Your goal is to be happy, so go, do whatever it takes to achieve it! I believe in you and I love you. You know it's true. If you read this, doesn't matter where you are right now on this planet, I wish you a wonderful night and a happy peaceful life where all your dreams become true.

Thank you, God, for what you have allowed me to experience in my life. The unconditional love of a wonderful father and mother, The strength and love, the laughter of the comedienne that was my big sister, The true love of a man that just took my breath away. The unconditional love that I have for my children and step-children and thank you God for the lessons you have delivered to me in my life.

Toni Muñoz Kaufman was born and raised in Mission, TX, and is known for her television production, casting, and entrepreneurial ventures. She is the host of the popular Radio Show and Podcast, The World Class Mentors. designed to highlight and honor the powerful influence of mentors in people from all walks of life.

Toni had the honor of being on the presidential transition team to bring home Former President George H.W. Bush and served as his personal technology instructor and staff support manager. Toni presented and was known as a technical evangelist for Microsoft products. And she was honored as Top 10 Women in Computing.

Toni's Productions and Casting Background (in English and Spanish) is famous for her discovery of international talent and beauty across the televised game show industry. She produced The Latin Grammy's, and many other popular Talent and Game Shows.

Scan the QR code with your smartphone to watch Toni's video message.

Or, follow this link:
https://youtu.be/4tu4ArkV8Ho

18

Don't Let Your Circumstance Define You!

......◆◆◆......

"When you can't control what's happening, challenge
yourself to control how you respond to what's happening.
That's where the power is!"

~Source Unknown

by
Melissa Blake

I struggled for many years in a frustrating, stuck place where difficult circumstances defined my world. I experienced others' deaths and suicides, rejection, Post Traumatic Stress Disorder (PTSD), and abuse. Today, as a coach and empowerment specialist, I promise you that you don't have to go through all the turmoil that I did! Here is how I wrestled with and solved this dilemma to create the fulfilling life that I desired.

The offshore breezes blew softly in through the window of my car as I drove leisurely along Ocean Avenue in Santa Monica, California. I was 30 years old, and I had just treated myself to dinner at a local restaurant. Although I had tried for years to make sense of my stressful family upbringing, I was holding it all together well.

Suddenly, out of nowhere, a man walked directly in front of my car. I froze in horror as I felt him hit the front of my vehicle and saw him bounce off the windshield. In a stunned panic, I immediately stopped my car and got out to help him. He tried to get up, but there was blood everywhere and I cautioned him not to move.

The police arrived before I knew it. They pulled me away from this man to question me, and I learned his name was Fred. After the police interview, I went home and contacted my mother and my best friend. They quickly arrived, and we went to the hospital to inquire about Fred. The hospital nurse took me into a room and informed me that he had been dead on arrival. I covered my mouth and screamed a loud bloodcurdling scream that could probably be heard for a mile. I was in shock.

The scream echoed another cry that had come from me 12 years earlier. I had just returned home from college after learning that my grandfather was ill. My grandfather was my hero, and the only man who had ever truly showed me any love. I needed to see him!

My dad met me at the Los Angeles airport baggage claim while my mom hid in the car. He had promised my mom that he would not tell me my grandfather—my mom's dad—was dead. But when he saw me, he sadistically announced, "Your grandfather is dead. He hung himself!" Then, too, with tears streaming down my face, I had covered my mouth and uttered a bloodcurdling scream while everyone around me just stared.

My grandfather's funeral was a major event in Oceanside, New York, where he had been living for about 50 years. He had started the local Savings and Loan in the 1960s and been its president until he died in 1978. He had built many homes for others, had been a prominent political activist and Freemason, and owned two commercial buildings at a major intersection in town. He was honored several times for his various humanitarian efforts. nd he had loved me.

So many people came to my grandfather's funeral that a lot of them had to stand outside in the rain. On the day of his funeral, the doors of his synagogue were opened to honor him as his hearse passed it. This gesture was extraordinary! Even though suicide is considered a terrible sin in Judaism, my grandfather had built this first synagogue in Oceanside and he had been its first president.

At the time of my grandfather's death, my parents were both consumed with their own feelings and had nothing left to spare for my debilitating sadness. My mother didn't get along with her own mother, and it fell to me to comfort my grandmother on my own during the funeral services. At the cemetery, I was crying so hard in the pouring rain that when it was my turn to shovel dirt onto the lowered coffin, I slipped and almost fell into the grave; I would have gone in had someone not grabbed my arm.

Soon after the funeral, my mom sent me back to our home in Pacific Palisades, California with my dad, where he almost immediately threw me out of the house for the perceived injustice of being minutes late to feed our diabetic dog, Coco. The dog was fine, but my father was obsessed with Coco and lathered affection on him to the exclusion of all else. He had never thrown me out before. I was devastated!

I was so upset that I called my mom. Rather than consoling me, and taking my side, she suggested, "Why don't you stay with my friend, Marsha, until you go back to school?" I felt abandoned. When I returned to the University of California at Berkeley, I was too overwhelmed with grief and rejection to function. I felt horrible despair about my grandfather's suicide, my father's all-too-familiar raging at and rejection of me, and my mother's failure to protect me from my dad or support me.

I had been a good girl who got excellent grades. During my childhood and young adulthood, I desperately tried not to disturb my parents. But, honestly, they were capable of deep cruelty in their words and deeds. They verbally shredded me to pieces regularly. I lived in constant fear; I never felt safe. I truly thought that they did not care about me at all. I also believed I was the problem.

Their behavior towards me finally motivated me to do the most rebellious thing I had ever done. I withdrew from school and went to live with a friend in Los Angeles. I did not tell my parents where I was nor that I had left school. And I returned to school within a year to finish my degree.

A dozen years later I contended with the shock of having been the instrument of a stranger's death. I struggled with undiagnosed PTSD. I kept subconsciously reliving the car accident. I kept wondering if I could have done something to prevent it. Was it actually my fault?

Have you ever blamed yourself for something you had no control over, then kept obsessing about it?

Many witnesses had confirmed to the police that I was not at fault. The police determined that Fred's death was a suicide, and I was never brought up on any charges. After interviewing me, the department of motor vehicles also decided that I was not to blame. Yet, my father was in such a fury about the fact that I had wrecked my car that he threw a chair across a room.

In 1990, very few people understood PTSD. My therapist kept telling me that I was an underachiever even though I had passed the Certified Public Accountant (CPA) exam and held down demanding jobs as a corporate accountant. I had chosen a career as a CPA because my parents had approved of it. I dreaded and hated the work, and the turmoil in my life showed up as debilitating back pain.

I sat on many therapists' couches over the years trying to make sense of it all, but retelling my stories just retraumatized me. At age 32 I married an accomplished older television director who was just another one of my many attempts to find a replacement for my grandpa. Like many first marriages, I had married someone similar to people in my family because I confused familiarity with comfort. My husband was verbally abusive and narcissistic. He was unwilling to work unless he thought the assignment was worthy of him, while he expected me to work at a job that I hated.

My husband had been a heavy partier, but no longer drank, and he regularly attended Alcoholics Anonymous meetings. I started going to Al-Anon, the 12-Step program for the family members and friends of alcoholics that are impacted by their disease. I went to meetings because I wanted to change my husband; however, Al-Anon did not help me change him at all. Instead, I began to learn that I had value separate from the people with whom I associated, and my parents' abusive treatment of me was about them, not me.

About nine years into my marriage, I joined a two-year program to study spirituality and Judaism after having a strong spiritual awakening during the Jewish high holy days. My parents had not provided me with any religious training. During my first year in the program, I was enjoying doing numerous Jewish spiritual practices. I would repeatedly say the 72 Hebrew names of God, talk to God while being in nature, and meditate daily with a Jewish mantra. I became very open from these practices, and many painful memories I had repressed came flooding back into my consciousness. Remembering was necessary because there needed to be awareness of the past for healing and change to occur.

As time went on, I was getting perplexing messages when I meditated. I discovered that I was experiencing a dark night of the soul; a period of desolation suffered commonly by mystics in which all sense of consolation is removed. It is a time where our old ideas and rationalizations no longer serve us. People in this state tend to feel alone and lost; they question everything, including their sanity and the existence of God.

Have you ever questioned everything?

Ignoring my own voice had ignited a war that waged inside me. My old beliefs were dying which made it hard to understand where I was going next. I felt more lost and confused than ever. I sat in a state of "bottoming out" and the related indescribable emotional pain for several months.

I divorced my husband, who disapproved of what I was doing. I did all the filings myself and sold my half of the house back to him. I booked a three-month stay at Life Healing Center in Santa Fe, New Mexico where I saw incredibly colorful sunsets. People came there from other recovery facilities to deal with their underlying trauma after getting sober from their substance addictions. I had no such substance addiction, but I was a recovering codependent who had enabled my husband's behavior in numerous ways. I had an excessive reliance on other people for approval and my sense of identity. I had believed I was special because of who my grandfather had been— until I was confronted with his suicide.

Going to Life Healing Center was a great investment. I received sessions of Eye Movement Desensitization and Reprocessing (EMDR), a light and sound therapy that makes you feel distant from the trauma you have experienced. My PTSD was largely cured by this therapy. From the deep work that I did at the center, I started to understand how my childhood trauma had defined me and my actions. My triggers were just growth opportunities. I realized that I had a choice in what I did and how I responded to events. I began to not only ask for inner guidance but to listen for the answers that came to me. I learned to trust myself and my deep inner knowing.

I continued my personal development work because I believe that if I am not growing, I am dying. I'd always been curious and loved to learn. I hired a physical trainer so I would be more aware of my body, less "in my head," and more physically fit. I got involved in medical Chi Gong, massage, and fascial stretch, which helped heal my back. I learned where my energy was stuck in my body, how to get the energy to flow, and how to manage my energy better.

I worked with many types of psychological therapies. Biofeedback taught me how to get into deep relaxation and other mental states that would help me solve problems by utilizing different ways of thinking. Cognitive therapy led me to begin to question and change thinking that was not serving me. I found that subconscious thoughts and programming run us, and I started to uncover and reprogram my thoughts. Through shadow work, I learned to own parts of myself that I had not been willing to accept.

My continued spiritual quest brought me to believe that there are many portals or spiritual paths to God and greater knowledge into which we can tap. I have found that all mystics, no matter what tradition they embrace, believe the same thing: that we are all one! This is what I believe too!

My experiences and my work on myself helped me to become very empathetic. I realized that kindness was more important to me than anything. I started to see how I had unconsciously learned from my parents to be unkind to myself and to use honesty as a weapon. I made a concerted effort to develop self-care practices and to speak more gently. Further, I came to realize how much self-love and self-acceptance are key to leading a fulfilling life.

I ultimately decided to go to a coaching school which overlooked the majestic Pacific Ocean in San Diego, California. I knew that I was a natural teacher since I had been asked to teach at UCLA and did teach at various points in high school and college. I was good at mentoring and creating a space for others' healing. I had sponsored people in 12-Step programs, trained in spiritual accompaniment during the earlier two-year spiritual program that I had attended, and spent years running accounting teams as the financial controller of various companies.

Coaching school was a true revelation! Through exercises the school assigned, I found that at the essence of my soul, I am effervescence, boldness, insight, curiosity, and devotion. The exercises also uncovered that my life purpose is the embodiment of ecstasy, which makes a lot of sense because I have a great ability to find, express, and bring joy.

I came to understand that the life story we tell ourselves and our mindset defines our lives; our beliefs and thoughts create our reality! I grew to comprehend that what we decide to think and do in the face of hard issues will define our future. I chose to reframe my mistakes, failures, and traumas into lessons for which I could be grateful

After I experienced people taking their lives through suicide, I came to believe that life is precious. I decided to focus my life on helping others empower themselves because I now have the skills and experience to do it. I specifically enjoy helping people find and live with authenticity and purpose so they can create fulfilling lives that lead to positive legacies for themselves and their families!

Are you living a completely fulfilling, purposeful life? If not, what are you going to do about it? What would the value be to you of accelerating your transformation with the support and accountability of a trained, understanding coach?

Authentic empowerment is possible. I sincerely wish you well on your journey to finding it.

Melissa Blake is an empowerment coach credentialed by the International Coach Federation who guides corporate, entrepreneurial, and private clients to achieve greater professional success, better relationships, enhanced well-being, and fulfillment.

A former C.P.A. and corporate controller, Melissa is also a trained Spiritual Director, and a public speaker, who provides heartfelt support to empower her clients to profound growth and change.

To learn how her proven strategies can assist you in actualizing your goals, Connect with Melissa at:
https://EZcard.com/melissablake,
text melissablake to 64600, or call/text directly to (415) 342-5985.

Scan the QR code with your smartphone to watch Melissa's video message.

Or, follow this link:
https://youtu.be/BN3uXeplQ3M

19

My Life as an Agropreneur:
From Country Lanes to CyberSurfer

··· ◆ ◆ ◆ ◆ ··· ·

*Entrepreneurship is living a few years of your life like most
people won't, so that you can spend the rest of your life
like most people can't.*

~Unknown

by
Brian Ludwig

Have you been dreaming of becoming an entrepreneur?

I sat in a sturdy plastic chair in the YMCA craft room and looked around at all the busy kids around me. I was four years old and restless, not a brilliant combination for a little boy who has been asked to create something clever out of paper, glue, and a little paint. My brother and I had been dropped off at the Y to learn how to make things that would look nice and give our mother a cute reason to brag about us. But the project work did not have a lot of appeal for me. Don't get me wrong, I appreciated a nicely glued paper shape as much as the next fellow. But the entrepreneurial wheels were turning in my brain even then. I had an idea.

My mother would give my brother and me a little bag of potato chips each for Saturday morning snack time, but rather than eating mine, I would sell a single chip to the other kids for a nickel apiece. At the time, a bag of chips cost only 10 cents. My mother laughs about it now, but at the time she was ashamed of my precocious "profiteering;" the other mothers, apparently, just figured that if their kids were dumb enough to pay me a nickel for a single chip, they deserved to lose a week's allowance. My little business came crashing to the ground a few weeks later, when the other mothers started to pack bags of chips for their kids, too, but I had learned a good lesson in the value of making a profit.

I didn't know it then, but that YMCA craft room was an early proving ground for what was to become my life's work. I grew up on a farm in rural Canada, where fields unroll in a rich carpet of food-to-be, and cows, pigs, chickens, and sheep haul farm family members out of bed before dawn to get the day's work started. Farming is hard work and hundreds of millions of people in North America even today rely on the willingness of countless farmers to supply grocery stores and restaurants with the precious food that keeps us fuelled up and motoring forward through our days.

At the same time as I was learning about how to run a farm, I was constantly surrounded by my father's entrepreneurial spirit. And I had a great love for science. All of which meant that at the end of high school, I had no idea what to do with my life. Like a lot of young adults at the time, I thought I had to have it all figured out ahead of time. After attending a one-week agriculture career camp, I was fascinated by a presentation from Agriculture Canada: they were launching a program to train and recruit hundreds of young people to become agricultural scientists, as they were facing a large wave of retirements in the upcoming years.

That sounded perfect for me! I went into Agriculture College and earned my Bachelor's degree and after that, I completed my Master's degree in Agriculture and started work on my Ph.D. Then, all of a sudden, Agriculture Canada made a drastic policy change and severely cut back its research program. All those jobs that they had been training people to assume were now gone. Permanently. I felt shocked! I'd been working for years towards what had seemed like a sure career that was going to suit me to a "T"!

Have you ever felt as though your future has been yanked out from under you?

Did you feel discouraged and confused, too?

Well, I didn't spend a lot of time wallowing in self-pity, since farmers are pretty used to the unpredictability of life and I had been raised to "make lemonade" when life hands you lemons. I decided to visit some of my old professors and colleagues from my first university to survey the job market. I thought they might have some ideas for me, but this turned out to be a dismal experience. Everyone I talked to complained about only having two-year contracts; they were constantly looking for new work.

I decided to plan out my Ph.D. research and training plan. I had been given a full three-year scholarship and so I consulted with numerous professors who strongly supported the research I wanted to do. The only problem was that the Ph.D. committee that had direct control over my studies was not supportive. One committee member came right out and said my plan was rubbish. Instead of focusing on agriculture research, the committee wanted me to become a molecular biologist.

Molecular biologist? I was in agriculture, for Pete's sake!

This was the last straw. I resigned from my academic pursuits and went back to the farm to work full-throttle on a small consulting and research business that I had set up a year or two earlier. I had had enough of letting others determine what was best for me. I was going to control my own destiny from now on. I was going to be an entrepreneur.

As far as I'm concerned, the entrepreneurial lifestyle is the way to go. There is no life like it. Yes, there have been rough times when I've wondered, "why the heck did I ever decide to do this?!" Then I think back to the times when I did have the occasional stint as an "employee" and realize that I was never truly happy at those jobs. Time and again, I've realized that my true calling is being an entrepreneur. I am my own boss. I am free to take any direction I want. I make my own destiny!

But there are three big lessons I've learned along the way that have made a huge difference in my success.

Lesson Number One: Stay on Top of Your Business Finances

Never take your eyes off the cash flow because it's the lifeblood of business

~Richard Branson

As I mentioned, I had actually started my first real business before I left my studies. I was testing experimental weed control chemicals on my family's farm. Like most aspiring business owners, I was focused on doing the work. I did not have much time for the business's numbers. After all, isn't that what my accountant was for?

I met with my accountant a year after I hired him, and he gave me two pieces of news that did not impress me. First, he told me that I owed a massive amount of tax money to the government. "How can I possibly owe that much?!" I exclaimed. I was a university student who had spent every dollar from my scholarship and lab instructor salaries on getting my business going. I had even borrowed $20,000 to buy some equipment. There was no spare money! What the...?

I quickly realized that my accountant had neglected to tell me a lot of things I needed to know. To add insult to injury, the guy handed me a $2,000 bill for the lack of advice he had given me throughout the year. "Thanks for nothing, buddy," I thought. This is when I realized that going forward, I had to take responsibility for my business's numbers. This was a key business lesson that I learned the hard way.

As a university undergrad in the pre-internet era, I had had a tough professor who taught me a valuable lesson. He told me that with a library at my fingertips, I could learn anything I wanted. Taking this advice, I took it upon myself to learn about business finances. I first started to learn about business taxes and how to reduce my tax bill. I learned to do my own taxes and I learned how to maximize my tax savings to keep more money in my own pocket. I also learned how to focus on key numbers from my business financials to ensure I was going in the right direction.

And then I didn't just look at my own numbers, I also started to help others with theirs as well. I learned that a lot of business owners avoid dealing with their business finances at all costs. I also learned that I had a strong skill in working with numbers. Best of all, I actually enjoyed working with numbers. And it made me feel really great to help other people make some sense of this vitally important part of their business.

This leads me to my second lesson.

Lesson Number Two: Be Prepared for Change

To improve is to change; to be perfect is to change often.

~Winston Churchill

Initially, my business was to be a private farm research and crop consulting business. But few producers were willing to pay for private consultants. After my incident with my accountant, I was already learning everything I humanly could about business taxes, and I began computerizing my accounting books. Not many people owned a personal computer in those days. But I soon learned to develop a computerized accounting system that I used to monitor my business financials and minimize my taxes.

I was completely unprepared for what was to come next.

I was at a farm show where I happened to meet an exhibitor while having a bite to eat. While talking, we happened upon the topic of computers. He was interested in the fact that I had a computer and was using it for accounting and financial analysis. As it turns out, that exhibitor was working for an Agricultural Tech School and he offered me a part-time position as a contract instructor. At that time, farmers were just starting to use computers in their operations and greatly needed help. Within three years, I was one of the school's key instructors, teaching farmers about computers, crop production, tax planning, financial management, estate planning, and business diversification.

It was a dream come true!

The funny part about this teaching position was that most people who knew me would have never thought I would be willing to take on a job like this. You see, I was, and still am today, an introvert. In a social setting, I will sit on the sidelines listening to everyone talk, unless someone asks me a direct question. Most people could not imagine me in front of a room teaching. But when it comes to teaching and presenting, I am fearless. I can get in front of a crowd of hundreds without breaking a sweat because I have a strong passion for training and mentoring others.

I continued to do contract work for agencies focused on agricultural business training for the next 10 years. At the same time, I was doing less crop consulting and more financial consulting. When I first started my business, I had no plans to teach or provide financial consulting. However, by taking advantage of trends in the marketplace, and being open to opportunities as they presented, I was able to capitalize on the skills that I had learned for my own business and use them to bring in additional revenue that allowed me to grow my business faster while helping others.

The changes kept coming

Over the next 30 years, I made several major business shifts. I obtained a Master's Degree in Distance Education as I was experimenting with providing agricultural training on this new thing called "the Internet." I became certified as a Microsoft programmer and developed some livestock financial analysis programs. Eventually, I was doing so much tax planning work that I decided to earn my professional accounting designation. To this day, I continue to earn a variety of certifications in business coaching, internet-based marketing, advanced taxation, cross-border taxation, and anything else that looks like it will help me serve my clients better.

More change is afoot. For years I have been dabbling with taking my business online, but the Covid-19 pandemic has shown me the need to get my business online much faster. By the time you read this, I will have launched the new online phase of my business and I will be serving a global customer base.

This leads me to my third important lesson: don't be afraid to get assistance.

Lesson Number Three: Don't be an Island; Build a Team

Great things in business are never done by one person,
they're done by a team of people.

~Steve Jobs

If you recall, I talked about a professor who told me I can learn anything with the right resources. and now, we have the internet, with its massive resources. Over the years, it has helped me develop a broad, diverse range of skills that allow me to better serve my clients.

Throughout most of my career, I have been resistant to getting consulting assistance unless I absolutely needed it. I've been determined to learn what I need to know and do it all myself. It saved me money and taught me a lot. However, looking back, I realized that learning on my own also took longer to implement my projects, and often, I would either lose interest or someone else would come to the finish line first.

I've actually been dabbling in my current online project and learning new skills to support it for the past three or four years. Then, a year ago, I enlisted the help of mentors and coaches. I quickly realized the key benefit of working with a coach is that I could learn the content faster and be able to implement projects in a fraction of the time that it would normally take me. Having a team has helped me grow my business much faster, and brought me to profitability much sooner.

Final thoughts

Thirty-five years ago, I could never have imagined myself where I am today. Despite all the challenges and changes that have occurred over the years, I can now offer my skills, service, and wisdom to a growing list of clients who want to grow, too.

My key message is that you need to focus on your cash flow. Cash is king! Without this one piece, your business will quickly close. I help my clients understand and use their accounting numbers to make management decisions *now* – not just to prepare a tax return the following year. I also help business owners maximize their tax savings so they can keep more money in their pockets, rather than sending it to the government. Finally, I work with businesses to understand their marketing and how to improve it, especially with respect to digital marketing. My overall goal is to help business owners increase their business success, so they achieve their ultimate life goals.

I've come a long way from that little kid in the YMCA craft room who sold potato chips to his peers in order to make money. And while I'm still not a fan of crafts, I do love to create successful outcomes on behalf of my clients.

 Brian Ludwig is a personal financial and business coach who works with small business owners to more effectively manage their cash flow and, ultimately, to put more money into their pockets at the end of the day.

He offers a complimentary membership site and phone app that has a wealth of financial and business information and short courses, a variety of advanced training programs covering different aspects of optimizing your cash flow, and a year-long mentorship program that provides personalized assistance to grow your business.

Brian Ludwig
To check out Brian's courses
Download my mobile app: Growing Your Business
www. brianludwig.ca
https://www.linkedin.com/in/brianludwigcpa/

Scan the QR code with your smartphone to view Brian's video message.

Or, follow this link:
https://vimeo.com/458226350

20

The Power of Uncertainty

···◆◆◆···

"Without sacrifice, the character of love does not exist."

~ Guruji Mahendra

by
Inthirani Arul

Growing up, I lived in an environment where I faced uncertainty, anxiety, and a huge responsibility. I felt like the weight of the world was on my shoulders. There are times when we can't see the end result because we are coming from a place of uncertainty. Everything we know can change in an instant. We lose that connection to our true self. When we live in uncertainty, we find ourselves living in stress because what we know is no longer familiar or in alignment with our truth.

There is a difference between worry and anxiety. Worry is about something that we refer to from our experiences from our past. Ninety-five percent of what we worry about never comes to pass, and the other five percent we have no control over. Anxiety comes from fear and uncertainty about what may happen in the future. There usually are three responses to anxiety – fight, flight, or freeze.

Notice where you go in times of uncertainty. Realizing the choices that you make moment by moment dictates your future outcome. Even when you feel everything is out of control and uncertain, it is essential to remember that you still have a choice.

Was there a time in your life you felt lonely and uncertain?

I was carefree as a child, as most of us are when we are young. I played in the backyard, watching my mother work in the garden, and I would even help her. During the hot summer weather, I would dash in and out of the sprinkler, and I even made a water slide out of plastic garbage bags. I was curious about the insects and even touched them. I enjoyed looking closely at nature, observing how the snow and rain fell, and also how peaceful I felt while I watched. I loved lakes and noticed how the shallow parts of a river all flowed in one direction. When I threw a pebble into the water, the sound of its splash fascinated me. I liked to watch the ripples in lakes and ponds where the water was more stagnant and the fish swimming. I even recall observing the chickens and ducks that my neighbors released in the evenings to roam their yard and how some would make their way under or come through the wire fence into our yard.

Now, when I look back, I can clearly see the certainty that exists within the principles and fundamentals of nature. When we lose that connection and move against the direction of flow, for example, when we go against the flow of a fast-moving river, we will face uncertainty, obstacles, and will eventually fall because we are going against the fundamentals and principles of nature.

Uncertainty comes from a place of fear and lack. This is where we lose that connection to our truth in our lives. When we don't trust or we lose trust, this leads to stress, which in turn leads to anxiety, low self-esteem, depression, lack of confidence, and other health-related issues.

At the age of nine, I was the oldest daughter in the family. When my father was at work, it was my responsibility to prepare lunch. My mother was a diabetic who also suffered from mental health issues and, at this point in her life, had been diagnosed as legally blind. One day I called to my Mom to ask her to come eat lunch. When she didn't respond, I went into her room and found her lying motionless on her bed. I tried to wake her by calling to her. My voice grew louder as I grew more scared. I even tried tapping her on her shoulders and moving her arms and legs, but she still wasn't moving or responding.

I could feel the adrenalin rushing through my body. I panicked, went into overwhelm, and thought the worst. She was dead! All I could think to do was to run outside and call for help. In an instant, everything was changing, and the future became uncertain. I could feel the anxiety pooling in the pit of my stomach, and my whole body was shaking.

My neighbor told me to run back inside and call 911. My vision blurred, and my hands shook, but I managed to turn the dial of our rotary phone and spoke with the operator, who reassured me that an ambulance was on its way. I even ran outside afterward to wait for the attendants so they wouldn't miss the house.

Once they arrived, they worked on her, and she regained consciousness. I was so relieved and could breathe with more ease again. I called my father, and then my mother and I traveled to the hospital in the ambulance, where my father met us. When I saw him there, I ran over to him, and he gave me a big hug and said, "You just saved your mother's life."

That day of great uncertainty changed my awareness forever of the gift that is human life. I also gained self-confidence, inner strength, a deeper inner and outer awareness, and a knowledge I hadn't possess before. It is indeed in those moments of uncertainty that we all face during our lives where we can gain the greatest gifts. In a moment of realization and heightened awareness, we know that everything is shifting.

What gift have you received from a time you faced uncertainty?

That day I found my mother lying unconscious on her bed, I felt myself physically going into flight and emotionally into freeze. Later I discovered that this often happens when people experience emergency situations. Physically I took action because my gut feeling, my inner knowing told me the truth, that there was something horribly wrong. I took flight, and I ran for help. But emotionally, I froze and temporarily lost connection to the truth and trust, only to feel them later on when I had unfrozen emotionally.

As time progressed, I learned how the anxiety of this day had become ingrained in me. It followed me wherever I went and showed up in social situations, especially when I was around other people. When I was sixteen years old, my high school offered me the opportunity to volunteer at the Vancouver General Hospital. I was so excited, but I had never traveled by bus by myself. I learned how to do it, but my anxiety was high every time. I thought everybody was looking at me as I boarded the bus, and I worried about what they thought of me. My heart would race uncontrollably when boarding or getting off the bus because I could see them looking at me.

On the day of my orientation at a long-term care ward, I walked into the women's ward. Beds were lined up along the windows in this long room. In front of some of the beds, patients were tied to their chairs so they wouldn't fall or walk away. I could hear some moaning, and one was crying, "I need to go to the washroom." She was squirming and trying to move in her chair. The nurses were busy, and as a volunteer, I wasn't allowed to walk her there for safety reasons, hers and mine.

As time passed and they grew to know me, the nurses gave me opportunities they wouldn't normally give volunteers. I was allowed to walk patients and feed them. I was so gratified to be able to help decrease the nurses' workload and to improve the patients' situation through engagement. I got to know many of the patients. I listened to the patients share their stories of pain, struggle, and triumph, and I learned how each and every person makes a difference in this world. I discovered that, when we give from our hearts from a place of true caring and when we share our gifts, time, presence, and life force, not only do we learn and grow and strengthen our connection to the flow of our life force, but we also begin to live from a place of certainty and truth. Through this awareness, we can impact the lives of those we serve and leave an imprint. We are guests on this planet, and we are here to leave this planet a better place than how we found it.

After I had been volunteering for five years, the volunteer coordinator told me that I was invited to attend a ceremony where I would receive an award for the highest number of hours of service by a junior volunteer. They wanted to interview me and take pictures for an article in the hospital newspaper. My heart was overflowing with gratitude because I really loved helping the patients and getting to know them.

A few weeks later, we had just returned from Malaysia, and there was a message on the phone to call the volunteer coordinator. When I did, she told me, "I have been trying to get a hold of you! Because you had the highest number of hours as a junior volunteer, you had been selected to have brunch with Prince Charles and Lady Diana who are coming for the opening of Expo 86. However, we had to give it to someone else because we couldn't reach you."

I had always admired Lady Diana for who she was and what she stood for and the humanitarian work she had been doing in the world. My energy suddenly shifted, and I felt sad and then angry with myself. This was an opportunity of a lifetime that I would never get again.

I share this story because, as we go through life, opportunities will be presented to us, and it is through awareness and quick action that we must take advantage of those opportunities, or we may regret it the rest of our lives. The truth is we all have opportunities that are presented to each and every one of us, and they show up in different forms. It is up to us to be aware of these opportunities and then decide what we will do with them.

I learned more about myself through the experience of being a volunteer which, in turn, gave me a greater awareness about this opportunity that had been made available to me and that I had lost. Now I look back and see a connection of a greater awareness I had as a young child who used to watch World Vision as tears would roll down my cheeks. I would also watch the Variety Club Telethons and even tape them as a teenager. This deeper awareness that has always lived within me opened another door that led me to become one of the Ambassadors with the Women of Global Change. I have served both in Mexico and Jamaica, where I had the privilege of participating in two humanitarian projects serving underprivileged children and their families where we refurbished schools and brought supplies and goods to support their needs. My bigger vision is to create scholarships to support orphaned and underprivileged children with their educational and extracurricular activities so they can live their most joyful and fulfilling lives.

Even in the midst of uncertainty, you have a choice by realizing that, in every moment you take action in your life and with every step you take forward, you are building your self-esteem and self-confidence. The choice you make determines your outcome.

There is a difference between worry and anxiety. Anxiety comes from the fear of the unknown, and when you recognize it, you are given a choice to move forward and thereby direct your future outcomes. The truth is every choice you make dictates your outcome and destiny. It is up to you to be conscious of your everyday actions, reactions, character, and behaviors that will affect the outcomes you want to achieve in your life; to become aware that you can create a ripple effect not only in your own life and the life of your family, but also in your community, your society, and even all of humanity.

Today, I am forever grateful and blessed because of the Trivedi Effect and the creator for all the opportunities I have had to learn and grow and for my very existence. I know for certain that when we take action in our own lives through our own assessment and self-awareness and by following the principles and fundamentals of nature, the universal principles, and ultimately our Creator who created each and every one of us, we can live a life of certainty and become the best person that we are capable of being.

As we grow in our own awareness, our life force strengthens us and elevates our connection to that awareness which, in turn, brings us closer into alignment with the truth of our very existence and the depth of who we truly are.

Inthirani Arul is a scientifically validated life force conduit, human relations leader, the author of four books, and the founder of SoulPathDiscoveryInc. She empowers single parents, health care professionals, teachers, and those who want to become authentic, heart-centered leaders to live their optimum life and unique purpose. She is a graduate of CEO SPACE and Peak Potentials Training and an ambassador with the Women of Global Change. Inthirani believes that within every person lives possibility and growth.

Inthriani Arul

To learn more about her, visit Inthirani.com or SoulPathDiscovery.com.

https://www.pinterest.fr/inthiraniarul/boards/
https://www.facebook.com/inspire88
https://www.facebook.com/Inthirani
https://www.linkedin.com/in/inthirani-arul-22013749/detail/recent-activity/
https://www.instagram.com/inthirani.a/
https://youtu.be/1pJxYUdPtz4

Scan the code with your smartphone to view Inthriani's video message.

Or, follow this link:
https://youtu.be/1pJxYUdPtz4

21

Sculpting Your Legacy

......◆◆◆......

by
Roger Killen

Clarity about the legacy you want to create gives you a North Star that guides you to a purposeful life. But how do you choose the legacy that's right for you? My selection process took 13 years and 3 game-changing epiphanies before it felt right. I hope that my story makes your selection process shorter and more linear.

It all began on Christmas Eve 2006. I'm sitting at my desk overlooking English Bay in Vancouver, British Columbia on the west coast of Canada. Everything outside my window is one shade of gray or another. I'm racking my brain for an answer to the same question that has driven me nuts at this time of year for many years – what should I give my Dad tomorrow as a Christmas present? I reflect on years of tools, ties, and trinkets. A little voice inside me is saying "Roger, you're a creator. You can do better." I decide to take a walk to stimulate my creativity. The Seawall around Vancouver's iconic Stanley Park is only 60 meters away. I walk briskly to stay warm and in 30 minutes arrive at Siwash Rock – a basalt sea stack that rises 15 meters out of the waters of English Bay.

I stare at Siwash Rock and have an idea. Dad has everything material that he wants. What if I give him an experience instead of a thing. But what experience? That's when it came to me. When I arrive home, I write in a Christmas card, "Dear Dad, My Christmas present is a gift of my time to help you write your autobiography. With love, Roger". I am excited because Dad will be thrilled with this novel gift... or so I thought!

Dad and Mum live a block from me on Beach Avenue. Our family tradition is for my older sister and me to gather at their home on Christmas afternoon to enjoy snacks and drinks and exchange gifts before dinner. My Mum is 84 and filled with vitality. Dad is 92. His body is frail. His once erect posture is stooped. His once brisk walk is a slow shuffle behind a walker. His once-bright blue eyes are tired. Every night, he has a pee, goes to bed, and falls asleep, but not always in that order!

We are in their living room. My Mum, ever the organizer, places a stack of gifts in front of each of us and invites us to take turns opening gifts one at a time so that we can experience each other's pleasure. After several rounds of gift opening, Dad pulls my card from his stack. He opens and reads it. His words haunt me: "Roger, you're a wonderful son but I'm done. Thank you, but you have better things to do with your time." Several reactions wash over me: I am sad that Dad has given up on life. I am upset that Dad has rejected my novel idea. I am confused as to what to do next – should I drop the idea or should I fight for it. I decide to fight for it. I also decided that I need to be strategic and that here and now is neither the right time nor place to counter-attack.

Overnight I develop a strategy and the next day revisit Dad and Mum. As Mum is in the kitchen making tea, I say to Dad: "Dad, you were born in 1914 and it's now 2006. I'd love to know how you lived those 92 years. Would you please accept my Christmas gift ... for me." I knew that Dad would never do anything for himself but would bend over backward for someone who asked for his help. He pressed me for what I found interesting about those 92 years. "Dad, you've lived through 2 World Wars, the Great Depression, man landing on the moon, the development of the automobile, aeroplane, radio, TV, phone, fax, refrigeration, vaccination, production line, microwave, Internet... and even sliced bread. You've lived through the most fascinating period in the history of mankind and I'd like to learn about it from your perspective."

Hesitantly, Dad agreed to give it a go. Yes!!!!!! Our game plan was to meet every Sunday night so that I could interview Dad. Our goal was to chronicle his life's milestones and then write the story of each milestone. Between my Sunday night visits, Dad would review his many photograph albums for more details. Initially, he struggled with faces and names and places and dates. My questions tickled his mind. What began as a trickle became a stream and then a flood of long-forgotten memories.

Dad remembered graphic details about his boyhood in a small rural town in Northern Ireland from 1914 to 1929. Dad remembered lusty details of his life and loves as an eligible bachelor in Belfast during the Great Depression. Dad remembered romantic details of meeting, courting, and marrying my mother during the Second World War. Dad remembered poignant details about first holding his daughter in 1948, and son, me, three years later. "Roger, for 9 years after you were born, I didn't have a good night's sleep," he told me... many times.

From these and many, many more memories, Dad and I gradually built an inventory of his life. As this inventory grew, Dad realized that his achievements defined a rich, full, and successful life. He realized that his contributions were the hallmarks of a good man, father, husband, employee, employer, and human being. He realized that his legacy was huge. With these realizations, some of Dad's self-confidence returned, his self-image rallied and his spirits lifted. As they lifted, he shuffled a little faster and he stood a little taller. His blue eyes began to sparkle again. He even began to flirt.

It took 2 years of Sunday evenings to chronicle Dad's milestones. But time was not on Dad's side. He died at age 94. His autobiography was incomplete. I deeply regret that we started it too late and urge you not to make this mistake with your special senior.

GAME-CHANGER #1

When Dad died in 2008, I was 57. I didn't have any children or grandchildren so hadn't given much thought to the topic of legacy. His unfinished autobiography and death caused me to reflect on my own life. I began thinking a lot about legacy. My reflections brought clarity about 3 things:

1. We influence people every day by what we say, do, write, record, and share, and all of that influence becomes our legacy.
2. "Yes", I want to sculpt my legacy on the hearts and minds of millions of change-makers.
3. I want the form of my legacy to be a massive digital collection of ideas that inspire change-makers to take action. This clarity became, and remains, my legacy, my purpose, my North Star.

In 2011, three years after Dad died, I turned 60, retired as a serial entrepreneur, and cast about for a give-back project that would allow me to sculpt my legacy. The following year, I attended a TEDx event and was smitten with the concept of "Ideas Worth Spreading." I thought that I'd discovered the perfect vehicle for my legacy.

I was inspired by the thought of a new TEDx event whose speakers and ideas would make action happen and change the world. I assembled a team of people - including Iman Aghay - and together we produced the first TEDxStanleyPark event. This event taught us many lessons – mostly of the "what not to do again" variety!

In each of 2015, 2016, 2017, and 2018 we produced a TEDxStanleyPark event. Every year was bigger and better than the year before. The 2018 event took place in front of over 2,000 attendees. All 13 speakers received a standing ovation. Their videos have since received nearly 40 million views.

Shortly after this event, an old friend and I are enjoying happy hour on the patio of Vancouver's Sylvia Hotel on English Bay. As we await our second bottle of Chardonnay, Brian leans in intently and asks "Roger, what action do people REALLY take after they hear your TED talks?" I am stumped. I cannot answer Brian. In the following few days I realize that "Ideas Worth Spreading" is a far cry from "Ideas Making Action Happen", I realize that the talks that I am producing are a blend of information and entertainment but are not triggering measurable action, and I realize that what I want to do with ideas – inspire people to take action that tackles humanity's pressing problems – and am doing – "infotaining" people – are as different as day and night. I had to fix this misalignment and get back to building my legacy - a collection of ideas that activate change-makers.

GAME-CHANGER #2

After much soul-searching, I made the game-changing decision to say goodbye to TEDxStanleyPark and create a new brand called Get Inspired Talks. These talks describe ideas that are not endpoints but are starting points for inspiring people to think differently and take measurable action that tackles humanity's pressing problems. I thought that getting each talk to trigger action would be easy. Right!

In your personal and professional lives, you often need to influence others to do what you want them to do. Are your children, partners, employees, contractors, and suppliers as responsive to your calls to action as you'd like them to be? Probably not. Imagine how your life would change for the better if they were. The stakes increase if you are the leader of a family, an organization, a community, or a country. Your ability to cause effective action to happen has massive consequences: your family will thrive or struggle, your organization will prosper or perish and your community or country will flourish or flounder.

If you are a speaker, the difficulty you experience persuading your audiences to take up your call to action is amplified by your lack of a personal relationship with them and by each audience member's ability to ghost you.

So what are ordinary people, leaders, and speakers to do to make audiences of one or many take action? I believed that the answer lay in a 4-part formula:

1. Build rapport by using "you-centre language" (you-your-we-our-us), self-deprecating humour, smiles, and eye contact.
2. Engage by telling personal stories and using simple language, short sentences, and vocal variety.
3. Inform with clear, relevant, and well-organized content.
4. Inspire with a precise and urgent rallying cry.

It's Saturday, October 19, 2019. I'm the MC on the Get Inspired Talks' stage at the elegant Playhouse Theatre in downtown Vancouver. Every speaker gave the talk of their life and received a well-deserved standing ovation from an appreciative live audience. Every speaker's video received over 10,000 video views within 30 days of its launch. Every speaker's talk was repurposed as a chapter in an e-book that became an Amazon bestseller and was then formatted into a paperback.

I dreamt of massive action happening. I had visions of fixing some of humanity's pressing problems. I had high hopes of each speaker receiving offers of highly-paid speaking gigs from around the world.

Did massive action happen? No, it didn't. I felt crushed. I felt that I had failed the speakers. I felt that my legacy was a pipedream. I surveyed the live audience and realized that what the speakers created was massive INTENTION to take action. Audience members stood, clapped, felt moved, and intended to take action. But after the event, life happened and the audience members' good intentions were replaced by urgent priorities and quickly faded. Clearly, the 4-part formula was incomplete. Something else needed to happen while the intention to take action was strong. My resolve to change the world depended on me figuring out what that something else was.

GAME-CHANGER #3

Countless hours of research later, I arrived at a game-changing truth – the only way to cause high-functioning, busy, time-starved audiences to follow through is to support them to take a small first step while their good intentions are fresh. When they experience positive early results, they'll keep going and complete the call to action.

To test this thesis I have done 2 things:

1. I directed upcoming Get Inspired Talks' speakers to split their call to action into 2 parts: a CALL and an ACTION. The CALL inspires a strong intention to take action. It is clear and expressed passionately. Its scope is big enough to cause transformation to happen but not so big as to be

overwhelming. The ACTION is a number of small steps that are easy to take, easy to measure, and easy to reward.

2. I commissioned the development of an app – called WinWin3 – to support Get Inspired Talks' listeners to take a small first ACTION step after hearing a speaker's CALL. Get Inspired Talks can measure each ACTION step accurately and reward its taker with points that can be redeemed for "feel good" rewards.

CONCLUSION

Get Inspired Talks is my legacy. Its potential to change the world inspires me. My vision is that Get Inspired Talks becomes a media empire with mass appeal, that it serves humanity as a beacon of hope, and that it elevates live and online change-makers to see beyond their self-interest, realize that they can make a difference in their own way and take effective action to make that difference happen.

In 2031 I turn 80. In that year Get Inspired Talks will produce 10,000 talks. Each will be seen, heard, or read 100,000 times to inspire over 1 billion actions that move the needle toward a better world.

Becoming clear about my legacy and how to sculpt it has taken me 13 years – from 2006 to 2019. It required 3 game-changing epiphanies:

1. Collaborating with Dad to write his autobiography and his death in 2008 made me realize that I wanted to create a legacy and define its form: to create a massive collection of credible ideas that trigger change-makers to tackle human-ity's pressing problems.

2. Building TEDxStanleyPark over 5 years into a wild success only to realize that "Ideas Worth Spreading" was not the same as "Ideas Making Action Happen" and then having to get back on track to achieving my legacy.

3. Believing that it would be easy for Get Inspired Talks' speakers to make measurable action happen was wrong-headed. Necessity has been the mother of invention and now I am putting in place a methodology that I believe will make this happen.

Standby...

Gaining clarity about the legacy I want to sculpt has not been easy but has been worth the effort. I now lead a rich and full life and have a North Star to guide my decisions. I hope that my story helps you discover your legacy faster and with fewer pivots. I assure you that your quest is worth the effort.

Roger Killen is from Vancouver, British Columbia, Canada. He helps business people gain impact and influence by teaching them to craft and deliver stories, talks, and presentations that activate people.

Roger is the founder and producer of TEDxStanleyPark (one of the world's largest TEDx events), the Organizer of Vancouver Business Network Meetup (the largest small business Meetup on the west coast of North America), and the founder and producer of Get Inspired Talks (like TED talks only with a focus on making action happen.

Roger Killen
Email: rogerk@getinspiredtalks.com
Website: https://getinspiredtalks.com/
Linkedin: https://www.linkedin.com/in/rogerkillen/

Facebook: https://www.facebook.com/roger.killen.7
YouTube: https://www.youtube.com/c/VancouverBusinessNetwork
YouTube: https://www.youtube.com/getinspiredtalks

Scan the QR code with your smartphone to watch Roger's video message.

Or, follow this link:
https://youtu.be/SS7WKgFrjEA

22

The Fire Walk

···+◆+···

*Our deepest fear is that we are powerful beyond measure.
It is our light, not our darkness, that most frightens us. We
ask ourselves, who am I to be brilliant, gorgeous, talented,
fabulous? Actually, who are you not to be?*

~ Marianne Williamson

by
Carol Chesney Hess

D id you know that eight out of ten women dream about writing a book, but less than two percent of them will ever see that dream come true?

That statistic keeps me up at night because I'm a book coach who specializes in helping women write their transformational books. I know how much the world needs the life-changing, inspirational words, and wisdom of women.

Can you guess what keeps so many women from writing their books? Fear. And that's why my first job as their book coach is to help them explore and conquer their fears.

And it's why my story is about the day I discovered how to conquer my fear. It changed my life.

⋯⋅◆⋅⋯

"You want me to do what?! You must be nuts!"

That was my initial reaction when my roommate Louise suggested I join her in a firewalk.

"No, really," Louise had explained in her most convincing and somewhat condescending tone of voice. "I think you're ready for a firewalk, Carol. It's a once in a lifetime experience."

"Tell that to my feet."

"You won't get burned, honest. I didn't."

"Right. Well, I'm not you," I had answered grumpily.

Sometimes I wished I *were* Louise. She didn't do anything she didn't want to do. She called it honoring her divine resistance. She didn't stress out about her perpetual lack of funds but calmly explained she was simply working off bad money karma from a previous lifetime.

As her roommate who frequently dealt with the mess in the kitchen Louise was divinely resisting cleaning or handled Louise's share of the rent her money karma prevented her from paying, I frequently complained about how convenient life was for Louise.

But as annoyed as I could get with her, inwardly I begrudgingly admired Louise. She was exactly who she was, not who other people wanted her to be. She wasn't intimidated by anyone, including her mother, who was every bit as intimidating as mine. Maybe it was the tarot cards or spirit guides she was always consulting. Whatever it was, Louise was very sure of herself. And she was never scared of anything.

"Honestly, Carol. You will face all your fears at the firewalk. You will come to understand that fear is an illusion."

Fear an illusion? I wasn't convinced.

"Once you've walked the fire," Louise continued, "You won't ever walk in fear again."

That was a pretty convincing argument. Who doesn't want to be fearless, right?

So three days later, I found myself in a car heading for New Hampshire with Louise and two other fire walker wannabes. That's when the butterflies in my stomach started. Not the polite butterflies of nervousness. These were the I'm-so-scared-I-could-puke kind of butterflies.

My companions didn't notice my silence. They were too busy questioning Louise, the veteran fire walker. I was busy questioning my sanity. While they were wondering how many times they would walk the fire, I was wondering if I would ever walk again.

Finally, I couldn't stand it one more minute!

"Isn't anyone else in this car as petrified as I am," I demanded to know.

Apparently not. This was all just a grand adventure to the three of them.

As we made the last turn to the site for the firewalk, I decided I would *not* walk the fire. I would be the dispassionate observer come to witness an interesting folk phenomenon. I would certainly not walk the fire. I would watch *them* walk the fire. And then I would drive them all to the hospital. Yes, that's what I would do.

Well, it didn't quite work that way. But it didn't quite work the way Louise said it would either.

After several hours of sitting outside on an uncomfortable log, staring at all the other crazies in the circle around the fire pit, listening to a lot of mumbo jumbo, and participating in even more mumbo jumbo, I came to a rather horrifying conclusion. I had changed my mind. I *was* going to walk the fire. Butterflies be damned. I was going to walk the fire!

I was? Hell, no, I wasn't walking that damned fire! Hell, yes, I was going to walk that friggin' fire! No! Yes! No! Yes! Definitely not! Absolutely not! Butterflies, stop already! Read my lips. I am definitely *not* going to walk the fire.

I looked over at the shaman who was leading the firewalk. At the moment, she was dancing around the six-foot flames of the bonfire we had built and lit earlier. Oh my God, she had just grabbed a can of gasoline and was throwing gas directly on the fire so the flames shot even higher! Didn't she know how dangerous that was?

I was astonished. Nothing disastrous happened. The fire didn't leap up the stream of gasoline to the can she was holding like I'd seen it do one time when my father was lighting the grill. Instead, the shaman calmly put the can down – way too close to the fire for my comfort – and then she pointed her fingers at the flames.

First, she moved her hand upward, and the flames shot skyward. She did a little jig. Then she pointed to the right, and the flames danced to the right. She danced with them. Then she pointed to the left, and the flames danced to the left. So danced some more. She lowered her hands, and the flames lowered. She raised her hands, and the flames rose up. It was quite the performance, and I was awestruck.

Then she sat down next to me and began a group discussion about fear. We went around the circle, each of us, in turn, naming out loud a fear we had. "Speaking in public." "Snakes." "Losing my job."

If it was a fear we shared with the speaker, we uttered "Ah-ho." I did a lot of ah-ho'ing. I didn't know I had so many fears – fears I had never thought of until someone else named them. But there they were, hidden inside where I usually didn't have to look at them.

Each time the fear-naming came back around to the shaman, she would say, "Dig deeper, people. What do you fear?"

"That my partner is having an affair." Ah-ho. "That my father is going to die." Ah-ho.

"That I'll end up a bag lady on the streets." Louise led the loud chorus of ah-ho's on that one.

"Dig deeper, people. What do you fear?"

"That I'll never discover the work I'm here to do." Ah-ho. "Letting go of control." Ah-ho.

"That my writing is no good." That one was mine. I was surprised how many ah-ho's it got.

"Dig deeper, people. What do you fear?"

"That I'm not good enough." A very subdued ah-ho. "That I'm not lovable." An even quieter ah-ho. "That I'm a mistake." The ah-hos were whispers.

Every fear and every ah-ho were attaching themselves to me, even the ones with which I didn't identify. They were combining, stacking up, and becoming a physical weight I could feel pressing down on my body. An oppressive, thick fear energy hovered over the circle. The weight and the energy became unbearable. Anything was better than this awful, sticky, heavy quicksand in which I was trapped and sinking deeper.

I had to dissipate the fear. I had to walk the fire! Oh shit! I was going to walk the fire! I had no choice. I had to. The butterflies went crazy. I had to walk the fire *now*!

Just then, the shaman leaned toward me and patted my knee reassuringly.

"Patience, Carol," she whispered. "You're ready, but the fire isn't. And the circle isn't. You must wait for the fire. You must wait for the circle. Keep your focus."

So of course I immediately lost my focus. How on earth had the shaman known I was ready? Well, I wouldn't call it ready exactly. I just wanted to get the whole damned thing over and done with.

I thought about my boyfriend. We were supposed to go dancing next weekend. Well, that was out. I'd be lucky if I ever danced again.

"Focus, Carol!" the shaman hissed.

I jumped. Right, focus. Easier said than done. Maybe the shaman knew what she was doing. Maybe even the circle knew what they were doing. But I wasn't sure I knew what *I* was doing!

"Trust yourself, Carol!" the shaman hissed.

Good Lord! Was the woman a mind reader?

Night was descending now, and finally the fire was ready. But I wasn't sure the circle was. The glowing red coals were reflected in every pair of unblinking eyes staring intently at the fire.

"Now let's talk about your fear of the fire, your fear of getting burned."

Oh my God! The shaman was relentless!

And so we went around the circle again – once, twice, three times. The fear energy got darker, stickier, more palpable, and more present with every chorus of ah-ho's. Silence fell. The only noise in the now pitch black clearing was the occasional pop and then hiss of coal. Each time there was a pop, someone gasped. Each time there was a hiss, someone jumped.

We couldn't stop staring at the coals. Whenever they started to turn gray, the shaman would rake them until they glowed fiercely red once again. Each time she raked, the circle gasped. As if it made any difference whether the coals were gray or red. They were hot. Very, very hot. Feet-burning hot.

Suddenly the shaman gave a whoop, threw down her rake, and walked across the coals. No warning, no fanfare. Just like that. One, two, three, four steps, and she was on the other side of the fire pit. She smiled, did a little jig, and with a motion of her hand indicated it was the circle's turn.

That's when it got weird – well, weirder. All of a sudden I was on my feet and walking to the head of the pit. As if from a great distance, I heard Louise exclaim, "Oh my God, it's Carol! She's going to walk the fire first. I don't believe it!"

I didn't believe it either. But as I stood looking down at the coals, I smiled. They looked like an enchanted fairy town. They twinkled and sparkled like stars fallen from heaven. They looked friendly, even inviting.

I took a deep breath, stepped high over some invisible barrier, and placed my right foot on the coals. Then my left. Uh oh. I was feeling warmth. Was I supposed to feel warmth? Louise had told me the coals would feel like popcorn or styrofoam peanuts. Well, I was feeling *warm* popcorn, *warm* styrofoam peanuts.

I looked at the shaman on the other side of the fire pit. She smiled and nodded encouragingly. I took a third step and then a fourth. I was out of the fire and on the other side of the pit, standing next to the shaman.

Oh, my God! I had walked the fire! The shaman grinned broadly, hugged me, and let out a startlingly loud whoop that made me jump.

Chaos erupted. The circle became individual people again. People jumping up from their log seats. People running to the head of the fire pit. People walking the fire. People laughing and crying and hugging and whooping.

The shaman kept raking the coals, and people kept walking on them or dancing in them or running through them arm in arm. It went on for a long time.

I walked the fire three times that night. I wasn't laughing or crying or hugging or whooping or dancing or running. I was in some kind of inner, alone, quiet place far from the chaos and noise and people.

At one point, Louise came up to me and said, "Dance the fire with me, Carol."

I just shook my head. This wasn't an experience to be shared with Louise or anybody else. This was for me to go through alone.

That night I didn't learn what Louise said I would learn. I didn't learn that fear is an illusion. I learned that fear is very real. So real it created a physical weight under which my shoulders bowed. So real it created an invisible barrier over which I stepped each time I walked the fire.

And I certainly didn't learn how to walk the rest of my life with no fear. I walk with fear every day. But I did learn how to step over my fear and keep walking, and that was a game changer.

Carol Chesney Hess is a book coach who encourages and inspires women to step over their fear and make their dream of writing a transformational book come true.

She offers do-it-yourself and group book writing programs and leads annual writer's retreats on the coast of Maine where she lives.

She is currently writing her own transformational book, *The Journey Back*, due for release in November 2021. For more information or to contact Carol, visit her website at www.carolchesneyhess.com.

23

Uplifting Your Life

·· ·+·◆·+·· ··

"We can do together that which I can't do alone."

~ Gary Neidhart, Author

by
Joey Nichols

It's commonly said that opposites attract, but I believe that this is incorrect. We attract who we are, we attract where we're at.

I've found that the most effective way to find high-quality friends and better opportunities in life is to focus my energy on becoming a better version of myself. By becoming a higher-quality friend and a more skillful and self-aware person, I also became someone who is attractive to those same kinds of people. When people work together to spread hope and kindness into the world then the opportunities for success are limitless.

The following story shares how I discovered this message of hope through the help of others, and how you and I can help make a positive difference in someone else's world:

I'm just a normal guy- a son, a creative person, and I was fortunate to have a good childhood. Even so, I started to struggle with depression, anxiety, and other mental health issues as I got older.

As a teenager, I experimented with drugs out of curiosity, as many teens do, but my experience was different because while most only find a temporary distraction and can "take it or leave it" when I drank and used I found what I thought was a solution to all of my insecurities and emotional issues. The substances seemed to give me the relief and self-acceptance I was always looking for. I became hooked on drugs and almost succumbed to the depression and anxiety that fueled the substance abuse, but eventually, I found recovery.

After working hard for several years to overcome my challenges with substance abuse and mental health issues, life was finally going smoothly. I moved from the suburbs to the city of Atlanta with some friends and I assumed that because I'd overcome my issues, everything would be okay and life would propel me towards my dreams, although I had no clue what they were.

I made new friends quickly after settling into my new location, and life was good for a time.

Although I made new friends quickly, I was surprised to discover that I was still lonely and felt like something was off inside of me. Some of those old feelings of anxiety and depression started to creep back in, but I told myself I'd get through it because this new life was great.

After a little while, the day-to-day routine started to become more familiar, and I started to feel uneasy and bored – like something was missing, and I wasn't sure what it was or what I should do to change it.

One of the principles I've learned is that giving back to others who are still trying to reach the level I'm currently at helps me to see the contrast between where I once was and where I am now. This contrast helps me stay grateful for what I have in the present moment. But even the lifestyle of service and introspection can become a routine, and at some point, there comes a time for us to grow again, to expand beyond our comfort zone without renouncing what we currently have.

And that's where I see so many people get stuck.

The issues that bring many people into early recovery are obviously destructive, and there are tons of resources out there to help people who are struggling with active addiction and mental health challenges. It's also easy to measure if someone has stopped using or is taking their medication and adhering to a treatment plan for aftercare.

This first phase of recovery is essential because without it usually nothing else is possible. So just staying sober is a huge success and many people are satisfied with that by itself.

But for others, "success without fulfillment is the ultimate failure" - (Tony Robbins), and for some people, myself included, there needs to be more growth in order to become aligned with their calling. It can be difficult to find guidance that takes into account the specific lifestyle and lived experience of people in recovery.

As for me, I became interested in personal development which led me to dive into books and I discovered tools and techniques that helped me to look inside and figure out what my passions were.

I tried many different things, with varying degrees of success. I was willing to experiment and try out new things, and my network of friends, family, and mentors gave me the strength to jump into the deep end- even when I was scared. I kept pushing forward and found new opportunities and new mentors. Eventually, I became part of a circle of entrepreneurs who showed me a whole new way of looking at what is possible in life.

As someone who exists in both the recovery community and the entrepreneur community, I would feel the frustration of wanting to help connect the two, but not knowing how to share what I discovered from amazing business coaches and life coaches in a way that was sustainable, and also respected the spirit behind many recovery communities: help is freely given to those who reach their hand out for assistance.

This was a frustrating predicament but I always felt like I would figure it out someday...

I started contracting as a writer with a team of my friends and mentors, and I was thrilled to be part of what was my dream company to work with.

And then one of my best friends overdosed and died.

And I saw friends on social media posting about their friends and their children overdosing and dying.

And I volunteered at an event to help families who had lost loved ones to suicide, and we had a memorial that was 10 feet high and probably 40 feet long that attendees had completely covered with pictures of their friends, children, and parents who had died by suicide.

I'd experienced many instances like these in the past, but they started to pile up and weigh down on my spirit. For all the beauty in the world I'm privileged to experience, there is also so much unnecessary self-destruction.

With all of this still keeping a spot in my mind, I kept pushing on. I continued to be part of both worlds. While I was growing my business, I was also volunteering in jails, and when I was traveling to new cities, I would share the recovery message wherever I could. The most rewarding experience during that period was sharing recovery in facilities for homeless teenagers. I loved helping all of these people, but I also felt limited in my abilities to bridge the gap between the two worlds.

Then the pandemic hit. I was in Las Vegas, headed to Los Angeles for a business event with the team.

The manager for my wellness company in Atlanta had left unexpectedly, so I was losing money back home in that business, and now with a virus spreading it didn't look good for the longevity of that company. After the event was over and the team went home, I stayed in LA to work with a life coach. But things were getting weirder every day with the coronavirus. My coach and I decided to cut our visit short.

I was torn about whether to go back to Vegas or Atlanta. I took a mentor's advice to go back to Atlanta so I could see family and friends. It was the right decision because days after I flew back home, we went into quarantine nationwide and almost all of the businesses shut down. When I spoke with friends and other people in recovery over Zoom, I saw just how devastating the pandemic was to my community.

People were overwhelmed, and scared, and unsure of what to do. I felt their pain because my wellness business collapsed during the shutdown, but thankfully I had another skillset so I was able to pivot. I was well aware that the only reason I was able to be so flexible was because of the business mentorship I'd had over the years and the network of entrepreneurs I had to guide me.

Every time I met with people they spoke of losing their jobs. I saw friends crying and the fear and uncertainty was palpable all over the country.

I saw a man who had helped me out years ago when I was early in recovery- a man I looked up to-.start sobbing from the stress and pain and fear he was experiencing and I watched him break down uncontrollably because he had been laid off and didn't know what to do. His tears were the embodiment of the pain of so many of my friends and associates.

I was seeing people who had worked so hard to overcome addictions and build a life for themselves lose it all. And now in addition to facing unemployment they were isolated and ashamed and facing the same self-destructive tendencies. I heard about people who survived the worldwide Coronavirus crisis only to die in their homes after relapsing on drugs and alcohol.

And at that moment, something inside of me shifted. The weight I carried with me from all of the trauma became too much. Something inside of me broke and I resolved to make a difference in the world.

I was done watching loved ones struggle. I was through with feeling powerless to help them get clarity, hope, and support. I was tired of my friends dying. I was done waiting for the perfect time to step up, and it no longer mattered how I made it happen, I just knew I had to do something.

In the past, I'd recognized that starting a non-profit might be a way to bridge the gap, but I had been stuck and never made it past the preliminary organizing phase. I wasn't sure where to start and the process seemed too complicated and difficult.

That didn't matter anymore.

I came across a colleague who had a coaching business helping people to start nonprofits. There were two options, the entry-level option to watch pre-recorded videos or the hands-on mastermind to work directly with the experts. Of course, the mastermind cost more, and if I joined then it meant pulling directly out of my savings.

But I came to the conclusion that if I'm not willing to invest in myself and my dreams, how can I expect others to invest in my dreams? And if I'm not willing to bet on myself as a person in recovery, how can I tell other people that they should believe in themselves enough to go out on a limb?

So I jumped in feet first and signed up for the high-end mentorship.

And it was the missing piece of the puzzle. The guidance was more helpful than I ever imagined.

Once I joined the mastermind on how to build a sustainable and scalable nonprofit corporation, things took off quickly.

I had renewed energy because I was in alignment with my purpose. Connections effortlessly fell into place. The IRS gave us 501c3 status in weeks. We were approved for our first mini-grant within a couple of months.

UpLift Your Life, Inc. was born.

When people in the entrepreneur space heard about our mission they were happy to offer access to their knowledge and expertise. We had our first person in recovery volunteer shortly thereafter, and we were able to hire another person in recovery to work in the nonprofit. We've partnered with an amazing heart-centered team of business people who are passionate about helping those who need guidance to create a new life for themselves.

At Uplift Your Life, we are dedicated to helping our communities and economy by empowering people in long-term recovery to learn entrepreneurial skills, to master their finances, and to become homeowners.

Whether they are starting a business, a side-hustle, or a passion project in their free time, we are here to help.

We do this through online training, personalized mentorship, media outreach, and live events.

Our message is that Recovery Is Possible, and people in recovery can overcome any challenge and create a fulfilling and exciting life for themselves. Their work uplifts society and positions them to become leaders for the next generation to come.

We believe that empowering men and women with these skills leads to self-worth, personal accountability, a sense of responsibility, and a culture of contribution that adds to their communities while reducing unemployment, relapse, suicide, crime, and recidivism rates.

We believe in those we serve and provide them with the mentorship and actual lived experiences that encourage them to believe in themselves.

Addiction, suicide, homelessness, domestic violence have all gone up. Instead of succumbing to the hopelessness we have instead stepped up to create a new generation of leaders who can use all of the amazing spiritual and personal development skills learned in recovery as a foundation to create businesses and projects that are heart-centered and focused on making a positive impact.

All of those involved with UpLift Your Life are leaders. We lead because "We can do together that which I cannot do alone."

I think that there's always good that can be found in almost any situation, it always depends on my perspective and how committed I am to finding the silver lining. If I can't find the silver lining, I can create it myself. And so can you. You can become a leader and share hope with others in their time of need.

You can get involved with our mission by:

- Spreading the word about what we are doing
- Connecting with us
- Connecting us with someone you know who has a platform to share our message
- Donating gifts or property
- Or by mentoring others in your own life and showing that hope and love are the norm, not the exception.

"I sought my God and my God I couldn't find; I sought my soul and my soul eluded me; I sought to serve my brother in his need, and I found all three; My God, my soul, and thee."

~ William Blake

Visit www.UpLiftYourLifeNow.org for more details on how to get involved.

Joey Nichols is an Atlanta-based entrepreneur and dream chaser. He started his first business at age 26 and over the next several years became an accomplished writer, life and business coach, actor, model, inspirational speaker, and advocate for suicide prevention and recovery from drug and alcohol addiction.

He's passionate about guiding people to discover their own inner freedom, confidence, and success, and sharing the message that Recovery is Possible, and people in recovery can create fulfilling and inspired lives through entrepreneurship.

You can connect with Joey and discover how to get involved in making a positive impact in people's lives by visiting

www.UpLiftYourLifeNow.org

Joey Nichols
YouRock@UpLiftYourLifeNow.org
404-793-6836

Scan the QR code with your smartphone to watch Joey's video message.

https://youtu.be/3TvwLWs82gw

24

All In...
The Journey from Impostor
to Authentic Leader

····•◆•····

"The authentic self is soul made visible."

~ Sarah Ban Breathnach

by
elan Bailey

You are the author, director, and lead actor of your own life. Yet how often do you find yourself living like an extra on someone else's stage?

What is the impact you're here to make in your lifetime? What's one thing you're committed to fulfilling in the next 12 months, no matter what? Regardless of who wins the next election. Or how long the Coronavirus is with us.

Now, what if you woke up one morning and realized that the only thing standing in the way of you realizing your impact and fulfilling your vision was your story?

I'd like to share with you what happened when I discovered this barrier for myself and how I used the biggest challenge of our lifetime to overcome impostor syndrome, carve a clear path back to my authentic self, and launch the next chapter of my best life.

2020 was going to be my year.

I have this ritual that I do at the beginning of each year where I sit and quietly tune in to my inner voice.

For me, this isn't about new year's resolutions or goals. It's about getting still and intentionally sensing what the year has in store. By all measures, my inner guidance system said 2020 was going to be a big year for me. In fact, the message that came through loud and clear as I indulged my new year's ritual was Big Energy.

What made this message so sweet was that it felt like the culmination and fulfillment of a journey I had begun almost four years before.

In 2016, I went through a period of major life transformation by choice. I ended a 7-year contract with an organization that did not align with my values, honor my worth, or amplify my strengths.

I made the official move to legally change my name to elan, a name that represents the passion and enthusiasm I live through my life. I lost 51 pounds and fixed my teeth, which had kept me from showing my full smile for over 20 years - longer than my son had been alive. And I made the move from being a long-time solopreneur to saying "yes" to my dream job as a Director in a software company.

2016 was the year of letting my inner compass guide me and I started to show up for my life in a very big way. I went from consistently taking on roles and clients as a behind-the-scenes contributor to being out in front as the director of my life and of a team that I adored.

During that year, I felt a strong call to action on my life and leadership. I would wake up every day between 4:00 and 5:00 am. I'd do some writing and yoga in the morning to prepare myself for the day ahead. I was in sync with life. Things were happening with ease. Yes, I was putting in the work, but I had let go of the effort and struggle that had been my modus operandi for the previous eight years.

At that time, my intuition was so strong that I felt like I had my own personal trainer who was challenging and supporting me to prepare for a significant life event. My own inner Mr. Miyagi. Except there was no "big event" as far as I knew. It was all just sensing and responding to life, with guidance coming from my inner GPS.

But within the first six months of being back in the corporate world, I could feel the old familiar challenges of trying to fit my full authentic self into someone else's vision and strategy. There I was trying to understand and implement decisions that impacted me but weren't made by me, while fitting into a structure and culture where it felt challenging to sustain the expression of my highest and best potential.

Within 16 months of landing my dream job, I got the news that I was being laid off. We were cash strapped as a start-up and I was expendable. I was heartbroken. I had spent so much time trying to live my vision through my work and had made heavy investments in the development of my team personally and professionally.

I had reduced team turnover by 80% and had helped many of my direct reports own their power and, launch the next chapter of their leadership by moving up or moving over to something else they were better suited for in the organization.

In my short time leading that team, it had awoken something in me. It had given me an access point to connect to the work I was most passionate about, people development. I was determined to make good on my own struggle to fit into corporate life, by helping others be their best selves at work.

Within four months, I leveraged that experience into my next opportunity, where returning to my entrepreneurial roots I went from doing people development on the side, to making it my central focus. Working with another start-up, I had the opportunity to take hundreds of employees through a development process of sourcing and sustaining their best selves at work.

I envisioned people development as an environment where people go to work as their whole authentic selves. Where they operate with a strong sense of personal responsibility for how they show up at work, rather than feeling victimized, as I had, by the system. A model where every person held themselves accountable for the impact they have on each other, the business, their clients, community, and the planet.

I was helping people full-time to live their best lives at work. And doing some of my best work in the process. But I was still doing it through the lens and constraints of someone else's vision. And this was start-up life after all, so it wasn't too surprising when six months later, my contract abruptly came to an end.

This rollercoaster ride was dizzying. It seemed that every time I got a taste of living into my vision the ride ended too soon. And I would find myself back on the ground, waiting in line for the next opportunity.

Shortly after my people development contract ended, I was recruited and signed on to work as an advisor with a consulting firm. I was nervous about sidelining my vision once again and going back to being an employee. And within my first three days on the job, my anxiety grew.

This was a competitive club, where my colleagues were ambitious and high-performing personalities with a long list of business accomplishments to show for it. I worried that I didn't have the extensive background or achievements to fit in with my colleagues or meet the role's expectations.

I felt like an impostor.

But I should be able to figure this out, right? Over the last ten years, I had learned the value of leaning into and showing up as my authentic self. I was scared but certain that by bringing my authentic self to this new environment, I would be successful.

The first five months were tumultuous. Here I was at an age when I expected to be hitting my stride, doing work that highlighted the best of my career experiences and skills, and enjoying my life outside of work. But when I turned 50 just two months into my new role, I was at the very bottom of the performance chart and battling the onset of a mini mid-life crisis.

So, when I got the Big Energy message in January of 2020, I decided to take my fate into my own hands. Rather than having to choose between my passion and a paycheck, I was determined to find a way to overcome impostor syndrome and incorporate my passion into my work. I set off to develop a whole strategy for how I was going to boost my performance by bringing more of my authentic self to my current role.

But by March, it was clear that Coronavirus had other plans. As the impacts of the pandemic swept across the globe putting increasing strain on my clients and the bottom line of my employer, the pressure I felt only intensified. And by the beginning of April, I was put on my first ever performance improvement plan.

How did I get here? How did I go from being the woman who had built a reputation for developing happy, healthy, high-performing teams to someone who was miserable, stressed, and under-performing?

Was this a cosmic joke? Was this what Big Energy really meant?

As I moved through the frustration and anger of losing my dream to Coronavirus, I was able to get quiet and still. As I did, I could hear the drum-beat of Big Energy calling to me. I realized I had taken the message of Big Energy and tried to strategize and manuever to make it fit my existing circumstances.

Have you ever done this? You get a clear message from your inner guidance system and then you sit and write a whole strategic plan around it to try to control the outcome. But things don't always go according to plans.

I was tired. I felt constant stress and pressure. My way of being was taking a toll on my relationship. And I felt deeply unhappy. I wasn't showing up as my best self in any area of my life.

I took a few days to consider my options. Should I keep fighting to hit the goal, ask for more help, or work twice as hard? Should I get off the ride and re-evaluate what I was doing with my life?

It was then I realized that I was choosing to hide in the shadows of someone else's vision, because I was afraid of my own - shadow, that is. It was clear that staying in this environment was costing me joy and fulfilment. And the longer I stayed, the longer I was putting off my own vision, under the guise of not having enough time, resources, or money to follow my passion. But now I wondered how much it was costing me in terms of expressing my full potential and having the kind of impact I was here to make.

It was then that I understood, Coronavirus wasn't a barrier to my vision. It was a catalyst. Once I made the decision to stop fighting to fit into a system that wasn't designed for me, the journey from Impostor Syndrome to Authentic Leader began in earnest.

As I came to an agreement with my employer to transition out. I started to think about what I was going to do next and how I was going to find a job, resume my old business, or start a new business in a pandemic.

I was scared and excited.

And as they say, when the student is ready, the teacher appears.

Three days later I received an email in my inbox that Iman Aghay was hosting a free webinar on how to build an online course.

I joined that webinar and decided to take Iman's course. Over the next eight weeks, I did the work to channel the Big Energy of 2020 into a platform for my new business. Ironically, I hosted my first BETA course on how to overcome impostor syndrome and lead with clarity, courage, and confidence in any situation.

Over the next few months, things that I had struggled with for the previous 11 months suddenly started to flow with ease. The right people and opportunities showed up. And I was able again to live my vision of developing others in their leadership, and in particular, helping women lead as their authentic selves.

Here are some lessons learned from the rollercoaster ride that has been my career and entrepreneurial journey that I'd like to share with you:

1. Never let anyone or any circumstance define your value. Define your unshakeable foundation, commitment, and values, and re-examine them yearly. Do things that honor your worth, align with your values, and amplify your strengths.
2. Follow your intuition. Strategic planning is a very masculine approach that definitely has its place in the world. But be wary of overusing it. If things are going sideways and not in

flow, look at your story first—your assumptions about what is true - and then drop your strategy and make room for intuition. Often, we're so busy trying to control our lives that we can't hear our inner guidance system. Give equal space to the intuitive parts of your being. You'll be surprised and delighted at what shows up.

3. Be willing to ask for and accept help. When I said yes to working with Iman, it was the first time in my career that I had hired a business mentor to help me go from idea to launch. The results have been phenomenal.

4. Never lose sight of your vision. Even things that you see as a threat or detour to your vision can be your greatest ally. When you see the world through the eyes of your creative potential, rather than feeling victimized by it, you can make something out of every opportunity. Look for what you can uniquely bring to every situation, and what you can uniquely gain from an experience without disconnecting from your inner compass.

5. We often think it's time, money, people, or resources that stops us from living our best life. But those things are "figure-out-able." If you're ever stuck in an area of your life, on a rollercoaster with lots of twists and turns but little fulfillment, look for the unexamined story that poses a barrier to your self-realization and connection with others. What are your stories costing you really? Every narrative serves us in some way for a time. But remember that you have the power to let go of or re-write any story that is no longer serving your highest and best expression.

Today, I coach women professionals, leaders, and entrepreneurs to reclaim the inner power to go "all in" on their vision, regardless of setbacks or circumstances. I challenge and support women to show-up fully and powerfully, communicate clearly, and make decisions with confidence, so they can finally make the impact they're here to make.

I also help organizations develop adaptive leaders and cultures where people of diverse backgrounds and cultures can co-create and thrive.

elan Bailey is Leadership Coach, Organization Development Consultant, and Founder of the UpLevel Leadership Academy. As a black woman, entrepreneur, and leader in male-dominated industries for over 25 years, she has learned how to navigate the intersection of age, gender, and race with power, love, and grace.

elan Bailey
https://uplevelmyleadership.com/
https://members.uplevelmyleadership.com/membership/https://
www.linkedin.com/in/elanbailey/
https://www.instagram.com/uplevelmyleadership/
https://www.facebook.com/uplevelmyleadership

Scan the QR code with your smartphone to watch Elan's video message.

Or, follow this link: https://vimeo.
com/458299214/e0f0e2749b

25

Cancer Was My Cure

·····◆·····

by
Paul Palmer

The consultant asked us why we didn't come earlier.

"We've been trying to get through the National Health Service process for a year."

"Well, you're lucky you got here because your partner only had another six months to live without treatment."

·····◆·····

I had always been a loner, or at least until I met my wife. In school, I avoided the bullies by spending time alone during breaks, keeping my head down, and studying. I have always been happy in my own world. In school, I had the nickname TTME, the thinking man's ecologist, I suspect because nobody knew what I was thinking. When I completed my Master's degree, my manager said, "Now you've proven you're a clever bugger," and laughed. I remember another manager asking me, "You know it all. Why don't you use it?"

That made me think a lot.

My first marriage failed because of my lack of communication skills. We never really had a conversation ever! We agreed what to do, I did it, she complained. Of course, life didn't make it easy. Five separate redundancies aren't exactly the career you expect.

When I'm in a room watching the television, even if the room is full of people talking and enjoying social activities, I can watch from across the room and remain focused. The activities going on around me do not distract me in the least.

Everything changed when I met Ausra.

I still do not really know why I wanted to get to know her. These days I say it was stalking, going to lunch when I saw her arrive for weeks. I asked her out at the works Christmas dinner and we've been together ever since, in sickness and in health.

Getting to know each other was interesting. When we met, Ausra routinely spoke Lithuanian. We communicated via Google Translate, a slow process as you might imagine, but it did mean we communicated and didn't just assume we knew what the other was thinking.

We had been seeing each other a few months, when Ausra said she couldn't cope with the travel any longer, that I was having to drive too much to go and see her. At the same time, her left side was becoming so painful that she couldn't sleep at night. There she was, working fourteen-hour days, and barely resting.

When we visited the doctor, we explained the situation, and she was referred for an assessment at the local hospital. They agreed there was a problem but that she had to be referred to another hospital with the capability of dealing with the issue. There was no mention of what that issue might be. I was quite disappointed with the system and the lack of communication.

In the meantime, I was continuing to work, travelling back and forth between the UK office and Denmark. I was in Denmark in November when I was told I was going to be made redundant, together with many others within the organisation. They apologised that my travel plans had not been cancelled since there was no one for me to talk to. I had a choice. I could turn around and go right back home to the UK or I could continue with the planned visit in Denmark.

I decided to stay but soon change my mind. I was stressed and worried, thinking about home and what was in store for Ausra. One of the people I'd been working closely with in Denmark offered for me to stay over at her house instead of alone in a hotel. I accepted her invitation, which helped take my mind off the situation and the uncertainty of what was I going to do.

I returned home with three months of gardening leave with full pay. (Gardening leave is when an employee is terminated and told to stay away from work for a certain period of time but remain on the payroll.) This was my opportunity to chase the NHS. We had already been waiting a long time for them to make any progress. Each time I called, I felt like I was being given an answer to go away. There was no offer to do something, no being helpful, no support whatsoever. I was alone again, just like I always had been my whole life.

I realised they weren't going to resolve Ausra's medical problem, that it was going to be up to me to do everything I could to ensure everyone knew what the problem was and to make sure someone actually dealt with the issue. I used my knowledge gained in the pharmaceutical industry to figure out who to talk to in the medical profession, how to communicate with them, and what was going to be needed.

Suddenly, I was communicating at a level with more interest than I had ever had before, spending time interpreting the words and the ferreting out the underlying meaning. When one hospital administrator told me the notes about Ausra's case had been sent elsewhere, I asked for all the details and the number to call. When I called, I discovered that the notes had been passed back to the previous administrator I had just been talking to. It was so frustrating, feeling like just a number in the system that had been placed on a waiting list. I'd heard about it from others, how you can go from the top of the list to the bottom, just by saying no once to an appointment.

I learned to play the game. This former self-appointed loner built a relationship with the different people I spoke to. I started to influence their behaviour to the point that one of them even called me back once to tell me that the notes had been passed to a new place – Guy's and St Thomas's in London. She explained that the reason no one locally had been able to take on Ausra's treatment was because of the complex nature of her condition. In this day of medical specialization, it's rare that one department within a hospital system is able to deal with cardiology, pulmonary, and orthopaedics as well as oncology.

I was shocked. Oncology. The word we all know and wish to avoid was out there in the open. Ausra had cancer. Should I tell her? Maybe she already realised, maybe not. I decided to keep it to myself, I did not want her to feel the stress that I was already feeling. I knew it could make things worse.

We travelled together to Guy's and St. Thomas's. I was driving of course; I knew we couldn't go all the way in the car so I chose the easiest station en route. Three hours later we arrived, a painful trip for Ausra but a positive one. In the waiting room, we both knew we were in the oncology department. I hadn't spoken to anybody. No one knew what was really going on. I was scared. What was the outcome going to be?

They started with the scans. Fortunately, the results came through in real-time. We didn't have to return for another visit. With the constant pain, I didn't really want her to endure another 6 hours round trip, she didn't complain but I could see her face. The consultant sat there, reviewing the data, looking at the scans, the x-ray, and the previous MRI scan. He explained to us what the situation was, that the cancer was growing and growing quickly, except he didn't call it cancer. He gave it a technical name that only I understood. Using Google Translate, I had to explain and describe the problem to Ausra. The consultant showed me the x-ray, explained how the growth was pressing on her lungs and potentially her heart although it wasn't clear.

That's when he asked why we hadn't come earlier and I replied, "We've been trying to get through the NHS process for a year."

He wanted another scan – a new MRI with higher resolution so he could be sure of the prognosis. I expected we would have to go away and come back another day. I was surprised when he said that he would arrange it there and then. That must mean it was serious.

We returned to the waiting room. Talking to Ausra without her realizing how stressed I was feeling was an effort. I tried to protect her, but it didn't work. She understood exactly what was going on with or without Google Translate.

After the MRI, we returned to the consultant's office. He wanted to schedule an operation, and of course, we agreed. I knew that smoking was unacceptable, so I had already warned Ausra that she would need to stop smoking and, if the consultant asked, she could tell him she had already stopped. During my numerous conversations where I had researched and investigated everything, I had also found out before we even got there that she would need to have somewhere to go after the operation with someone to look after her or they wouldn't perform the surgery. I arranged for her to move in with me so I could look after her afterward.

They offered a date in December just before Christmas for her operation, but Ausra didn't want her daughter to always be reminded of her mother's death at Christmas, so she declined the appointment. On 21st January 2011, the operation was a success, the lump was removed, and she started physical therapy in the hospital.

When they discharged her, they sent her home with a bag of medicine. The morphine pump was only available during her stay while she was recovering in the hospital. She liked it of course, and I knew the pump had a restricted dose, unlike the boxes of Oramorph she came home with. I looked after her at home, making sure she took the right tablets at the right time. I attended all the appointments everywhere – in the hospital for the check-ups, at the medical centre for the dressings. I explained to the nurse which dressings we should be using. After all, when I worked in pharmaceuticals in the past, I had been part of the team that developed cannula dressings (used for catheter sites to keep them dry) as well as those needed to absorb exudate (fluid that leaks out of blood vessels into nearby tissues). We got everything we needed, and the nurse ordered whatever she didn't have in stock.

Ausra's care went well. Recovery took time, but we had time. She was alive.

The experience changed me personally. I started to care what other people thought, what they said, what they did. I was no longer alone, and I never wanted to be alone again, not the way I had been before.

The experience changed me professionally. I started my own business because flexibility is key. I still need to be there when

I'm needed. I listen to clients, interested in what they have to say, interested in their needs and providing for those needs, whatever they may be. I communicate openly, clearly and not just by telling. It's important for me to understand first and apply my knowledge so I can help them solve their problems.

I've been anxious now for years – watching, looking for signs that the cancer has come back. I make sure I take notice. Is that a sign? Maybe. Soon it will be ten years clear, and the check-ups will be classified as routine, the same level of risk as anyone else. I'm happy, ecstatic, overjoyed, pleased I was there.

Ausra and I have been married now for five years. I'm no longer in my own world. I'm no longer happy to be alone. I really do feel cancer was the cure for my loneliness.

Paul Robin Palmer has been learning from his experiences in the Pharmaceutical Industry since the '80s, he started his consultancy in 2011 after his fifth redundancy.

Paul has a passion for automation, he has built numerous web sites, integrated them with e-commerce, and been promoting opportunities online for many years and now enjoys helping others do the same through another company he founded Business Strategy Training Limited.

Paul Palmer
www.paulrpalmer.com
www.busttr.com

26

Be The Change to Thrive and WIN

···•·◆·•···

"Only those who can see the invisible can do the impossible!"

by
Petra Contrada

I sat in the recliner chair in my living room with my eyes closed and my head sagging back into the headrest. I had dragged myself through another long day and I had barely been able to climb the steps from my car to my front door that evening. I was too tired and exhausted to move and, truth to tell, I was profoundly discouraged. Maybe you've had those days, too, when you have been so tired for so long that you can hardly hold your head up anymore?

In my case, most people would never have guessed what was really going on. At age 56 everything looked fine from the outside. I had a loving marriage and a successful six-figure business. It all seemed to be going well.

Yet, everything was extremely difficult and as I sat in my chair I realized that I was totally overwhelmed, overworked, and overweight. I was not so happy anymore. I was stuck. My life was not heading in the right direction, I was not fulfilling my destiny, and I felt no passion, deeper meaning, or purpose.

I have to admit that I had neglected many things that I had previously learned and implemented in my extensive professional and spiritual life. I knew better than to let myself drift this far off course. But somehow, I had. Yes, I am human, too, and you probably can relate. I had also foolishly closed my ears to my most trusted advisors, particularly to the advice my dear husband had to offer. My daily existence had become one that seemed purely to revolve around work and paying the bills, and fulfilling our everyday wants and needs.

Have you ever felt like you're running on a Hamster Wheel? Somehow, I had maneuvered myself onto one. The negative results were obvious. Whenever I looked into the mirror, I did not recognize the woman I had become. My face looked pale and puffy and there was no sparkle animating my eyes. Even my eyelids looked heavy—and could that be sadness peeking out from behind the grim set of my mouth?! I realized this was the price of having slipped into a spiral of damaging mindset, bad habits, and false beliefs.

I am sure you are not surprised to hear that I had become seriously ill somewhere along the way, as well. As I sat in that reclining chair that evening, I was still breathing with some difficulty, the relic of a bad case of pneumonia that had persisted for almost three months. I was seriously overweight, I had sleep apnea, I was on the brink of a full-blown case of arthritis, and I had high blood sugar, high blood pressure, and more.

The doctors tested for Lupus, Leukemia, and other diseases but couldn't figure out what was wrong with me. I got weaker and weaker, but as a strong German girl who had been born a Capricorn (what a combination!), I pulled myself together as much as possible.

Some days I could not push myself to expend even the minimum energy necessary to get through my day. Often when I came back home after meeting with clients, I had to hold onto my car for long moments before I could venture into the house, afraid I would faint otherwise. I thought I was going to die way earlier than I had expected and that I would not be able to do what I believed I was meant to do.

And, I was miserable.

How did I get to this point?

How had I let it all come this far?

I was devastated and very upset. I have always wanted to help others, to contribute to humanity, and to make a difference.

What was happening to my legacy?

What was I leaving behind?

How would others remember me?

Does some of this sound familiar to you? Have you ever felt that things couldn't go on any longer, and that you have almost wanted to give up?

I knew this could NOT go on any longer.

Yes, I was at that point. Then, one afternoon when I was feeling physically and mentally very weak and hopeless, and drowning in sorrow for myself, I decided to do what my husband had been recommending for quite some time, namely, to resume my meditation practices. He was convinced I would gain my mental and spiritual strength back. I had stopped meditation because I thought I was too busy, too ill, or subject to any one of a number of other excuses.

Very soon after I followed his suggestions something quite unexpected happened. I still remember the afternoon like it was yesterday. I sat in that recliner, barely able to cope, and meditated as I had begun again to do. I started praying to God, and said, "Dear God, I am too young to die and I believe that I have much more to give, and there is still much for me to do in this lifetime. Did I have all those amazing experiences, and accumulate all this knowledge over the years, just to bite the dust early? This cannot be all there is!"

I must have sunken into a deep doze, because suddenly I woke up startled, as I heard a deep voice commanding me to get up and **BE THE CHANGE** I wanted to see in my life. Chills still run down my back when I think about that moment. It catapulted me right up and out of my comfortable chair.

Instantly I knew that something fundamental had happened. I had gotten the "call," a message from the Universe, God, or one of his messengers. He had spoken to me loudly and clearly, and I realized that I had been barking up the wrong tree for far too long. Instead of seeking everywhere—and outside of myself—for answers to my issues, I now knew very clearly, that I had to start within myself. *I* needed to change. Instead of feeling sorry for myself and thinking about all my problems, I needed to take *action*!

After I heard "the call" I continued listening to the voice as it sprang forward into my consciousness at various times and in various places. I started following my intuition more and listening to my instincts. I examined the vast toolbox of past experiences, learnings, and lessons I had acquired and I started to take action. I was motivated and eager to get a grip on my life and to shape and change it on my own terms.

Looking back at my life, I realized that I was in many ways already an expert on the topic of change. I had lived quite an amazing and interesting life with plenty of the ups and downs that come with taking chances and thinking bigger. I grew up in Germany and lived for some years in Egypt before entering into a successful corporate career in sales, marketing, and training development. That phase of my career had lasted more than two decades, and it had been brimming with excitement, adrenaline, and achievement.

As Vice President of International Training and Business, I traveled around the world for many years. In the early 1990s, I was transferred to New York City, where I met the love of my life, Joseph Contrada. He invited me into a deeper version of who I was and who I am here to be and it was love at first sight. Now we have been very happily married for 25 years, liberated into deeper aspects of our relationship by the fact that together we have shared in the raising of a daughter who has surprised us, charmed us, and given us an experience of parenting that has made us connect even more deeply with our humanity.

By the year 2014, the year of my "recliner moment," I had been successfully running my own businesses for more than 17 years. But I was not well.

I have always been a curious student of life, and through my business experience, travels, learning, and coaching experiences, I had gathered a lot of knowledge and insight. I had also spent about four decades pursuing a path of spiritual and personal development. It was time to apply my wisdom and to create a new destiny. It was time to take responsibility, but all the ifs and buts on the back burner, and start to transform my life. Trust me when I say, I was ripe and ready for a change!

I love conscious change and the ability it offers to create the life we truly love, by the way.

That comes with the freedom to concentrate on your true purpose. To follow your passion. Like Steve Jobs said, "to make a dent in the Universe." I have not always liked change for the same reasons most of us don't. Change can be scary, unpredictable, and unpleasant. However, change is inevitable. Every day we experience change and often we try to avoid it because we are deeply stuck in our comfort zone. Life happens in cycles, we go through ups when everything is going smoothly, and then we go through, let's call them "stagnant phases," where things are not going as planned or expected. My life changed forever that day in August 2014, when I realized that I was solely responsible for the changes in me, with me, and in my life. That truly was the day I started to "*BE THE CHANGE*" to Thrive and Win.

Within one year I had completely turned my life around!

My first priority lay in gaining my health and happiness back. I almost completely changed my life and my lifestyle. I gained back my self-awareness and my self-confidence. And, over the next 12 months, I cut myself almost in half, dropping 100 pounds of weight and going from a size 20 to a size 6. Now in my early 60s, I feel younger and more vibrant than I did in my 40s and 50s. When I look in the mirror today, I see a much different woman than when I started my journey. I see the woman I envisioned when I was in my mid-20s when I worked for Parfums Christian Dior. At that impressionable age, I attended a training in Paris where I was very impressed with our trainer, who was in her 60s. She was competent, beautiful, and elegant, and she had an amazing presence. I wanted to look and be like her when I reached that age. And I can proudly and gratefully say, "mission accomplished" today.

But more than anything, I was deeply moved by my family's reactions. My husband, who never said a word about my looks, neither before nor after my transformation, looked deep into my eyes when I asked him what he thought about my changes and he said: *"Believe me, my dear, I am as happy as you are."* And my daughter looked at me and said: *"Mama, I am so proud of you, you look amazing. You age like fine wine that is getting better and better with age."*

What do the people who matter most to you think and say to you today?

But my efforts did not stop with my looks, my health, and my vibrancy. What I realized was, that I was not doing what I truly loved in the world, and that in order to live my legacy, and to fulfill my dreams and my destiny, I had to change everything I was doing.

I was shocked when I learned about some Gallup survey statistics that showed that worldwide almost 86% of the population does not like what they do. About the same percentage of the population report that they do not like themselves, either.

In the process of my own transformation, I discovered my true purpose and found my mission and vision.

I realized that I exist to be a guide for people when they are ready for the journey to their true destiny and for creating a happy, healthy, and successful life. I am here to help others to THRIVE and WIN on the front lines of life and business.

That's why I created my program for success called, "Thrive and Win."

It was born from my desire to fulfill my life purpose. After my own "divinely guided" life-changing transformation I asked myself the question, "How can I live my life with meaning and purpose, doing what I truly love?"

The answer was clear: my extraordinary and unique life and business stories are my message and my mission. The sum of my skills, experiences, and training, and my passion for spiritual and personal development, prepared me completely for my next life chapter. A new adventure has been added to my life, one where I can make a deep contribution as a success and fulfillment strategist, mentor, and international speaker.

I am now following my calling, applying my wisdom so I can have an impact in the world for others and all of humanity.

> *My vision is to build a future where people consciously create their destiny and enhance the way they think, act, and operate.*
>
> *While the vast majority of individuals strive to live, the truth is that we are sharing one united destiny and have it within us to live and work toward the greater good of humanity and for planet Earth.*

What made my transformational shift so rewarding and lasting was the realization that there are so many different angles and elements, "do's" and "do not's," in this process, that if you apply what fits for your individual design, you can, and will, prevail. As I developed my "Essentials for Change" formula and created the "Multi-dimensional Strategies"™ my clients use to power forward in their own lives, it became apparent that my success—my true, holistic, authentic success—was eminent. I started to *thrive* and *win* on the front lines of life and business... and so can you, too!

Conclusion: it is never too late to turn the ship around and change the way you look and feel. It is possible at any age and stage of life to shift and change and create the life you truly love. You need to start with yourself. You must be the change to thrive and win in all areas of life.

Welcome to my world: I invite you to be the change to thrive and win!

We are in this together... you are not alone!

Petra Contrada is the founder of Thrive and Win. She is an internationally renowned speaker, success and fulfillment strategist, spiritual Entrepreneur, and Rebel and also known as "The Queen of Change".

Today, female Entrepreneurs/Leaders/Business Owners hire Petra to Be The Change because most overthink, under-feel, and are forever missing key opportunities in life and business.

She is a guide for those who are ready to BE THE CHANGE to THRIVE and WIN.

Petra Contrada

Connect with Petra Contrada:
Website: https://www.petracontrada.com/
Facebook: https://www.facebook.com/bethechangewithpetracontrada
LinkedIn: https://www.linkedin.com/in/petracontrada/
Twitter: https://twitter.com/petracontrada
Instagram: https://www.instagram.com/petracontrada.bethechange/
Free Gift: www.ichange.live

Scan the QR code with your smartphone to view Petra's video message.

Or, follow this link:
https://vimeo.com/467130003/
a27d4f2e80

27

Not Good Enough

·····◆····

"There is no greater agony than bearing an untold story inside you."

~Maya Angelou

by
Cheri Merz

You know how people who have dyslexia talk about letters refusing to behave for them? For me it was numbers. I wasn't to understand spatial synesthesia for over six decades, but for me, numbers have always existed in a three-dimensional, irregular, virtual reality. Taken out of that context and made to sit in neat rows on lined paper, they meant nothing to me as a first or second grader.

I couldn't do arithmetic. If I had one penny and you gave me another, I knew I'd have two pennies. Put that simple arithmetic problem on a sheet of paper, and I couldn't answer it then. My teachers and my parents didn't believe that I didn't know the answers. To them, my wrong or blank homework pages implied that I didn't or wouldn't do the work.

My parents and teachers expected me to do well. It seems to me in retrospect they held me to a higher standard, maybe because I learned to read so early. In my parents' desire to see their little girl do well, they shared with me my teacher's assessment on my report card: I was an underachiever. Have you ever felt that you weren't good enough? How did that show up in your life? Did you refuse to compete because you knew you couldn't win? That was me.

I learned early that if I didn't want to be humiliated, I shouldn't aspire to something I couldn't achieve. Starting first grade three months before my sixth birthday, I was not only younger than the other kids, and not only smaller, I also wore glasses. In 1954, long before people like me were called nerds, I was a nerd. If that wasn't enough, something else set me apart. I already knew how to read. Maybe I was a little vain because of that, and maybe I showed it. In any case, I distinctly remember being socially awkward and not having many friends. My classmates ridiculed me when I was wrong or couldn't answer a direct question.

When I was eight years old, I read my first novel—Little Women, by Louisa May Alcott. While other girls my age or a little older were reading Nancy Drew and the Hardy Boys, I was reading classic children's stories from my mother's childhood library – The Boxcar Children and The Little Washingtons. By the time I was in eighth grade, I'd graduated to Earl Stanley Gardner mysteries – Perry Mason. I devoured Gothic romance books along with science fiction and horror novels in high school along with the classics assigned in English class. Victoria Holt one week, Edgar Allen Poe and H.P. Lovecraft the next, and then Ray Bradbury and Isaac Asimov, side-by-side with Charles Dickens and Herman Melville. I read everything I could get my hands on. I still do, though I draw the line at horror these days.

What made me feel safe and happy was reading. The characters didn't judge me, didn't make fun of me because of my glasses or my turned-in left eye, or because I couldn't interact unselfconsciously with others. Their worlds had rules that were fixed and reliable. And there wasn't any arithmetic! I fell in love with words and stories, and by the time I was a teen, I wanted to write for a living.

I wanted to write wonderful books that would transport readers to other times and places, like I was transported by what I read. Back then I wanted to write the Great American Novel. I didn't realize that was considered an impossible dream, though, or that there was no such thing as the Great American Novel.

At about 15 I saved my allowance and bought a correspondence course on writing. The first rule was "write what you know." So, I wrote a story about my church youth group. I lived in Utah and went to a Baptist church. Of course, everyone knows there are only Mormon churches in Utah, right? That's what my correspondence instructor knew. My grade for that assignment was an F; the instructor said I wrote a story I knew nothing about. Never mind that it was a true story – once again I was an underachiever. Even then I knew not to respond to a bad review, so I didn't explain. I just quit, and the idea of writing lost its luster.

I majored in English Literature in college, after learning I had no patience for small children and dropping Education. I learned nothing about writing or story structure. But I learned to write an essay full of BS, with well-structured and punctuated sentences. I graduated with a 3.5 average out of 4, without putting in much effort. However, I took ancient Greek in lieu of math. Math and I weren't friends. Underachiever. It should have been a 4.0.

At 20, three years after I started, I left college with a BA in English and promptly got married. I became a mother of two, then a divorcee. I got married again and had two more children. With six mouths to feed, my husband needed help earning a living, so, I went to work and forgot all about writing fiction. My business writing was great; it got my foot in the door and helped get me hired.

My life became a boring cycle of uninteresting jobs, though I loved taking care of my home, my husband, and my kids. Once I mentioned to my dad, who'd had a stroke a few years before, that I wished I could just stay home and be a mom and keep house, like my mother had when I was little. His lip curled and he replied with heavy sarcasm that he'd trade places with me any time I wanted. He longed to still be able to work, even though he was retired and disabled. At somewhere in my mid-forties, that made me feel like that little girl who was an underachiever yet again.

I never doubted that my dad loved me, except for one time, even though I only recall him saying it once. At times throughout my life, though, my dad left me with no doubt at all that I was a disappointment. Sometimes with a harsh word, other times just the weight of his disapproval. I never stopped wanting to hear that he was proud of me, or that he loved me. I knew it somehow, but I wanted and needed the words.

That one time I doubted came when I was 50 and my dad was 79. In 1999, my mother, brother, sister, and I gathered around what we hoped was not my dad's deathbed. He had bladder cancer, and though he was tired of fighting cancer on top of the aftereffects of his stroke, partially paralyzed and ready to let nature take its course, my brother had persuaded him to fight once more. He was scheduled for surgery at the VA hospital in Dallas to remove his bladder, but he had to wait for a surgical slot to open. While he was waiting, the cancer perforated through to his colon, further complicating matters. It didn't look good, but we clung to a thread of hope.

He was in pain, thirsty, and hungry while we waited for days. He couldn't have food or drink, because at any moment a slot for surgery could open. His medical team was feeding him through a PIC line, which didn't satisfy his hunger pangs, and we were only allowed to give him one or two ice chips an hour to moisten his dry mouth. Naturally, he was grouchy. Who wouldn't be?

I was the least adept at the ice chip transfer. With no depth perception, because I'm legally blind in one eye, I was slow. I didn't want to miss his mouth or ram the spoon into his lips. My dad finally lost patience with my awkwardness and snapped at me, "You're too slow! If you can't do it right, don't do it. Let Patti do it."

It felt like a physical slap in the face. I dropped the spoon and fled the room. Fighting public tears, I found a dead-end corridor and faced the corner, where I wept for everything I was losing and everything I thought in that moment I'd never had. Did he even love me? Had he ever?

A few days later, my sister and I had a return flight home scheduled, and there was nothing we could do to change it. Our dad should have had his surgery days before and be on the way to recovery. Instead, on the last morning, we were to be there, he had the surgery early and was barely conscious in the recovery room when we had to go. We were distraught, knowing this might be the last time we'd see him alive. I think back now and wonder why I didn't say to hell with my flight and stay. I wish I had.

It was a hard stretch for me, at 5'3", to hug him over the bars of the recovery room bed. I kissed him on the cheek and told him I loved him. He mumbled that he loved me, too, and that was the first time I remember ever hearing it. It was also the last.

Having awakened from the surgery to learn that he'd had his colon removed as well as his bladder, my dad lost the will to live and refused nourishment. He didn't want to see anyone, my brother reported when he called to tell me of our dad's decision. I respected his wishes, agonizing as it was to know he was choosing to starve himself to death without his family by his side. For a week, I thought of little else. When my brother called again to tell me he was gone, my first words were, "Thank God." I meant that his pain was over.

I understood immediately the blessing I'd been given, to hear those three all-important words before my dad was gone. I didn't understand until many years later the cost of those I didn't hear. I never heard that he was proud of me. What I knew was that I wasn't good enough, and I had known it all my life. Spoken words can hurt you. So can words unspoken.

It was another fifteen years, in 2014, before words, which had always been my forte, also became my vocation. As a kid, I'd wanted to write stories for a living. At sixty-five, I was finally given the opportunity to do so—pushed into it, in fact, by a client for whom I'd ghostwritten some nonfiction eBooks. In that first year, I turned out ten of the thirty-plus novels I would write over the next six years—more than 850,000 words that must have been pent up behind the dam of impostor syndrome – 'not good enough' syndrome.

The first book I wrote gave me joy and a sense of accomplishment, even though I still felt I could do better. I wrote another, and another, and before long I had evidence that strangers enjoyed my writing. Still, I kept thinking it wasn't good enough. One of my ghostwritten books even got to number nine in the entire Amazon catalog for a few glorious hours.

Last year, that client who had almost forced me to write fiction was able to stop looking for a job and live on the income earned by the twenty books I wrote for him. Because of our collaboration, he also had gained the confidence to begin writing his own books.

Combined with our backlist, his books continue to earn him a good living.

At times, I still struggle with impostor syndrome. I read the stories of authors whose prose is lyrical, and I despair that mine will never sing. I'm not alone. Many writers and would-be writers have the same paralyzing fear that they will never live up to their aspirations. Some also believe the time has passed them by. They mourn that their stories can't be told now – they believe it's too late.

Only you can tell your stories. If you're still breathing, it *isn't* too late. You can write even if you have a day job and caregiver responsibilities, or don't know how to start. You can write even if your grammar and spelling suck or English is your second or third language, and yes, even if you have impostor syndrome. If you have a story to tell, don't wait six decades or even six months. Johann Wolfgang von Goethe supposedly said, "Whatever you think you can do or believe you can, begin it. Action has magic, grace, and power in it." I say do it whether you believe you can or not. Set your stories free. I did.

Because words can heal, too. First, they can heal you. Authentic words from the author's heart can also lift someone from despair to knowing they aren't alone, and there is hope. Well-crafted words of fiction can give a little girl refuge from criticism or capture a little boy's imagination to make him believe he is powerful enough to fight the battles he must fight to survive. Our stories are important to someone, even if it's only ourselves. That's why I now coach aspiring writers to let their words flow, to find the time, and learn the habits that will let their words be seen.

To learn how I can help you, book a discovery call, contact me through my website, or ask to join my Facebook group, The Write Expert. You can also find me on LinkedIn.

Cheri Merz is an author and coach who guides coaches, entrepreneurs, and aspiring writers to write and self-publish their books using her six-step process.

Cheri has supported authors earning up to mid-six-figure incomes. She has written over thirty novels under pen names. Cheri holds a BA in English and coaching certification from Eben Pagan's Virtual Coaching program.

Outside of the passions of writing fiction and coaching, Cheri loves hiking, gardening, cross-stitch, and reading.

Cheri Merz
Online Contact Details
Website: https://metaprosperity.org
Facebook Page: https://www.facebook.com/wewritetobreathe/
Facebook Group: https://www.facebook.com/groups/thewriteexpert/
LinkedIn: https://www.linkedin.com/in/cheri-merz-689b07176/

28

Turn Your Biggest Challenges into Your Greatest Gifts

···•◆•···

by
Jennifer Eastwood

Have you ever had a moment when life knocked you down so hard that you had no idea how you would get up and go on with your life?

July 24, 2019, was one of those days for me. As I was walking out of the hair salon at 4:18 PM, I received a call from an unknown number. Generally, I do not answer my phone when I do not know the caller, but for some reason that day I answered. It was the manager of my husband, Mark's, apartment complex asking if I had heard from him that day because a friend of his was concerned about him. I had not heard from Mark, so they asked me if I would call the police to request a welfare check.

As I drove home, I called one of Mark's coworkers, who had not talked to him that day. I then called daycare to see if Mark had picked up our daughter. He had not. At that point, I was very worried. As I walked into my house, Mark's friend called. All his friend said was, "He's gone... he fucking shot himself in the head," before hanging up. My heart dropped into my stomach, and my world spun out of control. I grabbed my keys and purse and jumped into the car trying to get to Mark's apartment as fast as I could. I tried to stay calm as I drove and kept telling myself, "No, this can't be true. This isn't happening—not to me, not to my kids." I pulled into Mark's complex behind several fire trucks. It felt surreal – like I was in some crazy movie. The fire trucks were blocking the entrance, and I started to panic. I wanted to get to Mark and see him, so I could prove this was not true.

When I arrived at Mark's apartment, there were cops everywhere. I jumped out of the car and started running, but a cop stopped me. I told him that it was my husband and asked if I could see him, but the cop would not let me. I thought, "Oh my god, it *is* true. How am I going to tell my kids that he is gone?" The pain in my chest and my gut was so intense, I bent over as hysterical sobs began. When I finally stopped crying, I felt numb.

My life had forever changed.

I met Mark shortly after I learned that my husband at the time was having an affair. That marriage ended in divorce. Mark and I connected immediately as he was going through something very similar. We became friends, sharing our experiences, and helping each other heal from past betrayals. Our friendship grew and evolved into a romantic relationship. Mark made me feel special and safe. He had a huge heart that he shared freely. He was constantly telling me how amazing I was and how much he loved me. He supported me and went out of his way to do things for me that made my life easier. He loved my kids as if they were his own. Mark made me feel truly loved unconditionally. He listened to me in a way few people had. For one of the first times in my life, I truly felt both seen and heard. I felt like I mattered. We were soul mates.

We married three years after we met. In the first several years of our marriage, we faced some challenging times, as Mark was laid off and went to school to change his career. While doing this, we had a baby, and he became Mr. Mom, which was a struggle for him. Mark was clearly unhappy and depressed. He would get angry at the littlest of things and lash out. Yet, we were always able to work through our challenges and get back to the way things were at the beginning of our relationship. However, as the years went on, Mark seemed to become angrier and angrier and was lashing out more frequently. I never knew what would set him off, so we all walked on eggshells. It became exhausting trying to manage everyone's behavior.

Mark slowly stopped doing the little things that made my life easier, and he no longer helped with the household chores. When he was home, he was not engaged. It became harder and harder to get back to the way things were in the beginning. The man who had made me feel like I mattered was gone. And in his place was a man who seemed to see me as his worst enemy. It was confusing, and I did not understand what had happened. No matter what I tried, things continued to get worse. This left me feeling powerless and a victim of his actions or inactions. Five years into our marriage, I was miserable and beaten down. I was angry, resentful, and I blamed my husband.

One day, as I was getting ready for work, I looked in the mirror and found myself staring at a woman I did not know, a woman I did not like. That day I made a decision. I had let the challenges pull me down enough. It was time for me to take charge and turn my tragedies into triumphs, my obstacles into opportunities. I realized I could no longer rely on my husband to make me feel like I mattered. If he was not going to see me, hear me, and make me feel loved, then I needed to see, hear, and love myself. I needed to fight for me and my survival, as I had three children relying on me and looking at me as their role model. With this realization, I began focusing on how I could feel like I mattered. This gave me focus. I began feeling more in control and therefore felt less like a victim.

Less than six months before Mark's death, he was diagnosed with Borderline Personality Disorder (BPD). We finally understood what we were dealing with. However, things between us had become so toxic that we agreed to separate and see if distance would help us work things out. Part of working it out included him going to therapy to deal with the symptoms of BPD. However, he had lost hope and did not think there was anything he could do to save our marriage and keep our family together. A couple of months after moving out, he gave up, spiraled out of control, and took his life.

As we were still married when Mark died, I was responsible for cleaning out his apartment. The morning after he died, my sister and I met with the property manager of his apartment complex. As we walked up to his apartment, my heart was racing, and my hands were shaking. I was scared to go into the apartment where my husband died. My sister and the property manager went in first to assess the situation and cover up what they thought I would not want to see. It only took a couple of minutes, but those minutes felt like hours. Everything in me wanted to run away, yet I knew I could not. When I finally walked into Mark's apartment, it was so quiet. It felt somber, a little eerie even. There was a trace of an unpleasant smell. There was a sheet covering the couch and a small decorative pillow on the back of the couch covering the wall. Have you ever seen a bad accident you just cannot look away from? That was how I felt, I could not take my eyes off the couch where he died. I could see a splattering of stuff on the wall, not blood but his brains. It made my stomach churn.

When I asked about the pillow, my sister said it was to cover the bullet hole. All I could say was, "Oh," as I had not thought about there being a bullet hole in the wall. I could not move the pillow to look, so I walked into my daughter's room, which was on the other side of the wall. My eyes were focused on the wall, where there was a quarter-sized hole. As I moved closer, I could see where the bullet had hit the tv hanging on the wall. The bottom left corner was mangled. I looked down and saw drywall and several small pieces of the tv on the floor. The violence of what had happened shook me to the core.

I looked around the rest of the room. Everything else looked the same. The bed was made and the room clean, like everything was normal. Yet, nothing in my life was normal. My entire world had shifted and spun out of control. At that moment, reality hit me. It was gut-wrenching. I lay down on my daughter's perfectly made bed, feeling the cool softness of the comforter against my skin as big tears rolled down my face, leaving a wet spot on her bed. I curled up into the fetal position as sobs wracked my body. My heart hurt, and my stomach was in knots. The feelings were overwhelming. I was lost. My sister lay down behind me, wrapping her arm around me and just held me as I cried.

As I lay there with my sister, all I could think about was my husband holding a gun to his head and feeling all alone. It is such a violent way to die. My heart was breaking for all of us, and my thoughts were swirling. I realized that my husband made this decision not only to eliminate his extreme pain, but he made this decision for us, too. Mark knew there was something wrong with him and that his actions hurt us. He loved us so much and did not want to hurt us anymore. He wanted to be with us, yet he believed that he had too many demons to face, which were impossible to beat. In his mind, he believed we would be better off without him. At that moment, something within me shifted, and I knew deep in my soul that Mark made the decision he did because I mattered more to him than he mattered to himself. He loved me and the kids so much that he was willing to die to set us all free. In his eyes, he was giving us a gift, the gift of freedom. The question was, could I accept Mark's gift?

As the minutes turned into hours, hours into days, days into weeks, and weeks into months, I found it challenging to hold onto this thought and accept the gift that he gave us. Grieving is not easy. It hit me in waves, and I never knew what would trigger a wave or how big the wave would be. There were times I was blindsided by one. One minute I was fine, and the next minute I was not. I had so many emotions, and sometimes I had conflicting emotions that went through me at the same time. I was angry at him for leaving us, angry at myself for my actions. I felt guilty that I did not see or understand the signs. I had so many *if only's*. If only I had done this, not done that. If only I had understood what we were dealing with before it was too late. I blamed him. I blamed myself. I was relieved he was out of pain and relieved I was not going to co-parent with him. And then I felt shame for feeling relieved. All these emotions and thoughts are part of the grieving process, yet I judged myself for feeling them. I should not feel this way. I felt knocked around and battered.

I had to find a way to feel grounded in the midst of chaos, so I could ride the waves as they came. I kept coming back to the thought that, in his head, he gave us all the gift of freedom. And I needed to find a way to accept this gift. I did not want him to die for nothing. And then I saw the following post in a suicide survivor's Facebook Group: "What no one tells you about grieving is that you will mourn two losses: 1) the person you loved and 2) the person you were." I knew I couldn't bring Mark back, but I could make sure that I honored his wishes by focusing on the opportunity. Who was I going to become because of his gift?

Although I was still processing the grief, my focus began shifting to the opportunity I had. I realized that although our journeys looked very different, my husband and I both had struggled with feeling worthy. We were each looking to the other to *make* us feel worthy. I knew that I could not accept his final gift if I did not love myself and believe that I was worthy of it. With this realization, I began focusing on who I wanted to become and continued my work towards loving myself and believing that I mattered. This gave me something I could do, something that gave me a sense of control in a world where I felt I had no control.

I focused on seeing me and my truth, listening to my inner voice, loving myself, and believing that I am worthy. I began working on increasing my awareness of my thoughts and feelings, shifting my anger and blame to forgiveness, my criticism and judgment to gratitude, my resistance to acceptance, and trusting that everything happened the way it was meant to happen, and it was happening for me.

Have you heard the saying, "What doesn't kill us makes us stronger?" This is so true. The experience with my husband pushed me beyond what I thought was possible. It required me to rise up and find the courage to continue to put one foot in front of the other when I did not think I could even stand. And as a result, I am stronger, wiser, and a more authentic version of myself.

Sometimes our hardest moments and most challenging people in our lives turn out to be our greatest gifts. My husband was one of the greatest gifts of my life, as he was the one that led me back to me. I will forever be grateful for who he was, what he taught me, and the memories we made. I think about him every day and wish I had the opportunity to let him know exactly how much *he* mattered, how much *his life* mattered.

Whether you are struggling with the stress and challenges of daily life or you are facing the pain from a life-altering traumatic event,

you too can turn your pain and challenges into an opportunity to not only bounce back but bounce forward into a stronger, wiser, and more authentic version of you. If you would like information on how I can support you, send me an email at jenn@jennifereastwood.com with the subject Game Changer or click on the link to schedule a complimentary discovery call:
https://calendly.com/jenneastwood/game-changer

During her long career as a Certified Public Accountant (CPA) and auditor, Jennifer Eastwood found herself increasingly obsessed with understanding what inspired and motivated people to overcome and bounce back from both personal and professional challenges.

Jennifer is no stranger to the challenges professional women face as they try to juggle their personal and professional lives perfectly. She has also experienced significant pain from life-altering events including infidelity, divorce, abusive relationships, chronic pain, and losing her husband to suicide. In each challenging situation that Jennifer faced, she focused on the opportunities.

Jennifer left her safe career to become a Certified Fearless Living Coach and follow her passion for helping women turn their pain and challenges into opportunities and not only bounce back but bounce forward into a stronger, wiser, and more authentic version of themselves.

To learn more about Jennifer, visit www.authenticallyyou.com.

You can also connect with her at:
https://www.linkedin.com/in/jennifereastwoodcpa/
https://www.facebook.com/jennifer.kirbyeastwood/

 Scan the QR code with your smartphone to watch Melissa's video message.

Or, follow this link:
https://youtu.be/eDVJtos3MCk

29

Hurricane Season

···◆◆◆···

*"Shoot for the moon. Even if you miss, you'll
land among the stars."*

~Norman Vincent Peale

**by
Deneene Collins**

During a smoldering 107-degree day in the driest of deserts, I write to you from the eye of my hurricane. It is a calm place amid chaos. I've been blessed to find this sanctuary of sanity with an eye that allows me to see that even when storms in life are raging; we can choose to view the beauty of what is to be rather than the current calamity. I am no stranger to hurricanes. While you may have never physically been in one, entrepreneurship can be a hurricane itself at times. When we erect our dreams on solid foundations that come tumbling down because they cannot withstand the perpetual hard rains, destructive winds, and devastating floods in the business world; we are in a category 5 business hurricane. This is the story of my real life and business life hurricanes.

In 1997 a friend of mine was working for a job placement agency in midtown Houston, TX. She encouraged me to register for the agency saying I could only take the jobs I wanted and reject the ones I didn't want. I decided to go in and take their assessment tests just to see what might happen. Even though I had never taken a computer class in my life or had any formal technical training, I scored so high on their assessment tests; they placed me in a job on the computer helpdesk at PG&E Gas Transmissions Texas. I was working for one of the largest energy companies in the nation. Before long, I became the lead helpdesk agent and then I was promoted to a technical liaison position. Next, the PG&E Energy Trading division wanted to hire me to work procurement and vendor and asset management. Inside of two years, I went from being an unqualified helpdesk agent to ordering the computer equipment for the entire company and managing all their software licenses.

My salary jumped $10,000 in under two years and I was sitting on top of the world. At that time, I was living in Houston, Texas working in the downtown energy corridor. The building I worked in at 1100 Louisiana Street was pretty much right across the street from Enron before that great and tragic day it went down. My work life was as routine as the rising and setting of the sun until one very dark day when a company-wide meeting was called. The employees were split into two different groups for the meeting, and no one knew what was going on. I wasn't laid off that day, but one of my mentors from my helpdesk days was. I didn't know what to say to him as I watched him pack up his desk and the last several years of his life he had given to a company that was not going to do anything to help him secure his future. He neatly positioned everything into a little brown box making room for his pictures, papers, and desk trinkets that no longer held meaning in that space where he and his title had meaning. He wasn't crying, but I could see the tears on the backside of his eyes welling up like floodwaters in an internal hurricane.

"Goodbye," was all I could say. I wish I would have said more. He was the one who taught me how to be what I was within the company and recommended me for the great new position I had. I don't curse out loud, but in my mind, I thought silent profanities. This was a good man who didn't deserve this!

Not many days later the company had another meeting. This time they announced they were going to relocate the company to Bethesda, Maryland. If you could not go or if you were not chosen to go, you would get a six-month severance package all in one lump sum. That is when I decided I would use the money to start my own business. When you work for someone else, your destiny is in their hands, and your destiny should only reside in the hands of those who have your best interests at heart. You and God, hand in hand, are the safest and best gatekeepers of your destiny.

The company made me work for months during the relocation transition. During that time, I researched businesses I could start and came across an article about a man who had made $30,000 in one month. I contacted him and when my last day at the company finally arrived, I flew to San Francisco to meet him the very next day. This man was conducting seminars in the vacation business space making tens of thousands of dollars with every seminar. This guy was making crazy money as an entrepreneur, and I wanted in on his secret.

When I flew out to San Francisco to meet him the weekend after my last day of work, I didn't even get a hotel room. We met at a restaurant where he explained his business process to me. It was then that he told me that if I set up a seminar he could speak at he would split the sales with me. The rest of the day I walked Pier 39 and ended up at the Sheraton Hotel in front of the fireplace in their lobby. There were people there from all over the world I was able to chat with. No one knew I wasn't a hotel guest. I went to the front desk to mail some letters. Next, I went to the concierge to request a shuttle to the airport.

The moment I arrived back home in Houston; I began to plan my first seminar. I reserved the hotel meeting room and booked flights and a room for the millionaire speaker I had met in San Francisco and his wife. I recorded and ran radio ads, put in a second phone line at my house to take calls, and created reservation cards to send out in the mail. The event was a huge success until it happened. Everything I did for my new business was a huge success, I just didn't realize the person I hired to help me, and my new mentor was a terrible speaker with a stuttering problem. As I listened to him present to the audience I had gathered together, I wondered how he had become a multi-millionaire with such poor speaking skills. I guess that didn't matter because he was super successful. I took notes on his presentation and realized I could do it myself. I thought to myself, "I can probably do this presentation better than he can."

Between 1994 and 1996 I worked for a seminar company. I sold business packages for them, went on location to their various business seminars, and even ran their business consulting support line. I learned so much from this company that I was super ready when it came time to run my own. I put together my own events where I was the main speaker and before long, I was grossing a minimum of $10,000 in two hours on a Saturday. My business was a dream come true until I faced two hurricanes back-to-back.

My first hurricane was Tropical Storm Allison causing nearly $4.8 billion in damage. During this storm, I lived in the Inwood North subdivision in Houston, Texas where my street became a river. A woman I didn't even know got washed up into my driveway and had to spend the night with me and my children. My lawn was gone, and the front of my house was damaged. FEMA was my only hope for much-needed repairs. Three months later there was an entirely different type of hurricane; the twin trade towers came down in New York as a result of an act of horrific terrorism. I was living in a house gutted by the works of Allision and my travel-related seminar business was brought to a halt by 9/11.

What do you do when your dreams are nothing more than a pile of rubble? You rebuild, and that is exactly what I did. I got a job, but not until I had been unemployed for 18 months. Someone hired me over the phone, and I built his business to magnificence. When I left that company, another one hired me, and I worked with them to put together 50+ million-dollar deals. During this time, Hurricane Katrina demolished New Orleans, Louisiana, and changed the face of Houston, Texas, and other places flooded with Hurricane Katrina refugees in August of 2005. This aqua-logical tragedy changed many businesses, cities, and communities forever.

Little Miss Hurricane Rita was nothing more than a windy party girl that scared everyone. After Katrina, Houston authorities didn't want to risk the same type of devastation Hurricane Katrina caused, so evacuation was issued once there was the word of the coming storm. I was in the evacuation which was also known as the "Texadus".

The mass evacuation from Houston was being compared to the Exodus in the Bible of the Children of Israel leaving Egypt. My family and I survived this evacuation while experiencing depletion of supplies, no available gas to refuel vehicles, and many people with broken down vehicles on the highway to San Antonio, Texas that became a parking lot. We heard stories of lives lost during the evacuation to other cities like Dallas, TX. There were even people walking along the highway faster than cars were going. Stores were emptied of water, batteries, and other emergency supplies making the entire experience surreal. If you've ever seen a show on television about a zombie apocalypse, what I witnessed was close to that. It was *Book of Eli* type stuff.

And then there was Harvey! He was a devil of a fellow. Without even asking me on a date, I went straight to him. I don't always watch the news, so I didn't even know about Hurricane Harvey. My children's grandfather on their dad's side of the family passed away which is why I decided to drive to Houston with my son. He was going through a bad time emotionally, so it was like I had a hurricane as my passenger already. The closer I got to Houston, the worse the weather became. I gripped my steering wheel so hard my fingers began to cramp. Tall walls of water splashed over the freeway partition in the horrifying darkness as an 18-wheeler ran me off the road. I was afraid to exit for fear of flooding on the feeder road. Every inch of the road felt like miles where I was stuck in a place of possible death.

Hurricane Harvey was a beast, but I survived it. I even went to a funeral during it seeing a truck spin and hit a concrete wall on my way to Port Arthur, TX. How do we survive storms like this? I believe it is only by the Grace of God and the divine plan we are a part of. During Hurricane Harvey, while watching the news I saw a man catch a fish with his bare hands in his own house. I saw and personally knew people who were rescued by helicopter and boat. I've seen houses and businesses destroyed, but I've also seen survivors and cities rebuilt.

There are 365 days in every year in which we can do business, and out of those 365 days, 183 of them belong to hurricane season. Even if you've never gone through a physical hurricane; at some time in life you and your business will probably experience a metaphorical hurricane. That is when it is time to hunker down. I've been through both and I've had to rebuild each time. Horrible endings are nothing more than opportunities for beautiful new beginnings. It has been said that you can plan the perfect picnic, but you can't control the weather. The only thing you have control over is how you prepare for the storm and how you react to it once it comes.

As a business and real-life hurricane survivor, my advice to you is to wear a raincoat, carry an umbrella, make your boots on the ground galoshes, check the weather forecast for your niche, and always have an emergency backup plan for yourself and your business. After Hurricane Harvey, I finally went skydiving and Hit #1 on the Amazon Bestseller List. After Hurricane Harvey, I decided that living my purpose was more powerful than dying in my fear.

I AM Dee Collins and Entrepreneurs, Authors, Speakers, and Coaches hire me to unlock extraordinary income-earning opportunities in their businesses through profitability partnerships and publishing projects because most lack the inside information, decisive direction, and authentic action required to do so. For this very reason, I help them create, customize and communicate their message in highly impactful ways showing them that the bottom line is, every single day they do business; they must magnify their message so they can maximize their monetization. Palm trees have deep roots so even in the fiercest of storms when they bend to the ground, they will not break. It might be hurricane season in your life from time to time, but it is also a season where the storms you go through can make you better. Every fruit-bearing tree starts as a seed that needs to be watered. If that water is a flood, it will dissipate eventually, and the harvest will emerge.

I'm a survivor. You are a survivor. We are Game Changers!

Deneene A. Collins is the Founder of Success Creation Academy, Inc. and the CEO of Collins Consulting, LLC. She's an internet entrepreneur that publishes content with purpose who has helped key clients make upwards of $500K in under a year with strategic marketing methodologies.

Dee is a 3-time International Amazon #1 Bestselling Author that catapults aspiring authors into published status through her online courses and coaching techniques. Her latest book, *"Muscle Memory Millionaire" The Hidden Secret to Automating Your Success*, is changing the business landscape for many aspiring entrepreneurs and has given her notoriety in the areas of Business Mentoring and Coaching and Starting a Business.

http://deneenecollins.com/
http://successcreationacademy.com/
https://www.facebook.com/deneene.collins
https://www.facebook.com/deecollinsofficial
https://twitter.com/DeneeneCollins
https://www.instagram.com/deneene_collins/
https://www.linkedin.com/in/deneenecollins/
http://bit.ly/DeeCollinsYouTube
dee@successcreationacademy.com

Scan the QR code with your smartphone to view Deneene's video message.

Or, follow this link:
http://bit.ly/DeeCollinsVol5

30

Never Give Up!

....◆◆◆....

"Never, never, never give up!"

~Winston Churchill

by:
Chuck Sutherland

When life knocks you down with a sucker punch, fight the urge to stay down. Get back up and start taking one step forward at a time.

I had completed a Bachelor of Business Administration with a focus on real estate from the University of Michigan. When I returned home to Wichita Kansas, I wanted to get into the real estate business more than anything. Back then, the State of Kansas gave me a broker's license based solely on my college transcripts, counting all my real estate courses. In one day, I became a real estate broker. I thought I was something special!

I got married and we quickly had three kids in 6 years.

I started buying and selling houses and duplexes; I also built some buildings with my dad, who was a commercial builder. We built a small apartment project and a commercial building. And I learned a lot.

But then, a deep recession hit the country and I struggled to make enough money to take care of my family. As the recession grew in intensity, I had to invent new ways to make money. And banks were not lending money, so I had to get creative to make any kind of real estate transaction. As a result, I learned a lot of ways to finance property transactions and how to make real estate deals with nontraditional financing.

Back then, my best friend and mentor owned a local real estate brokerage and investment company with his brother. They had several offices in the Wichita area and owned multiple investment properties.

Among those was an old hotel near the city's downtown center and he approached me to buy it. I did not have much cash and the building was unlikely to get financed. But I saw an opportunity in this old hotel, and I was ready for a project that would prove my abilities and capacities to make money, manage construction, and turnarounds. I knew the property had been poorly managed, needed remodeling, but it was in a good location to make an excellent income while we owned and ran the hotel, fixed it up, and made it more valuable. Then I could sell it for profit. That was my plan.

And, most importantly, I thought I could make a decent income and take care of my family.

So, I got creative. I offered to buy the property for $1,250,000. I raised the down payment by giving my friend's company some small properties I owned as a down payment and then a $950,000 mortgage for the balance. His company was going to be my bank, and I would make regular payments to him – he was giving me seller-financing.

I wrote up the contract including the seller financing provision. Then, I added a "brilliant" clause.

In layman's terms, I would give him the notes, but then he would pledge back to me as collateral for the promises of things he would do after that closing. I thought I was so brilliant!

My attorney drew up the legal documents and we closed the transaction.

Later I learned I had made several critical and costly mistakes.

The first indication of a mistake came with the notification that my friend's company had filed for bankruptcy. I was notified when the bank holding an underlying mortgage on my property filed a foreclosure for the mortgage owed by my friend's company. They filed it on the same day!

I was traumatized! What was happening? I was so confused and uncertain; I did not know what to do.

And I did not know who could help me figure it out.

I felt completely alone.

The second mistake was that I trusted a man who intentionally betrayed my trust and put me and my family at risk to save himself.

During the bankruptcy and foreclosure proceedings, we all learned that my "best friend" "collateralized" my note and mortgage I had given him. What this means is that he simply made photocopies of the notes and gave them to two other banks as collateral as if they were originals. These were the same notes he also pledged to me as a guarantee for his promises.

Two things:

First, I think we could have figured out how to solve his problem if he had been open with me about his situation.

Second, I also think we could have figured out how to solve the problem if there just been one underlying note owned by the bank I had worked with. But in the bankruptcy proceeding against his company, additional fraudulent banking was revealed on my former friend's company.

There seemed to be no way to save the hotel or my finances. I felt hopeless!

It took a few months, but in the end, I lost the hotel because of the bank's foreclosure against my friend's company and I was able to reclaim the small properties I had given as a small down-payment.

I felt that my "friend" had ruined my life! I lost my down payment, the potential income to take care of my family, my credibility in the community, and my best friend!

This was one of the most difficult periods of my life.

I felt betrayed by my best friend and that shook my confidence in myself, my abilities, and my ability to do "due diligence," which is the process you use to validate if the property you are considering buying is as good a purchase as you think. This can take weeks to review all the relevant documents, understand the human motivations of all involved in the deal, and all aspects of the property that could negatively impact your plans. Could I trust my ability in planning and strategizing in the next deal?

More importantly, and more immediately, it impacted my ability to take care of my family, pay the rent and bills. When I think back to that time, I am sure subconsciously I felt I was something less than a man because a man would take care of the family; he would be able to bounce back quickly.

And certainly, a man could not show feelings. I had learned from my dad that to do so would be a sign of weakness. A sign of incompetence, or worse—mental or emotional Instability. If I showed how I felt, or even allowed myself to feel these painful feelings, it would show a lack of resilience when dealing with adversity.

When I was about 20, I had started listening to motivational recordings, encouraging success thinking, and a positive mental attitude. Speakers like Napoleon Hill, Dr. Norman Vincent Peale, and Earl Nightingale spoke to me.

But now I was struggling to keep it together and rebound. I knew I had to restart my perspective. The negative conversation I had with myself had to stop. I was focusing on what I did not want, what was missing.

I started to focus on what I wanted, what I could do, and what I knew and could leverage. Employing every bit of positive thinking and uplifting self-talk, I slowly regained my balance.

I started going back to what I had read about creating a "positive mental attitude". It was an hour-to-hour, day-to-day effort to set aside my negative thoughts and feelings to create a positive outlook. It took everything I had to just take the next positive step

I still had to find a way to pay the rent and feed my family. I needed to restart my career.

I knew I could do consulting—although I did not truly realize what that that would look like at the time. But I had learned a lot about real estate, appraisals, and property development over the previous ten years. I did not have any track record at all in consulting. I didn't have one area where I was an expert, but I knew something about several kinds of property and types of deals. But every day, I set out from my house with one goal—walk into somebody's office who might need some real estate consulting for something they were working on. I started by calling on real estate people that I personally knew. I made a list.

I found one person who need population information for an area of the city. They were developing a commercial building and wanted to know how many potential customers might be in the area. I had my first paying client.

Then I just continued putting one foot in front of the other. I showed up at the office of the next person on my list and asked if I could speak to them, and see how I could help their company.

I would review the newspapers and if I saw a company that might need help, I sent a letter. I probably got one out of ten consulting jobs I had from those letters. With consulting I did not need to have good credit or money, I had my knowledge to sell and if I did not know how to do a job, I learned. One job at a time.

Then there was a day when I got a glimmer of a whole new possibility. Financial recovery would not be instant or easy, but I could consult others on development or projects. I could analyze sites, guide the rezoning, or utility availability. Theoretically, I knew the processes, and I could obtain practical experience.

With that glimmer, I began to restore my faith in myself.

And the more I called on people, the more I found "synchronicity" in my visits with them. That instilled me with enough confidence to call on even more people. The more people I called on, the more projects I got. It became a self-fulfilling prophecy.

Need help with analyzing a property or a market, perhaps handle a labor situation? Sure, I can do that. Need somebody to put together information on the property they already owned? Sure, I can do that too.

Sowing seeds that produced good results landed me other opportunities. Satisfied clients introduced me to more consulting customers.

My market was expanding, and I was able to start over again.

The biggest lesson I learned was my reaction to life's experiences is what mattered the most. If I had stayed home and considered myself a failure, then the more that would have become a reality. On the flip side, the more I got out and had creative conversations, the more opportunities appeared.

The more business I got, the more money I made, which enabled me to meet the obligations of my family. Activity with the right intention breeds success.

This game-changer was not some "lightning bolt" moment wherein a single instant everything is perfect but instead, the "game-changer" was the clarity to keep going. To get better every day, to add one more step every day, to meet one more person every day.

This uplifting attitude of "one day at a time" made me see what was possible. I could see what I could accomplish.

I discovered this shift of perspective turned my failure into a success. Not overnight. But I learned I could get up off my knees, stand on my own two feet. I could take one step, then another, and stand up taller each day.

Momentum increased my ability to formulate plans to meet more people and find ways I could support them. With that foundation, I was able to rebuild my business.

The lesson I learned—it is never too late!

Get up, move forward, and do not stop. I felt a little bit like an old movie "Rocky," where the actor, Sylvester Stallone, was beaten, bleeding, barely able to stand up but he got up again and again. He survived one more round then another until the end when he and his opponent both went down. Rocky drew a draw—a tie. Sometimes a tie is all you need to get back up again and fight another day.

Then, one day, Rocky won. He became the heavyweight champion of the world. But it all started by stepping back into the ring ... one boxing round at a time ... and never stopping!

And one day, I won, too. One of my clients invited me to partner with him and I said "Yes"! But that is another story!

So, keep moving forward with all you've got until the end of the day. Then get up the next morning, keep moving forward, and "Never, Never, Never Give Up"!

It was the game changer for me, and it can be for you too!

Chuck Sutherland has been in the real estate investment business for over 40 years. He has been involved in the development of single and multi-family residential, commercial, retail, industrial, hospitality, and mini-storage projects. As either an investor/developer or consultant, Mr. Sutherland has participated in the completion of over $200 million in real estate transactions and developments.

Mr. Sutherland has also been a development consultant, conducting feasibility and market studies for industrial, commercial, hospitality, retail, min-storage, mobile home, and housing properties throughout the United States.

His course on Creative Real Estate Formulas has been used for over ten years as one of the fundamental creative real estate courses for several national real estate organizations.

Chuck Sutherland is also the author of three real estate books: *Creative Seller Financing, Creative Down Payments, and Advanced Creative Real Estate Financing* now on Amazon via ChuckSutherlandOnAmazon. com.

Contact Information:
E-Mail: Chuck@CreativeRealEstateNetwork.com
Website: https://CreativeRealEstateNetwork.com

Scan the QR code with your smartphone to watch Chuck's video message.

Or, follow this link: https://vimeo. com/461628959/c29ee2862d

31

Mortality, Eternity,
and the Path to Publication

· · · + + ◆ + · · ·

*In the face of mortality and eternity, writing my book was
actually more important than ever.*

~Susan Crossman

by
Susan Crossman

I stared at my husband in furious disbelief as he crossed his arms
in front of him and virtually dared me to contradict him. We
were squaring off in our ensuite bathroom as we prepared for bed,
the cause of the conflict having been his curt announcement that
we would not be going to his company's Christmas party the next
night. I was outraged. This was a party I had been looking forward to
attending for months. My husband had become reclusive over the
previous four or five years and we almost never went out anymore.
He worked hard, for sure, but he was drinking a lot and he had
become cranky and unpredictable.

I, on the other hand, was desperate to get out of the house and have some fun.

This was a second marriage for both of us and at the time I was home with three of the five kids in our blended family. The two children my husband and I had made together were still very young and we had decided that the family circus needed a full-time ringmaster; we had agreed that I was better equipped to handle the job than he was. I left my career as a freelance writer and editor and dedicated myself to keeping everybody on track and on focus as we careened through some very challenging years as a family.

My entire world now revolved around cooking, cleaning, looking after our kids, and keeping my husband productively focused on his career. We had moved a dozen or so times in our 16 years together, and my life revolved around finding movers, packing our belongings, unpacking them at the other end, and laying the foundation for a new life for all of us in our most recent new neighbourhood. It was exhausting.

I had been trying to write a book for 10 years by this point, and I was ever on the verge of giving up. Who takes a decade to write a book? Completely unsympathetic to the realities of my life, I felt like a failure. Prior to embracing the challenges of full-time motherhood, I had been successful in my work. I'd had great jobs and I had developed a solid freelance writing business that had carried me through five years as the single mom of the daughter I had created with my first husband.

My lifelong dream had been to write a novel. But I didn't know how to write a book and I didn't know how to get it published. I was full of self-doubt, too: who was I to think I could become a published author? Who was going to even read my book? What's more, it was hard for me to justify spending time on something that was not going to contribute any income to our struggling financial situation.

Although my second husband had consistently cheered me on in my book writing endeavours, his growing emotional neediness meant I spent all my time either with him or with my kids. Although I loved them all wholeheartedly I felt lonely and isolated, tearful, and vulnerable. My husband was all I had. I had set my book aside for the time being and decided I would finish it "someday."

Was I wrong to want more?

Have *you* ever wanted more?

I felt my sense of personal outrage rise as my husband scrunched his eyes and curled his lip. He was actually trying to stare me down! "Good luck with that," I growled to myself. I was determined to enjoy a night out. I had bought a new outfit, complete with a pair of gorgeous three-inch heels. They looked completely out of place on the floor of my closet beside the beaten up mom-flats I usually wore…but they tethered me to a world outside my normal life that felt cheerful and light, hopeful, and fun. Those shoes were pretty much begging me to dance. I prepared for battle.

Truth to tell, I wasn't sure what made me angrier: the fact that my husband was dictating my schedule, or the fact that I was not going to get a chance to slip into those beautiful shoes and play for an evening. I was the mother and step-mother of five children, and I was tired of struggle, moving, sacrifice, and exhaustion. I wanted to soar.

The years leading to this moment in time had been marked by four custody fights over the kids we had brought into our marriage, and the legal bills had been ferocious. In the fallout from the last legal battle, my second husband had started a business and it had failed in grand and dramatic fashion. He had been downsized and right-sized numerous times over the course of his career and he had been unemployed for a year-and-a-half once, during which time I had optimistically given birth to our youngest child. I had been a great wife. I had been loyal and supportive to a husband, who was, truth to tell, a good man and a loving father. He had a wonderful sense of humour and a strong sense of honour. I loved him.

But I had had enough. I needed some fun!

I was about to unleash a tsunami of vitriolic words when the man I had married calmly leaned over and vomited a gutful of deep red blood into the bathroom sink.

We both stared at the blood in dismay as it glided silently towards the drain in the bottom of the stark white bowl. The argument and the shoes were forgotten, although an angry, resentful part of me felt this was an awfully convenient way to get out of arguing over a long list of injustices I had been mentally nursing for months.

More blood spurted out of my husband and streamed through the drainage system of the fractured house we shared together and eventually—refusing all help, and stubbornly dedicated to fixing the situation on his own terms—my husband took himself off to the hospital in a taxi, a large Ziploc baggie on his knee. Numerous tests ensued. Was it gastritis? Colitis? An ulcer?

The diagnosis of terminal stomach cancer hit us hard. He'd get a year, at most, the doctor said.

We crumbled together in shock. It was unthinkable. He was the 49-year-old father and step-father of five children. He had so much to live for! I was devastated. Our children were traumatized. He felt gutted.

He got his affairs in order and said his goodbyes before sliding into a painful decline that ended with his death three months later. He had a gracious and gentle end.

As one would imagine, my world exploded into splinters of heartache I had no idea how to resolve. I was emotionally devastated and rudderless, trying to cope with an impossible reality I had never considered even remotely possible. My life had become deeply intertwined with my husband's over our years together, and now I had to invent a new me. What was I going to do with the rest of my life?

I cried endlessly, at first.

With my oldest daughter away at university, and my step-children living across the country with their mother, I moved out of my home with my two youngest children—then seven and nine years old. I found more modest accommodation. And I set out on the debilitating task of determining how to support my little family. Writing a book just did not seem like an important task in the face of mortality and eternity.

Or was it?

As I sifted through the ever-shifting sands of my new life, I thought about what was important to me, and looked at what I truly stood for. I ultimately realized that in the face of mortality and eternity, writing my book was actually more important than ever.

I had been assuming I would finish my book "someday." What if I died before Someday arrived? What if I *didn't* actually have enough time left to finish that book?

And so, I started writing again, diligently this time, and with a steady commitment to the goal of completing the manuscript. I wrote consciously, with the dream of expressing myself into the world courageously, no matter how vulnerable it made me feel. I had two struggling children to support and nurture, and the snarling threat of bill collectors required the emergency resurrection of my freelance writing and editing business. I was emotionally worn out and physically exhausted.

But I was motivated now. I was hungry for the completion of that book, a book that represented something creative and real, something I could call my own. I tore myself out of bed early every morning and sat down in front of my computer to go over that manuscript, and I wrote like the Goddess of Vengeance was after me. I poured myself into the project and after I completed my novel I polished it, lovingly and carefully, over the course of many months.

It was agonizingly difficult to be growing a business and supporting my children at the same time, but I did it. I hired an editor. Two editors. And I kept working relentlessly on that book.

Finally, 13 years after I started writing it, I obtained a traditional publishing contract and my precious book—dedicated to my late husband—hit the bookstores. It was the proudest and most bittersweet day of my life. I DID IT! I wrote a book that had made me proud.

Since that glorious day, I have written four more fiction and non-fiction books, and there are others clamouring to make an appearance. I have raised my children, purchased more great shoes, built my business, and discovered the joy of helping other people write their books, so they can share their messages and make the difference in the world that only they can make. I have finally found my place.

And I wonder if the writer in you has found its place, too?

Are you yearning to unleash the story you've been given to tell?

Are you letting it play happily with your future?

Or have you struggled with the self-doubt and uncertainty that afflict so many people whose dearest wish is to write a book? I believe that writing a quality book is an act of courage. And it requires a massive amount of determination to see the project through to the end. As a book coach and editor, I work with people who become emotional and intellectual warriors in the campaign to create of their story a published book that will change people's lives.

If you haven't yet finished that thrilling journey, take heart: you've got this!

And it doesn't have to take a family tragedy to catapult you into massive action. None of us knows how much time we've got left to cruise around dear old Planet Earth. But none of us gets out of here alive. One day, the jig is guaranteed to be up. Will you have finished your book by then? Will you have gone on to complete the book that might possibly follow the first one? And, perhaps, one after that? Writing books can certainly become part of what you do in the world, but you can't write the later ones until you've completed the first one!

Having had such a difficult path to publication myself it gives me great joy to help other people get there as easily and gracefully as possible. When my clients take delivery of their books, I am filled with pride at their achievement. It doesn't take magic to finish a well-written, high-quality book. But it does require us to step up and into a higher vision for our lives than we ever thought possible. The journey can be terribly challenging. But your readers are waiting!

Susan Crossman is a book coach, editor, and five-time traditionally published author who is passionate about helping clients harness the majesty of a good story to their dreams of making a difference in the world. She has spent decades wielding the "power tool" of language on behalf of coaches, consultants, innovators, and others who seek to write powerful books that will support their business while sharing their message.

She has developed a suite of programs and courses that help people start and finish writing the books only they can write, and she is available on a select basis to work 1:1 with clients as a book coach and editor.

Susan Crossman
susan@crossmancommunications.com.
Website: www.awakeningauthor.com
Linked In: https://www.linkedin.com/in/susancrossman/
YouTube: https://www.youtube.com/user/CrossmanComms
AmazonAuthorPage:https://www.amazon.com/Susan-Crossman/e/
B008D60YDQ%3Fref=dbs_a_mng_rwt_scns_share

Scan the QR code with your smartphone to view Susan's video message.

Or, follow this link:
https://youtu.be/RCKHpUw-YhM

32

Tomorrow is Today

· · · · ◆ ◆ · · · ·

"Don't take any shit from anyone."

~ Billy Joel

"Put your own oxygen mask on first before helping others."

~ Your Flight Attendant

by
Catherine Cohen

When Barry and I met, I thought he was the goofiest guy I knew. And it turns out he was. Barry always had a smile on his face. He was always making a joke, always seeing the lighter side of life. For 25 years, Barry and I laughed and smiled and chuckled through good times and the bad.

Barry was planning to move to Arizona when we met. I was fine with that because, as I told him, I was not looking for a long-term relationship. I had just come through a bitter divorce and I wanted to find myself again. But as the time drew nearer for Barry to move, I said to him, "you know what? I think I'll come to Arizona with you."

Barry's reply: "I don't remember asking you to move out with me."

I let him know I was not going to wait for him to ask. I'm no fool, I knew a good thing when I saw it. Soon after we moved to Arizona, I was ready to move back to New York. I hated being away from everyone and everything that I knew. And while I was crazy in love with this silly, funny, amazingly sweet and genius man, I had never moved far away from my family.

"I love you," he said to me. "You can't move back because I love you." That was enough to keep me in Arizona and build our lives. We decided, actually, I decided then informed him, we were to get married. We phoned his parents and my mother to figure out a date to fly back to New York for the wedding. On September 1, 1996, we were married under the chuppah in a not-so-traditional Jewish ceremony. Toward the end of the service, the Rabbi held up the wrapped glass for Barry to step on. Even though the true meaning is to remember the destruction of the Temples, our rabbi gave it a different meaning. The wish of all gathered was that our marriage should last as long as it takes to put the pieces together. Neither he nor I were in a hurry to put those pieces together.

Over the next nearly 24 years, Barry and I would be together 24 hours a day, seven days a week. And we loved every minute of it. We were both entrepreneurs and supported one another in following our dreams. Soon after we married, I left my job and became a massage therapist. Barry started a small website design and computer repair company that would soon become his full-time business.

Sometime in 2003, we created a barter exchange. Premier Barter became the first of three businesses we created together. Each time we decided to morph and build something new, it started on a whim, created out of frustration, researched then developed, followed by a launch filled with tons of love, a prayer, and fingers crossed. And, we always had a plan of action.

Creating a business with your spouse is neither easy, nor one of the smartest things one can do. If your marriage is not strong, seriously strong, there are two things you should never try to save your marriage. The first thing, never have a child to save your marriage. The marriage will fail, and the child will need many years of therapy. The second thing, never go into business with your spouse or significant other. The stress is unbearable. It is constant, there is no getting away from one another. Both Barry and I had parents who went into business together. Even though my father passed away young, my parents still had a strong, amazing marriage while running a successful shoe store. Barry's parents, currently retired, spent many years in business together and remain happily married. They were exceptions.

I could never imagine not having gone into business with my beloved. It was only natural.

Premier Barter became a well-respected exchange that we built and eventually sold. We then partnered with a friend to create software for the barter exchange industry. It was both our most successful venture and our biggest failure. Lessons learned included really know your business partner, do not let Yoko into the relationship, and Barry and I should only ever go into business with one another.

We moved on and created our most successful venture, Cohen Coaching. Barry and I made an amazing team. Our skill set was such that pairing up was a natural. After being in an industry for nearly 14 years, it was difficult to decide what we were going to do next. So we did exactly what we do for all of our clients, we went through our strengths and weaknesses, we listed all the qualities of our ideal client, we drank some wine, we ate something delicious

- the best decisions are made on a full stomach. And, we figured it out. Cohen Coaching was born and it took two years to mature, to really create our identity, our niche market, our offerings, and our business.

December 31, 2019, at midnight:

5, 4, 3, 2, 1 – Happy New Year!

We kissed and hugged. "I love you."

"Love you, too." We proceeded to hug and kiss all our closest friends. The people who meant the most to us. The people who I would refer to as "The Inner Sanctum". It was 2020 and our lives were beautifully laid out before us. Everything was coming together.

January 2020 proved to be our most successful month ever. New clients came on board, we updated our courses. We just came off a series of one-day workshops, ready to create a weekend event. This was going to be our year.

At the end of January, we were scheduled to attend a three-day event in Las Vegas. We were going to hone our coaching skills and choose refinements to our direction. We scoped out coaches and programs. After all, in order to have a great business, you need a great coach. And in order to be a great coach you need to have a great coach.

On the last Wednesday of every month, Barry attended a networking event he created. Men only. Cigars. Drinks. Networking.

I could either use the opportunity to hang out with friends, attend networking events of my own, or just sit home and catch up on some television show Barry was uninterested in watching with me. He surprised me by coming home early.

Barry just found out his father had cancer at 86. Barry kept saying, "my dad is going to die." What was going on? Our lives were laid out before us. This was supposed to be our year.

Within days, Barry was on a flight to New York to be with his family while his father went through two surgeries. The first, remove the myelomas that had developed in his legs. The second, replace the hips. The prognosis was good. My father-in-law would be fine. It was a minor hiccup. Our lives were still beautifully laid out before us. This was still going to be our year.

Barry met me in Las Vegas. We attended the event, saw old friends, and made some new ones. He had a slight limp–must have been the flights. We took pictures, laughed, joked, created new connections, and reinforced old ones. We were in our element. We were among like-minded people. Our lives. Our year. February faded into March. Business was good. We chose our coach. We decided on a plan of action. We were excited. Everything was proceeding just as we had planned it. Barry had a weakness on his right side. First in his arm, and then in his leg. Stress. He likely bent wrong or strained something when we were gardening. I worked on his muscles. We went to the chiropractor. We can fix this, because this is going to be our year.

At the end of February, we went to our favorite annual event, the Arizona Renaissance Festival. Once again, we were with our closest friends. The Inner Sanctum. Barry had trouble walking. Something was wrong. Barry was walking with a walking stick. He was weak. What could go wrong? Our lives...just in front of us. It's our year. Isn't it?

March meant Covid-19 hit hard. Getting to a doctor, to the right doctor, was not easy. Barry was sent for a series of painful tests and MRIs. Our doctor could not make sense of the results. There was a subluxation, a bone out of place on the left side of the spine. But it was the right side that was getting weaker and weaker. The last tests came back. It wasn't the test the doctor actually wanted. It took several more weeks to get into the neurologist. Barry's walking was increasingly labored. The look on the doctor's face said everything. "I need you to go for an MRI tomorrow. It could be a stroke. It could be something else, something more serious." We prayed that it had been a mild stroke. WE PRAYED IT WAS ONLY A STROKE! Because our lives were supposed to be before us. This was going to be our year.

On April 6, 2020, we received the news. Barry had a glioblastoma multiforme. When you look it up, the research says, "Glioblastoma multiforme is the most common and most aggressive type of primary brain tumors. Despite improved surgical techniques, therapies, and radiotherapies, the prognosis for this type of pathology remains very poor: most patients die within 12–18 months from diagnosis." His life, our lives, were over. This could not be our lives, my life. But here it was. Talk about a game-changer. Many thoughts went through my brain. None of them can be repeated here. No future? No happily ever after? This could not be real.

Within a month, just before treatment was supposed to begin, Barry fell into a coma. On the day Barry fell into a coma, we started out laughing for the first time in a month. We talked, had a delicious breakfast, and were looking forward to the next week when treatment would start. As we did for nearly 25 years, we said I love you over and over again. Within a few hours, he was in a coma.

We brought him home. On May 16th, 2020 my life changed forever. The love of my life, my best friend, my business partner, my partner in crime, Barry, took his last breath. It was 25 years to the day of our first conversation. Almost 25 years to the day of the first day that we met in person. My world, my life, everything I knew, ended in the moment he died. Our lives were no longer before us.

I sit here writing; it is raw because it's been only 4 1/2 short months while at the same time it feels like forever. In the one month, we had together following the diagnosis, there was not enough time to talk about the future. We thought we could beat the diagnosis, at least for a little while, so we didn't talk about it.

In 25 years, we never fought. We had disagreements, usually about business, which made the disagreements fun in a way. We said please and thank you. We understood what the other person needed and wanted. There were no secrets, there was mutual respect, and there was deep love and incredible passion. We lived in now. We took amazing vacations and created the memories I will treasure until Barry and I meet again. When we could have gone out, we stayed in and hung out together. When we should have stayed home, cleaned, or taken care of something, we went out and hung out with family or friends. We laughed. We cried. We lived.

And that was my past. On May 17th, 2020 I woke up knowing that I did not want mine to be a life that I did not want to live. But here it was, a new life laid out before me. The possibilities we were supposed to have-gone. The dreams we were supposed to make come true together held in my heart and mind. Where could the story go from here?

I do not know where it goes from here. One moment. One diagnosis. One last breath. And the whole world changes. My whole world changed.

This couldn't be the end of the story. In fact, this had to be the beginning of MY story. I never wanted a story of my own. Very soon after we met in 1995, I believed my story would always involve this goofy, sweet, brilliant soul, Barry Cohen. When you move forward in life, you cannot move forward with regrets. You cannot move forward with what-ifs. You cannot change yesterday. We have this moment and only this moment. The infinite now. Starting right now, tell everyone in your life how much you love them.

And now begins my story.

This is what I know to be true - my life is laid out before me. I am now at choice. Being at choice can be exhilarating or trepidatious. I have both. And, I have steps.

Step 1: Before the shitstorm starts, and there's always a storm, create a strong group of people around you. Remember the Inner Sanctum? They have become my strength. They are my way forward, personal friends, and professional allies. No one is an island. Not even you.

Know your strengths. Embrace your weaknesses. And then find a support team to shore up all those weaknesses. Chief cook and bottle washer is not a term you should embrace. Learn to rely on others. Create a team.

Step 2: Develop resiliency. To be resilient is the ability to recover quickly from difficulties and difficult situations. It is not a coldness, nor is it a lack of feeling. It is simply the ability to move past the current situation to a place where you can begin to make things better for yourself and others.

Step 3: Be grateful. In every moment of every day, there is something to be grateful for. When I had to make the decision to take my beloved off life support, I was grateful for the family and friends that held me up. When I knew Barry would die, I was grateful for my dearest friend's efforts to bring my husband home to die in my arms. Find the silver lining in every situation. It may be hard to find, but you must. Otherwise, life is nothing more than a miserable existence.

Step 4: Live in joy. Happiness comes and goes. Joy, along with gratitude, are a state of being. In the worst of conditions, in the most difficult of circumstances, joy transcends everything. If you find a joy-filled attitude difficult to achieve, you can do one of two things. The first way is to find something to be joy-filled about. Go play with a child. Or a puppy or kitten. Fly a kite. Spin around and around until you collapse in a heap of laughter. The other way I call "there but for the grace of God." Think your life is shit? Trust me, there is someone who has it way worse. Not my favorite way to achieve a state of joy, but sometimes it is the only way.

Step 5: Live in now. There is nothing harder for a widow than to NOT live in the past. But my life is not in the past. My beautiful, precious memories are there. And I enjoy them. But I do my best not to live there. This moment is the ONLY moment you have. There is no past or future. The eternal now is all we get. Your next breath is not guaranteed. This is liberating. Because it reminds you to do what you want, when you want. You are always at choice.

Step 6: Know you have choice. You are always at choice. Every moment of every day. Your choice can only happen in the eternal now, in this present moment. This is my moment, your moment to move forward. The past shapes our future. But in this perfect, present moment, your choice shapes tomorrow. For me, the love, joy, and beauty of the amazing and perfect 25 years I spent with the love of my life will shape my future. I choose to take the love Barry and I had and bring it to my future. I choose to take the love and joy, be grateful, and plant it as a seed for my future.

The beauty of your past can become the beauty and joy of your future. If you choose it to be so in this present moment. In the now. The only thing you have is this moment. The eternal now, the perfect present. In this moment, you are at choice. Choose wisely. Choose your people. Choose joy. Choose gratitude. Choose love. These things make you resilient. These things allow the silver lining to come through.

Close your eyes. Take your breath. Be in the moment. Make your choice.

Catherine is the co-founder of Cohen Coaching. A more creative force, Catherine is the ideas person. Ideas and inspiration seem to just come to her. Her specialty is taking a client's talent, experience, desire, and skills, and reworking them into new offerings, laying out the groundwork to get a new business started, or creating a path of growth and renewal.

Catherine enjoys crafting solutions that make sense to each client's unique situation. She is all about attracting the right clients to a business, so businesses grow organically.

Catherine is also a Sci-Fi fan, (Star Wars more than Star trek) a Billy Joel fan (don't get her started) and attempted piano lessons in her youth. She also loves reading everything from Arthurian fiction to business books and a lot in between. She is not a fan of romance novels.

Even though she is a bigger Star Wars fan, Catherine had the United Federation of Planets logo put onto the train of her wedding dress in honor of her late husband.

Catherine Cohen
www.CohenCoaching.com
Cat@CohenCoaching.com
https://youtube.com/c/CohenCoaching
https://www.facebook.com/CohenBusinessCoaching

Scan the QR code with your smartphone to watch Catherine's video message.

Or, follow this link:
https://youtu.be/J9GBXVZG98A

33

The Healing Power of Story

·· ·+ ✦ +· ··

"Life is like photography... we develop from the negatives."

~ Ziad K. Abdelnour

by
Becky Norwood

Life has prepared each of us with unique experiences, well-earned wisdom, creative talents, and treasured gifts. I have learned that the only real failure in life is the failure to grow from what we have gone through.

Let me share my story to give you perspective as to how I discovered my life's work.

From my earliest beginnings, my voice was silenced. I grew up in a devastatingly abusive environment with a father who was broken. Sexual, physical, emotional, spiritual, and mental abuse was a daily occurrence. As a young adult, I seemed to attract what I was accustomed to believing was normal. Gradually I discovered my voice, and an inner strength I did not know that I possessed. Eventually, I discovered the amazing power of authentically sharing my story. Countless stories of my childhood and young adulthood are incredibly difficult to share, but it was in the sharing of those stories that I found myself.

What is interesting about sharing stories like this is that there is healing power in putting pen to paper and articulating the story, and there is even more incredible healing that comes from releasing it out to the world. In so doing the intensity of the "story" that once held me hostage, lost its power, and was replaced by the ability to tell a new story. It paved the way to lead in a new way, to grow, and serve in ways that impact the world.

In my youth, hiding the truth was painstakingly drilled into my psyche. The fear of exposing the truth and being killed for doing so was very real. Combine that with the required "telling the truth" of every conversation be it with classmates, teachers, or adults... in minute detail to an obsessive, mean spirited, abusive father who was paranoid that his true colors would be exposed, and you have the resulting pain, confusion, and disillusionment of the victims.

As I stepped into adulthood, I was completely conflicted, confused, and certainly on a path to attract all the good my heart desired. Indeed, my healing journey has not been on a straight path, it has taken many twists and turns, and I suspect it will continue to do so.

I became a single mom when I was six months pregnant with my second baby, the oldest of the two was just 13 months old. I had married a man who was just like my father. However, having my children was the catalyst to the awakening that there was more to life than what had gone before, and I was determined that my children would have a beautiful life.

I began reading and searching for something... and that something developed into my traveling from Arizona to Arkansas to attend a week-long power of thought school. That week my heart was open, and my mind was exposed to incredible new ways of thinking. Oh, the things I learned! Bolstered, excited, and inspired with what I had learned, I returned home with a newfound awareness, of my self-worth, my inner strength, and goodness.

By that time, I had had my fill of what had happened to my siblings, my mother, and myself, what we had endured, and I was determined that it would stop. While I still trembled with fear, I knew what I had to do.

After returning from my trip, I went to my father's home and asked him to join me on the patio for a conversation. During that conversation, I told him how his abuse had affected me, and that while I was no longer under his roof, his abuse had left an indelible mark. I reminded him that he was still abusing my mother. Much was said that fateful evening. As we spoke, he became increasingly hostile and angry. Finally, I told him that it was time for him to leave. He could pack up his belongings, take what money he needed, take his jeep, and camp trailer, and go find his happiness. I told him how sorry I was that none of his family had brought him joy, but it was time for this to end. I told him I would seek out protection for myself, my daughter's, and my mother if he chose not to leave peacefully.

He was not a happy camper.

A few days later he knocked on my door saying he needed to speak with me. I was reluctant to talk, even more so to let him into my home. I stepped outside, fearful of what he was going to say.

These were his words, "Becky, I am so proud of you."

Shocked by his words, I asked why he would say such a thing. He responded, "Look what you have done. You have broken the pattern of abuse that has happened for generations of our family. Look at the way you are raising your children. You are good to them, you treat them with respect, and discipline with kindness. Look at what remarkable young women they have become."

As I stood dumbfounded and in tears, I said, "Dad, abuse does not work. It does not produce goodness." He said, "I know. You have taught me that." That was his greatest gift.

Three weeks later, he did leave, but with none of his belongings. That night, he did not return to his home. The next morning, I went to the sheriff and reported him missing. For the first time in my life, I shared my story. The Sheriff, who sat in disbelief, questioned, and double questioned. He knew my father, knew he was a difficult man, had even served on the City Council with him, but had not known the full scope of just how difficult he was. I cried and trembled my way through the story, insistently demanding that my mom and daughters, and I have complete protection. I asked that we be given new identities, because, although I suspected what he had done, I could not be sure, and his repeated threats kept ringing through my ears. I also begged the Sheriff not to make public the fact that he was missing because of my being in so much fear of the repercussions.

Two weeks later, the Sheriff insisted that it had to be broadcast on the news, and though they had searched to no avail... they could not wait any longer. I consented, and just hours after it was broadcast, someone reported having seen his vehicle about 50 miles out on a remote area of the desert.

He had taken his life the day he left.

While the news was a relief, the flood of emotions that ensued took many years to recover from. As my siblings and mother and I came together, we discovered many atrocities each of us had suffered but never spoke about to each other. As painful as it was, as the truth surfaced, we each processed in different ways.

Initially, I blamed myself for his death, even though I knew that it was a blessing for our family. He had come from a family of horrible abuse and I was aware of his pain-filled childhood and the atrocities he had gone through.

His pain was also now over.

From time to time I reflect on the little four-year-old me, the little girl who knew she did not want any part of the abuse and whose failed attempt to escape by running away resulted in a broken spirit for many years. I remember the pain, the fear, the feelings of unworthiness, and the perpetual sadness I felt. Those feelings stayed with me long into adulthood. Had I not had my children whom I deeply adored and felt responsible for, I likely would not be here today.

It has been quite a journey to wholesomeness and emotional wellbeing. I found that buried deep within me was the fire that prompted that four-year-old to attempt escape by running away from home, and it was that fire that has also led me to the healing that continues and the sacred work I now do in helping others discover the healing power of story.

The biggest step I took in my healing was writing and publishing my book, "The Woman I Love." That woman was ME!. For a fact, until I could love myself, all the dreams, wishes, and desires I held in my heart would not come to me. What transpired from publishing my book which became a #1 International bestseller is that paved the way to the discovery of my life's work.

In essence, my story became the gateway for conscious growth, a pathway for sharing, and brought healing for myself and others. It became the thread that has woven the tapestry that would lead me to become an advocate for courageousness and the freedom that sharing our stories brings. It became the discovery of my treasured gifts and my life's work. In sharing my story, the pain of the past lost its fire, and I am no longer THAT story. It is interesting how that works.

Today, I am a book publishing expert who values the incredible power of a story well-told, and I am consistently inspired by the stories of wisdom that springs from the authors I have been privileged to serve. As I work with authors to tap into the incredible power that emerges from storytelling I am humbled daily by the stories I hear. It brings me such deep joy to witness others showing up in the world with raw vulnerability sharing their stories. Just as I had experienced, by saying YES to sharing the painful stories of our past we discover special gifts we never knew existed.

In my case, accepting my own story, allowed me to release the story, to let it go, and no longer hold power over me. It opened the door to possibilities beyond my wildest imagination. In time, I learned that owning my story would amplify the special gifts I had no idea I possessed. My own sordid, painful stories lead me to discover my life's purpose.

Now, through the processes I have developed, I help others become their own story whisperer, expressing the value of their own life's lessons.

In so doing, each of these "storytellers" creates a magnetism that comes with an awareness of their unique individuality and the work and gifts they bring to the world.

As I work with authors to craft the words of their life's journey, I am constantly reminded that I did not hold a corner on the market for troubled times. What a delight to work with so many from incredibly different backgrounds who have withstood incredibly tough situations. They have found their way and now serve as teachers and leaders in our world, standing up, sharing their stories, their wisdom, and their expertise. There is not one of us who can escape life on this planet without earth-shattering events that rock our world.

Storytelling can bring to light untapped wisdom.

Storytelling can heal lives.

Storytelling can transform the heart.

Story is the gateway for growth.

It's a path for sharing.

Story is what brings us closer to one another.

And it's through the threads of our stories that we weave together an empowered new world.

In vulnerably sharing our stories we become...

Advocates – Truthtellers – Unifier's – and Wayshowers
How? You ask...

Let's take the word ADVOCATE.

An *advocate* is someone who can help you speak up so that your needs are heard, your rights are understood and your problems are resolved.

So, I ask:

How would telling your story move and inspire others?

What would sharing your story do for you?

A truth-teller communicates and does not hold back. A truth-teller looks for solutions, and create an environment where people feel it's OK to mess up and make mistakes. They cultivate an environment in which owning up to our ugly stories, and mistakes is OK, and it's safe to fail.

A truth-teller eliminates barricades. Should we decide to become a leader, we have the power—and the obligation—to get rid of anything that prevents people from performing at their best. We don't allow barriers that keep people from telling complicated or unwelcome truths. Celebrate the truth by speaking the truth as their leader.

A truth-teller gives us reasons to be better than we are. The remarkable power in telling the truth is to let people know they can be part of the solution, and they can be part of something bigger than themselves. As a leader, you can provide them with a compelling vision that gives them a reason to be better than they are.

Great leaders are remarkable truth-tellers. They know that honest hearts produce honest actions.

> How can you break free of any resistance to telling your story?

> It is said that "The truth shall set you free." In what ways could that freedom bless you?

> In what ways could it bless others?

Unifier – the definition of a unifier is a person who unites people to others for a common cause.

An example of this is Nelson Mandela who was renowned as a unifier and lover of family, friends, people, community, society, and humanity in general. He is an amazing teacher and you can be as well.

> How could attracting the strength of like minds serve to help you grow?

> What role could uniting shoulder to shoulder with others willing to share their stories of courage and resilience play in creating a better world for future generations?

> How would the power of story impact your world?

A **Wayshower** is one who guides other people on moving onto their path, just by living an inspired and authentic life which acts as an example and motivation for others to follow. Wayshowers are infused with the highest virtues and live their lives in a **way** that always keeps the highest interest of all beings.

The greatest gift we can give ourselves is to love ourselves.

The greatest gift we can give our families is to love ourselves.

The greatest gift we can give the world is to love ourselves.

We do not owe our past a place in our future.

Brene Brown says: *"The irony is that we attempt to disown our difficult stories to appear more whole or more acceptable. But our wholeness, even our wholeheartedness actually depends on the integration of all of our experiences, including the falls."*

Our stories are our connectors, and as such, a well-told story can have a huge impact on transformational change in others.

Shame, guilt, and fear are life's destroyers.

I was so ashamed of my deep dark secret, that as an adult I kept it hidden away. Yet, it ate at me. The shame kept me from stepping into my greatness. It kept me in a near-constant state of depression, that was a constant fight to stay on top of.

I remained a single mom for 20 years, unwilling to once again attract the same kind of people and situations into my life especially where my daughters were concerned.

I also felt unworthy of being loved… and was too afraid for many years to open my heart. The guilt kept me from feeling joy and accomplishment in life. Fear that I would be discovered and snubbed or rejected was constant.

The amazing thing for myself and so many others is that owning and vulnerably sharing our stories allows us to release the awful and ugly stories and opens the door to the dreams we dared dream but never thought attainable.

For me, it created a new story... one I happily accepted and stepped into.

How can you bring your sacred gifts to the world?

What special strength would you share to make an impactful difference in our world?

I ask you...

What is your story?

#1 International Bestselling author, speaker, & book publishing expert, **Becky Norwood** is CEO of *Spotlight Publishing™*. She is widely recognized for the empowering 'story whisperer' intuitive way she passionately guides others to become their very own story whisperer. She incorporates her methods with sound marketing that is the pathway for business expansion and audience growth.

Becky has brought over 350 authors to #1 bestseller. Countless listeners have heard her live online interviews of both authors and experts offering sage advice. She offers an extensive catalog of services supporting emerging and established authors.

Becky Norwood
www.spotlightpublishing.pro
https://www.linkedin.com/in/beckybnorwood/
https://twitter.com/urbizspotlight
https://www.facebook.com/SpotlightBookPublishing
https://www.instagram.com/beckynorwood_spotlightbiz/
becky@spotlightpublishing.pro

Scan the QR Code with your smartphone
to view Becky's video message.

Or, follow this link:
https://youtu.be/ozG4CPq5YHs

34

What if You Fought City Hall!

·····◆◆◆·····

"The brittle hopelessness of the Humpty Dumpty Effect
crashes into obstacles
and turns the world end up, like Titanic after the iceberg.
Why did the Big Egg fail to anticipate his plight?
Why did his own experience, academic theories, and
training let him down so hard?
Was he so arrogant he thought himself unsinkable?
Were his messengers afraid to deliver bad news?
Might they actually have enjoyed his tumble?
Or was he simply not listening to them?"

~ Christopher C. Cowan
Spiral Dynamics: Mastering Values, Leadership, and Change

by
Natasha Todorovic-Cowan

"You can't fight City Hall," 'they' say. It's a common trope for a reason. But that's what I was doing anyway.

It was a cool morning, and I'd walked the three-quarters of a mile to get here. I sat on a low wall across the street from the police station at eight o'clock in the morning. The marine layer was in, and that made it gray, quiet, and a little sticky in our coastal town in California. I was fidgeting and kept checking my phone. I did my best to not bend or damage the sheet of paper I'd carefully carried over with me. It was a foreign object that I desperately wanted to dispose of. It sat there on the wall, close enough to rescue if a breeze saw fit to move it, far enough away to buffer my discomfort.

Across the street, up the stairs, and at the entrance to the police station, a homeless man ranted into the intercom. The front door of the station was locked and inaccessible without an appointment. You had to call in advance, and the homeless man didn't have a phone. He was maskless, unlike the few people wearing masks appropriately in a time of Covid-19.

A couple started up the steps. Seeing the barefoot man clenching a blanket around his shoulders, they paused midway. Hearing obscenities hurled into the black box on the wall, they were hovering momentarily on the step and reconsidering their errand. They wisely aborted their morning's mission.

Fighting entrenched powers, historically rooted in a political, bureaucratic, staid, and immovable institution, is akin to banging your head against a brick wall. It's a masochistic act. Expect pain, disappointments, frustration, and, the lucky avoid the traps of cynicism and despair. I didn't blame the homeless man for his frustration. I wondered how he had gotten here and whether anyone would respond or if he'd be hauled away.

Mine is an incredibly diverse neighborhood. It runs the gamut from our "unhoused neighbors," as some charitably call the people inhabiting our streets, back alleys, and dumpsters, to the Latino workers who man our restaurants, tend our gardens, clean our homes, work in government, and teach our children. Most of the workers do their best to eke out a living in a very expensive part of the world. While the city struggles to get sufficient workforce housing, millionaires and Hollywood stars inhabit our town.

My husband and I once found ourselves behind John Cleese in the supermarket checkout line. We loaned him our rewards card since he'd forgotten his. He and my husband exchanged a Ministry of Funny Walks moment. Julia Child secretively shared her favorite Mexican restaurant with us -she didn't want to play favorites publicly. Kirk Douglas ate at a nearby table while we had dinner one evening. Sue Grafton signed a book to my mother-in-law who was a fan. While waiting for our burgers, our friend said, "Hey, I think that's Brad Pitt."

Looking over, I replied, "Can't be. He's too short." The man stopped, turned red, and stiffened. My friend was probably right. I'd inadvertently slighted Brad Pitt.

As I said, mine is an incredibly diverse neighborhood. In a single day, you can bump into a star or watch a crazy person rant and rave. Today it was the latter.

In exactly eight days, I would be presenting my case to a judge in an online, quasi-judicial hearing. I wasn't a lawyer and didn't want to hire one. Over the past four weeks, I had had to rapidly learn dozens of things that had nothing to do with anything I did in my real life.

My situation was disconcerting. I had customer projects demanding completion, deadlines looming, an inbox brimming with unanswered emails, calls needing to be made, programs needing to be finished, and product delivery needing to be completed. Yet, here I was, sitting on a wall, waiting to serve a subpoena to the chief of police's right-hand man.

"How did I get here?" I wondered.

Hannah Arendt's term, "the banality of evil," flitted across my mind as the barefoot, bearded man across the street grabbed a fistful of papers from the opposite wall and threw them down the stairs in a fit of rage. The relevancy of Arendt's term becomes apparent to those confronting the nameless, faceless walls of government institutions holding the faceless people behind those walls. They make policies impacting the lives of people oblivious to those policies. The unremarkable people merely do their jobs and try to hold onto them. They keep their heads down, doing normal things, following rules once created to serve people but now serving to create more paperwork for more unremarkable people.

If I pursued this quest of mine, would someone be sitting on this wall one day, watching me? Would the immovability of these institutions have me screaming vulgarities into a banal box on a wall at an anonymous person, with nothing but the clothes on my back, a blanket, and frustrated rage? Isn't that what fighting City Hall gets you?

This particular cascade of events began with a sign in the window of our local CVS, a drug store, and convenience store. It was an application for a liquor license.

My home is just a few blocks from the beach, to which a diverse range of human beings are attracted. We're a tourist town attracting people from around the world, beckoning them to frolic in vacation bliss mode. We're a student town, encouraging them to enjoy their educational years, take a break from study, relax, and find fun with friends on the sand and in our restaurants, bars, and wineries. We're a retirement town where older folks stroll along, watching the waves and the gulls. We're a family town, where hard-working parents take their kiddos to the beach to make sandcastles and paddle in the water. We're a wedding town where couples walk hand-in-hand while they make sand footprints that disappear when the next wave washes in.

My life is blessed with perpetual blue skies, palm trees, and beaches. And while I appreciate this slice of paradise in which I live, my eyes and mind track for different things – the weak signals of emerging cultural shifts, seemingly vague "disturbances in the force," ripples subtly building social tides. Along the coast from Mexico to Canada, particularly in southern California, an underclass of the ignored, the broken, the desperate, and the defeated marches in droves to the temperate climate of our oceanside towns. Wealthy, celebrity-filled California contains twenty percent of the nation's homeless within its borders, thus representing the full economic disparity of our society from the top to the bottom.

Imagine getting up on the perfect morning on a perfect day with a trip on the calendar. It was early enough in the morning and I wanted to walk to the bus to Los Angeles International airport. As I pivoted my rollaboard onto the sidewalk, the temperature was a perfect caress on my skin. The flowers and the ocean scents hung in the air and I took a delicious inhale.

Several steps took me around the corner onto the main street. One of my "unhoused neighbors" was passed out across the sidewalk in front of the CVS bottle in hand. Winding the rollaboard around him, another 50 steps took me to a couple in front of the liquor store. She weaved back and forth angrily castigating the man on the curb arms wrapped around the trash can like a long-lost lover. He sang with joyful, drunken abandon. Avoiding them, I slowed behind another homeless man teetering side to side heading towards the same corner as I to cross the street. Two feet from the trash can, he bent over and vomited on the sidewalk. I narrowed my nostrils to the sickly-sweet contents of his stomach hanging in the air.

"Another day in paradise," I said it out loud.

This scene was altogether too common. Our wine tasting, our craft beer breweries, the rented student homes on the cliffs by UCSB where they party, fall down those cliffs and 6-8 students die each year.

In fact, if you're a Californian living by the coast, lengthy discussions with complete strangers over the topics of homelessness and alcohol problems come easily. It's a commonality that joins people. Discussions abound about the homeless who make their encampments in our backyards, in our driveways, on our beaches, along the train track, about those who congregate in alleyways behind businesses for drug-dealing and prostitution, causing patrons to think twice before going into establishments thus depressing business.

If change is going to happen, someone had to do something. One day that someone became me.

Three years earlier, I had filed a protest to the Alcohol Bureau of Control (ABC) regarding the CVS liquor license, which I'd completely forgotten about until a letter arrived in the mail. It announced a hearing date three weeks later at the end of June. Suddenly, I found myself preparing to present my case at the CVS liquor license hearing.

I was out of my league. I didn't know where to start. I didn't know what to do. I didn't know what to argue. I didn't know the process. And I didn't know what kind of evidence was needed. I needed to make motions, get a continuance, and compel the other parties to share their discovery. The CVS lawyer had forty years of specializing in these issues in the state of California. He owned the largest law firm in the state serving businesses with liquor licenses. He could run circles around me. Everyone and anyone who had any experience with the ABC and these issues told me, "Natasha, expect to lose."

We were days away from the hearing when I learned that our room hadn't been cleared nor was the building open due to Covid-19. The CVS lawyer wanted to go ahead. The ABC lawyers didn't care. But I had immune compromised witnesses, so I filed a motion for a continuance and held my breath. A conference call was organized. The line was silent as the CVS lawyer, the ABC lawyer, and I waited. The judge got on. Within five minutes my motion was granted. There were three more weeks to prepare for the virtual hearing via Zoom.

It was analogous to cramming for a test, research for a dissertation, and preparing a client proposal at light speed. I learned new acronyms, new concepts, new language, and a new appreciation for legal practices. I collected my exhibits. I began to practice phrases like "under section 61.4 ..." and "Your Honor" and "public convenience or necessity."

In our city, a liquor license can be delayed if the police department doesn't grant a "public convenience or necessity" (PCN). I discovered a discouraging pattern on the part of the police department. They would deny the liquor license applicant a PCN, then later on make an about turn and grant it. In other words, protest it and then rubber-stamp it. They did this because they believed they had no power over what the ABC wanted. The ABC did little or nothing to enforce the conditions outlined in a liquor license no matter how many pictures or letters of complaint were submitted. Unless an applicant had felonies, there wasn't a liquor license that the ABC or our police department didn't like.

Although the ABC argued that my concerns were not supported, my outreach and conversations established that the problem existed in other states. Researchers had mapped the detrimental effects of alcohol in communities and had discovered a correlation demonstrating that, with every 10% percent increase in the availability of alcohol, a concomitant rise of 4.2% in alcohol-related crime followed. The various effects rippled through neighborhoods, including young people drinking at younger ages. My job was to show how this specific license for CVS would increase crime in our specific neighborhood.

A friend made a public records request and received all sorts of information. We spent a weekend slicing, dicing, crunching, and digesting the police calls for service in front of CVS, down the block, in our neighborhood, and on the adjacent city blocks – calls that the ABC and the police department willfully ignored. I produced a chart showing a steady increase of crime year over year using police data.

I worked day and night to prepare. I was ten days away from the hearing date, and time was running out for me to submit my discovery documents. It became clear that if the neighborhood was to have a fighting chance, I needed the police chief to rescind her letter granting the PCN to CVS. I imagined it could be a gamechanger.

Focusing on that goal, I learned that the Chief's right-hand man was one of the state's most knowledgeable experts in this area. It was one reason why the city had hired him. The police chief had brought him with her from San Diego due to their work together on these issues. He declined my invitation to appear as a witness. I either had to subpoena him or have the chief remove the letter or both. I chose to focus on both.

So many people stepped up to support this protest. They made calls, agreed to be witnesses, shared, and practiced their stories with me, and gave me expert guidance and advice. Progress happened because they stepped up.

It was Monday, a week and a day away from the hearing. I had failed to successfully serve the subpoena to the chief's right-hand man. I was walking home, furiously trying to figure out another solution, when my phone rang. A reporter for the local news channel wanted to meet me for an interview in the CVS parking lot in an hour. Practicing safe social distancing, I shared the story with her. Her next visit was to the chief of police's right hand. The story aired twice that night on the evening news, and I did an interview for a local paper the next day. A second local news network picked up the story and aired it Wednesday. A few calls came in from around the state - others who had tried to push back against the ABC, a well-funded liquor license applicant, and the entrenched bureaucracies in their cities and who had failed.

I beseeched two city council members to ask our city administrator to ask the chief of police to rescind the letter. I called the city attorney and city administrator to highlight the hole in our local policy depressing economic development.

Tuesday was consumed by confirming and finalizing my witness list and completing discovery by a five pm deadline. At 4:55 pm, I sent 199 pages of exhibits, pictures, evidence, and crime data to the CVS and the ABC lawyers. The file was so large the email bounced. I scrambled to break up the exhibits, compress them, and resend.

Wednesday went to confirming my thirty-two witnesses—residents, business owners, heads of nonprofits serving the homeless community, a council member, a former councilmember, and an expert witness.

Confirmation came that a subpoena had been served to the mysterious consultant the ABC had hired – tick that off my list. The Chief's right-hand man had also been served. Tick that off my list.

Friday night at 5:45 pm, four days before the hearing, an email with an attachment from the Chief's right-hand man appeared. It wasn't what I had hoped for. The police chief hadn't retracted the letter. However, conditions had been placed on the CVS liquor license. For the first time in our city, the police department had placed stringent conditions upon a national retailer. We awakened the department to an awareness of a power they hadn't known they held.

Saturday and Sunday I spoke to every single witness. Wrangling thirty-two witnesses wasn't easy. Some were frightened and couldn't sleep. Some were frustrated with the situation. Some wanted to tell their story and be heard. I repeated information about how to use Zoom controls over and over and over.

Sunday night I received a personal email from the CVS lawyer following his request for a continuance to the Administrative Court which he had copied me on. His client hadn't had a chance to review the conditions.

Lunchtime on Monday, we were on a call with the judge. The CVS lawyer agreed to the police department's conditions. The judge said, "Whatever agreement you reach must be acceptable to the Department (ABC)."

Three important things changed. City Council was willing to study "public convenience or necessity" and look at why the police department was making land-use decisions. We called on our council members to take back control of the alcohol licenses since a city exerting local control can override the ABC. And CVS changed their district policies to ensure staff policed the perimeter and asked drunks and vagrants to leave.

Today I walked through the neighborhood. The area around CVS is quieter and looks better already. It turns out you can work with City Hall after all. And that's a game changer.

Whether it is resistance to change, cultures in conflict, or dysfunctional teams, Natasha Todorovic-Cowan supports leaders and their teams to strategically architect transitions, pivots, and avoid meltdown through change from C-suite to shop floor.

Rooted in 70 years of research & application, Natasha Todorovic-Cowan has more than 25 years of experience applying SPIRAL DYNAMICS® tools/programs to reveal the root causes of people problems to organizations.

With clients on 5 continents, she is the world's leading expert in this approach and helps leaders, teams, and organizations achieve their vision.

https://www.linkedin.com/in/dr-natasha-todorovic-cowan-mba-a5470719
https://www.facebook.com/spiraldynamics
https://twitter.com/SpiralDynamics

Scan the QR code with your smartphone to view Natasha's video message.

Or, follow this link:
https://youtu.be/E8SfqR9AQXc

About Iman Aghay

·····✦·····

Compiler and Inspirer

Iman Aghay is a serial entrepreneur, international speaker, and 6-time #1 best-selling author.

He is best known as the founder of Success Road Academy and has created over 50 courses that help coaches, authors, speakers, and entrepreneurs grow their business aligned with their life purpose.

In 2010, Iman founded Success Road Academy, which has become an industry leader in online marketing and training. Through Success Road Academy, Iman has worked with over 150, 000 business owners, in various niches, and helped them expand their business and impact. Iman is also the founder of Entrepreneurs International Network, which has a community of over 150, 000 members in 5 countries. Iman is also part owner of JV Insider Circle, the world's leading community for entrepreneurs to find partnerships and deals, by utilizing community and connection. He continues making an impact through using community to connect entrepreneurs to their life purpose, and the people who can assist them.

He has become widely successful by helping other people to achieve greatness in their own lives.

Iman's TEDx talk is one of the world's top-rated speeches, which focuses on how to live a life with no regrets.

Iman has mastered creating a successful heart-centered business. He believes that all entrepreneurs can build a business based on their life's purpose. His vision of having a massive positive impact on 100 million people has fueled his love and passion for guiding entrepreneurs to success.

As the Leaders' Mentor, Iman's focus was and always is serving his clients and community with the utmost excellence and integrity.

Have you enjoyed the game-changing stories in this book?

We invite you to leave a review on Amazon or other online book stores.

Be sure to check out the other books in this series:

Book 1
https://amzn.to/2GWjBAz

Book 2
https://amzn.to/3lH35mS

Book 3
https://amzn.to/3iSXDvv

Book 4
https://amzn.to/3lLNJOa

Also, check out Iman's other books:
Ultimate Course Formula – How to Create
and Sell Online Courses in 60 Days or Less
https://amzn.to/34NNzP6

Leaders Success Journal
https://amzn.to/2SOQth6